Warplanes
Lost & Found
in
The Bahamas

Warplanes Lost & Found

in

The Bahamas

how unlikely volunteers found
ten historic aircraft
in a year

Eric Wiberg

Island Books

by the same author:

Bahamas in World War II
Mailboats of the Bahamas
U-boats in the Bahamas
U-boats off Bermuda
U-boats in New England
Swan Sinks
Round the World in the Wrong Season
Tanker Disasters
Boston Harbor
First Fifty in Fifty
Published Writing
Juvenilia
Åke Wiberg (co-author)
Napoleon's Battles (co-author)
Travel Diaries
Yacht Voyages

First in a Series

Print ISBN: 978-1-7356324-2-1
e-book ISBN: 978-1-7356324-1-4
Library of Congress Control Number: 2023904029

Layout and editing by Abdul Rehman Qureshi, writingpanacea@gmail.com
Cover by Caitlin D. Fitzgerald

Dedication

for Dad, for inspiring and supporting me

-and-

for Joanne Green, niece of aviator Jack Wood

special thanks to those who loaned their boats to this quest

Howard Story, *Parole* for an entire month
Amanda Lindroth, *Schooner Queen*
Eric Cottell, *TT Providence*
John Wiberg, *Shoal Shaker*
Rich Ashman, *Kimber-L*
Phicol Wallace, *Lost Key*
Denis Galipeau
Ulric Williams, *Yisel*
Toby Smith, *Da Skiff*

In Memoriam

In memory of Alistair Grant Cleary of Christchurch, Canterbury, New Zealand, 1922–1943. From his nephews Grant, Steven, Graham, Anthony, and Stuart Cleary, and great-nephew Ethan Cleary, who were never able to meet him. Alistair joined the RNZAF and died five miles northeast of Morgan's Bluff Andros when his B-25 ditched at night on May 21, 1943. Although the aircraft's wheel and life raft were recovered, none of his remains or those of the five other officers and crew were found. Alistair was 21 years of age and known for his sense of fun and mischief; at one point he was reprimanded for jumping over the tail of an airplane.

World War II Aircraft

Martin Baltimore

Grumman FM-2 Wildcat

B-25 Mitchell

Martin B-26 Marauder

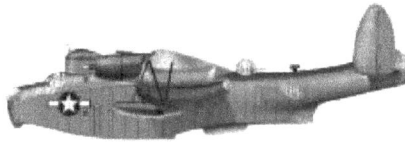

Martin PBM Mariner

de Havilland Mosquito

Douglas SBD Dauntless

Avro Lancaster bomber

Boeing B-17 Flying Fortress

Grumman G-21 Goose

Consolidated B-24 Liberator

Douglas A-20 Havoc

Consolidated PBY Catalina

Charts

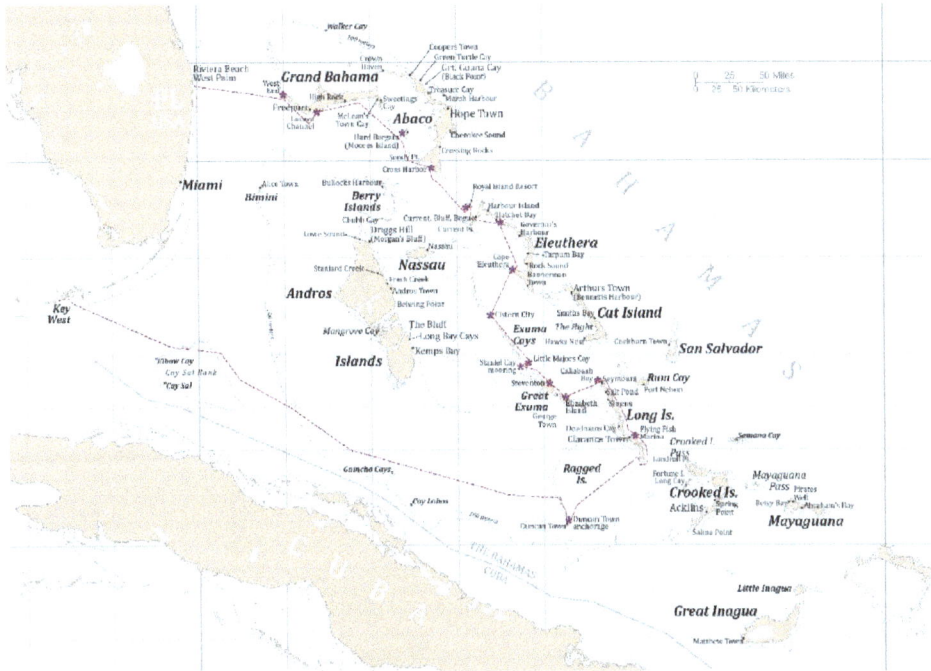

The track of 59' S/Y *Parole* in January, 2003 1,200 nautical miles through Grand Bahama, Abaco, Eleuthera, Exumas, Long Island, Ragged Island, the Great Bahama Bank to Cay Sal Bank, one of the largest atolls in the world. By Robert Eller Pratt.

The Royal Air Force standard, draped over their *Book of Remembrance*, at Christ Church Cathedral in downtown Nassau. This unique record of all casualties of aviators who flew in or through the Bahamas was researched and the hand calligraphy entries made possible by the Erickson family active in Inagua.

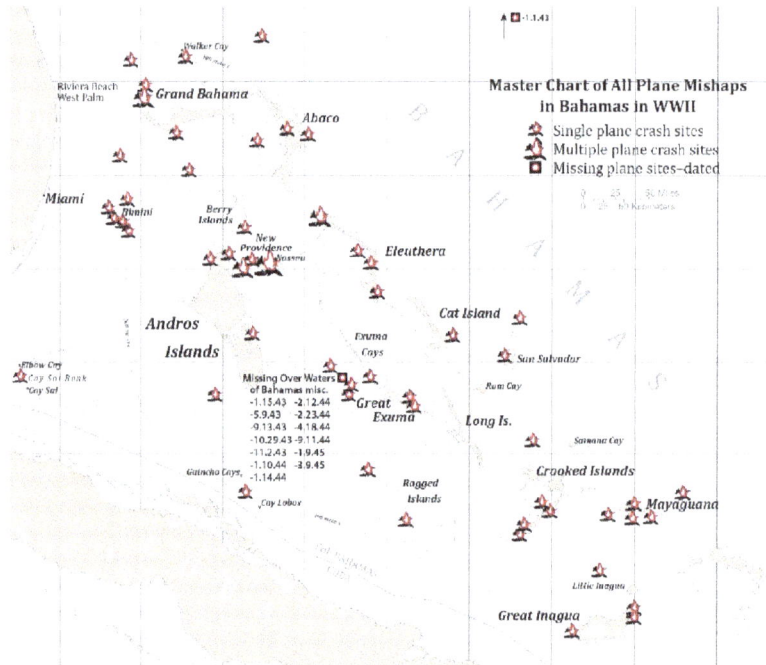

Overview of Allied plane wrecks and accidents in Bahamas in World War II.

A long line of B-24 Liberators preparing to take off from Oakes Field during World War II, from the Australian War Memorial in Canberra. This illustrates the many thousands of aircraft which lifted off from New Providence, before factoring the many thousands more which transited over the Bahamas from the US, mostly towards Trinidad in World War II.

Contents

Forewords

The dedicated research undertaken by Eric Wiberg over the years on the history of The Bahamas is extensive. This latest herculean undertaking of *Warplanes Lost & Found in The Bahamas* builds on his work of *Bahamas in World War WII*, the relatively unknown military history of the islands. This factual edition provides a wealth of information on many levels: for readers of history, military history, and expanding to family history—which is where my gratitude lies—in being able to make a personal connection to my late uncle, F/O Jack Wood, RCAF whose B-26 crashed near Cable Beach in 1944.

I had looked at my uncle's military file in the Canadian Archives, before it was online, and tried to understand the accident report, but had no context for an event that happened almost eighty years ago in another country. Ten years later, I received a message on Ancestry asking if I was any relation to the pilot from Eric, who was then researching the event. This began what was to become a wild ride leading to the discovery and recovery of Uncle Jack's and Maurice O'Neill's crash site near Eric's family home in The Bahamas.

We all have the benefit of the author's broad approach, connecting with others through time and space, and in my case, to have tangible evidence of my uncle's service and final resting place. Eric submersed himself (literally) in determining the background, connections, locations, and retrievals of the island's aviation history for the descendants of the servicemen. He also shares stories relating to those living on the islands at the time with his own personal journey.

I am grateful for the care, dedication, and effort that it has taken to bring this book about and how Eric's path as a young man crossed that of my uncle's plane wreckage so many years ago.

Joanne Green, family historian and
niece to F/O Jack W. Wood, RCAF
and on behalf of all the Wood
Family descendants,
Guelph, Ontario
March 2023

Anyone interested in world history, and in particular World War II history, owes author Eric Wiberg a debt of gratitude for his contribution. Only the rare combination of bold explorer, tireless bibliophile, keeper of local knowledge, and dedicated scribe could forge the key to unlocking this treasure trove of otherwise forgotten history.

Eric is that man. What he has uncovered in the present book as well as his *Bahamas in World War II* is a world of conflict, chaos, uncertainty, conviction, hope, and fear. Far from being the backwater where "nothing happened," Wiberg gives us The Bahamas as a microcosm for the global cataclysm out of which the world of today was born.

In these pages, Wiberg documents and returns to human memory the people and events caught up in that maelstrom who deserve far better than to be forgotten, and without whose sacrifice our lives would be poorer and our world much dimmer.

Readers with a family connection to those who served should find in these pages a welcomed remembrance. All of us will find in it something of an education. Read on and remember.

Robert Rydzewski
Aviation radio historian and writer
Newark, California
March 2023

Dr. Grace Turner and fellow archaeologists and staff from Bahamas Antiquities, Monuments and Museums Corporation accept the parts from the B-26 Marauder found in Delaporte Bay, Cable Beach, in November 2021. Author and father at right. The parts are being conserved at AMMC on Shirley Street, downtown Nassau.

This book brings to light previously little-studied or new facts about events that occurred in The Bahamas and would have remained unknown until Eric Wiberg uncovered them. His curiosity, interest, wide and deep reading, research in archival microfiche files and genealogical sites is backed up by his captain's knowledge, instincts, and swimming prowess. He actually found metal and wrecks under the sea by paddling a $50 inflatable pool raft he named *Clementine* as a tribute to Winston Churchill's wife, and for longer explorations he was loaned small motor boats by friends.

Eric displays impressive knowledge of aircraft and military units along with intimate geographical knowledge and persuasive techniques to utilize local volunteers. He was assisted by almost 100 eager amateur historians from every corner of the vast Bahama Islands. In individual chapters he portrays stories of land and sea ditching, crashing and explosions from Delaporte, Clifton Bay and other locations in New Providence; Tarpum Bay, Bannerman Town and Royal Island in Eleuthera; Castle Island in the Crooked Island Channel, Moore's Island, Abaco, Great Exuma, Ragged Island, Inagua, Grand Bahama, Mayaguana, Andros, Bimini, Berry Islands, and little-visited Cay Sal Bank.

At least 170 allied aircraft had accidents on airfields, in the oceans, and on the islands of The Bahamas during World War II. Eric tells stories of bravery, fear, dread, motives, ambition, survival, and lonely deaths. One of the most horrific tragedies that affected Bahamian residents was of a mother who died of asphyxiation. Her baby's head was crushed by a plane crashing into the home, and the husband was burned. Eric tells of the deaths of young pilots and air crew and the devastating effects upon their wives, families, friends, and communities.

The buildup of New Providence led it to become the hub of all South Atlantic air deliveries to the Allies in Africa, the Mediterranean, Middle East, and Far East. The Bahamas were the headquarters of the Allies' trans-South Atlantic aircraft delivery system during that war, a critical hinge in the aviation supply chain. The RAF instructors trained over 7,000 students for the front, and pilots, navigators, copilots, and radio operators moved over 9,000 aircraft to Africa between August 1942 and late 1945. Of great benefit to The Bahamas was that roughly a third of the population of New Providence were Royal Air Force or in their employ. As well as Windsor Field, they were employed in dozens of World War II sites, docks, facilities, buildings, hospitals, and hotels, most of which are still visible today. Sadly, many graves are too.

In this book's conclusion, Eric gives would-be writers great advice: "Research the hell out of the topic in every database and archive you can, get to the site and ask as many people as you can about what they know—often what they don't know is more informative that you are in the wrong place—and finally, get dirty, get wet, and get cut up. If you don't, you probably won't find the plane, or what it is you are looking for."

Drawing on Goethe, he exhorts: "Whatever you dream you can do, begin it!"

Jim Lawlor
Vice President and Corresponding
Secretary, The Bahamas Historical Society
Nassau, NP, The Bahamas
April 2023

AUSTRALIAN WAR MEMORIAL   P01367.001

An incoming group of aviators and trainees, from the Australian War Memorial, which titled it "members of the 1943-06 intake of navigators into No 111 (C) Operational Training Unit (OTU), at Nassau." A comparison of names given with casualties thankfully provides no matches: all survived the Bahamas.

Preface

Picture this: you find a piece of twisted aluminum a foot long in the sea, and it has the paint of a plane's tail number on it. You don't know much about that type of B-26 airplane, or any airplane for that matter. In trying to single-handedly pull 45 pieces of it out of the seabed and onto a surfboard, into a car and a back yard, you damage your lower spine so badly that walking and sleeping are difficult. That winter, neurosurgeons in Boston declare you unfit for work or lifting: disabled. Yet within a year, with the help of many others, you have found so many other aircraft that the largest organization globally for the B-26 Marauder invites you to be the keynote speaker at their annual conference. It is on an airfield in Ohio. That, in a nutshell, is this story.

Perhaps it is inevitable that, after over four decades of writing, a tactile historian might become part of the fabric of the story. Though a blurring of boundaries between subject and chronicler may be troubling to a journalist, for a memoirist and war historian who has never served in a military force, keeping the two apart was not difficult. Though I often visited sites depicted in more than half a dozen history books covering The Bahamas, my inclusion in written accounts was often limited to obscure endnotes, to verify sites, for example.

In the events of this book, however, my role is intermediary between two groups: the men who often sacrificed their lives, or at least their aircraft, to bring the war from the Americas to Europe and beyond; and the men and women who volunteered their time, knowledge, and watercraft towards finding what remains. And those remains are scattered throughout the length of the Bahamian archipelago.

To paraphrase Captain Willard in the film *Apocalypse Now*, "There is no way to tell their stories without telling my own." This is because I appear to have been the first to both find and publish the original ORB's or Operational Record Books from two primary RAF bases in Nassau, as well as from US Navy bases in Exuma and beyond. One reason publishing them took 75 years was censorship (they were sealed until at least 1972, when I was aged two), and another appears to be a lack of broad interest. In bringing these records to the surface, and to general readership globally, I became a self-anointed guide. As a full-time writer, part-time teacher, and captain who was often on a tight budget, I found myself relying on the generosity and enthusiasm of others. Convincing others of the veracity of the aircraft locations, and the novelty of finding them, thus became part of my overall campaign.

Fortunately, like-minded family and friends stepped forward, in some cases having heard of my efforts independently. One contributor who I'd never met called and said bluntly: "I've been given coordinates for a lot of stuff that turned out not to be there. I'm turning to you because I understand you deliver results for what you go after." That, of course, was immensely encouraging; and indeed, we found the targeted aircraft on the first day of his and my diving together.

To tell this story, I—we—needed to go into the field as well as the archives and microfiche files, and find the metal under the sea, in the mangroves, and in the ubiquitous bush. Splashing into the water and hopping ashore between November 2021 and February 2023 allowed a myriad of insects to extract their dues, and the poison wood and sea urchins to do their work on dozens of eager amateur historians from Hard Bargain Moore's Island Abaco to Duncan Town Ragged Island, Castle Island, and Acklins Island. And these adventures have yielded tangible results. This book represents a blend of narrative perspectives which I believe readers will enjoy.

There are three pillars, or themes, to this text:

- Volunteerism during World War II by Allies serving in The Bahamas
- Action and accident, focusing on the debris—and graves—left behind
- Volunteerism in The Bahamas since, to find remnants and families

The numbers are mesmerizing: over 170 air accidents have been stress tested and confirmed from 1942 to 1946, as well as an outlier civilian craft from 1930. In order to find those aircraft, owners of nine boats provided their vessels free of charge. But this is not a list of accidents nor a drum roll of the deceased, nor a battle standard for aircraft found. Together we will discover not just what happened and how the crash sites were found, but who participated, was wounded, died, rescued, mourned, and who found and buried the dead.

The stories ahead aren't focused on steel and the limestone, coral, and mud the planes crashed into; they are the stories of human flesh, fear, dread, motives, ambition, success, survival, and often horrific, lonely deaths. Indeed, the non-aircraft fatalities alone would be enough to fill volumes with woe, including over 30 incidents of harm befallen on roads, sailboats, trucks, operating tables, in bars, by propellers, disease, friendly fire, and sometimes by the deceased's own hands.

Step one to find these planes and their crew was completed with the 950-page tome, *Bahamas in World War II* in 2020. That in turn was the result of over a dozen years of paper-chasing by me and people spread across the globe in numerous archives, libraries, and databases, primarily in North America, Europe and Australia.

Step two was finding physical traces of the planes: pieces of metal mostly. For that, I had to rely on the logistics, finances, and safety in numbers which only a team with guides and local knowledge can provide. And more often than not this was on a shoestring budget.

As a result of nearly 100 different volunteers from all over pitching in together, ten planes were either found or their losses were accounted for; as in having an eye-witness point to the spot. Often, the primary tools of discovery were ears used to listen, heavy-duty boots, a swim mask and a snorkel. I didn't use drones or SCUBA gear. Some of the participants and I had sailed together 30 years ago and reunited for this task, others I arranged to meet from Boston, and still others, like a couple of journalists based in Berlin who I met in Acklins, were just friends made in the field. I thank each and every person who contributed and committed time, funds, energy, and good wishes, starting with Felix, my son of 16 years who filmed my *TED Talk* video at the outset.

This entire effort began soaked in salt water—tears, in fact. In November of 2021, our mother was gravely ill, and I was home in Nassau for the longest time since I had left 40 years before. As a way to cope and process her suffering, I manically swam at sea every day. My target area was in front of the family business—Cable Beach Manor—as it was being torn down by the new buyer. It was winter, and I was terrified, yet I found my first World War II plane: a B-26 Marauder. My motive was simple. I had just published the first book detailing the locations of all the World War II aircraft wrecks in the Bahamas. This made me realize: *"Now I've given anyone enough information to find these planes themselves, before I do!"*

My early success made me want to find more aircraft. Since I had already catalogued over 40 parts of one, I set out to find all of the B-26 Marauders lost in The Bahamas; I accomplished that in less than a year. Then I set out for a month on a 59-foot sailing yacht with a centerboard, a diver, a mechanic, a wounded war veteran for a captain, and a technology expert who ensured we had internet so that we could consult experts worldwide the whole time. In three weeks, we found three aircraft and figured out the locations of three others, for an average of two planes a week.

The rest, as they say, is history. And don't worry—there are still unseen relics in Bahamian lands and seas for others to find.

ETW, Boston
June 2023

Support Vessels

Clementine, inflatable pool raft, Eric Wiberg, Delaporte Bay, Nov.-Dec., 2021, Clifton Bay, Nov., 2022, Exumas, Jan., 2023. Used to find two B-26s and for training.

Da Skiff, Toby Smith, Delaporte and Cable Beach bays, 2021. Grid-searched for the first B-26 Marauder.

Denis Galipeau's boat, with Henrik Gedde Moos, Delaporte Bay, Nov.-Dec. 2021.
Diving trip to snorkel in search of the first B-26 Marauder from Sandyport.

Yisel, 26' Eduardoño, Ulric Williams, Delaporte Bay, Dec., 2021. Good Samaritan.
Rescued me holding a large engine cowling, tied it up, and towed it to shallow water.

Shoal Shaker, 23' Mako, John Wiberg, Delaporte Bay, summer, 2022, Clifton Bay, Nov. Pinpointed the site of the first B-26, towed me behind to find B-26, Clifton Bay.

Schooner Queen, 32' Stuart Angler lobster/picnic boat, Amanda Lindroth, Clifton Bay, Nov., 2022. Towed behind by John Wiberg to find B-26 which Stuart Cove found in 1983, believing it to be a different type of aircraft.

Kimber-L., 48' DeFever trawler, Rich Ashman, Clifton Bay, Nov 2022. Support boats in Clifton Bay for B-26 Marauder.

TT Providence, 30' Scarab Sport, Eric Cottell, Findlay Cay, White Banks, Dec 2022. High-speed voyage to area of White Banks near Finlay Cay to investigate a false hit for cruiser wreck, which turned out to be seagrass.

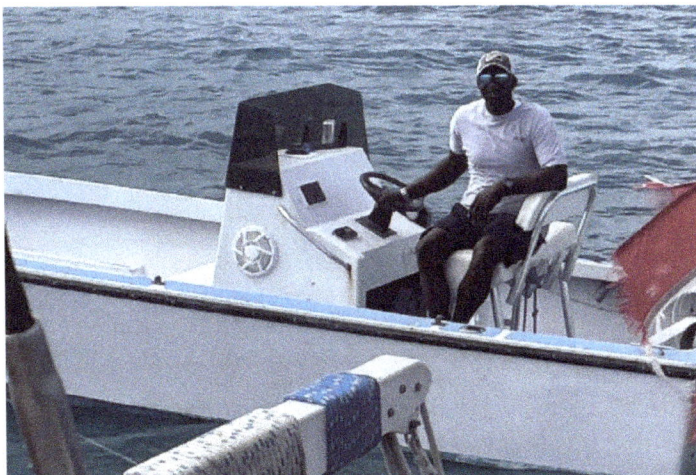

Lost Key Lodge Skiff, 24' fishing guide boat, Phicol Wallace, Ragged Island, Feb 2023.

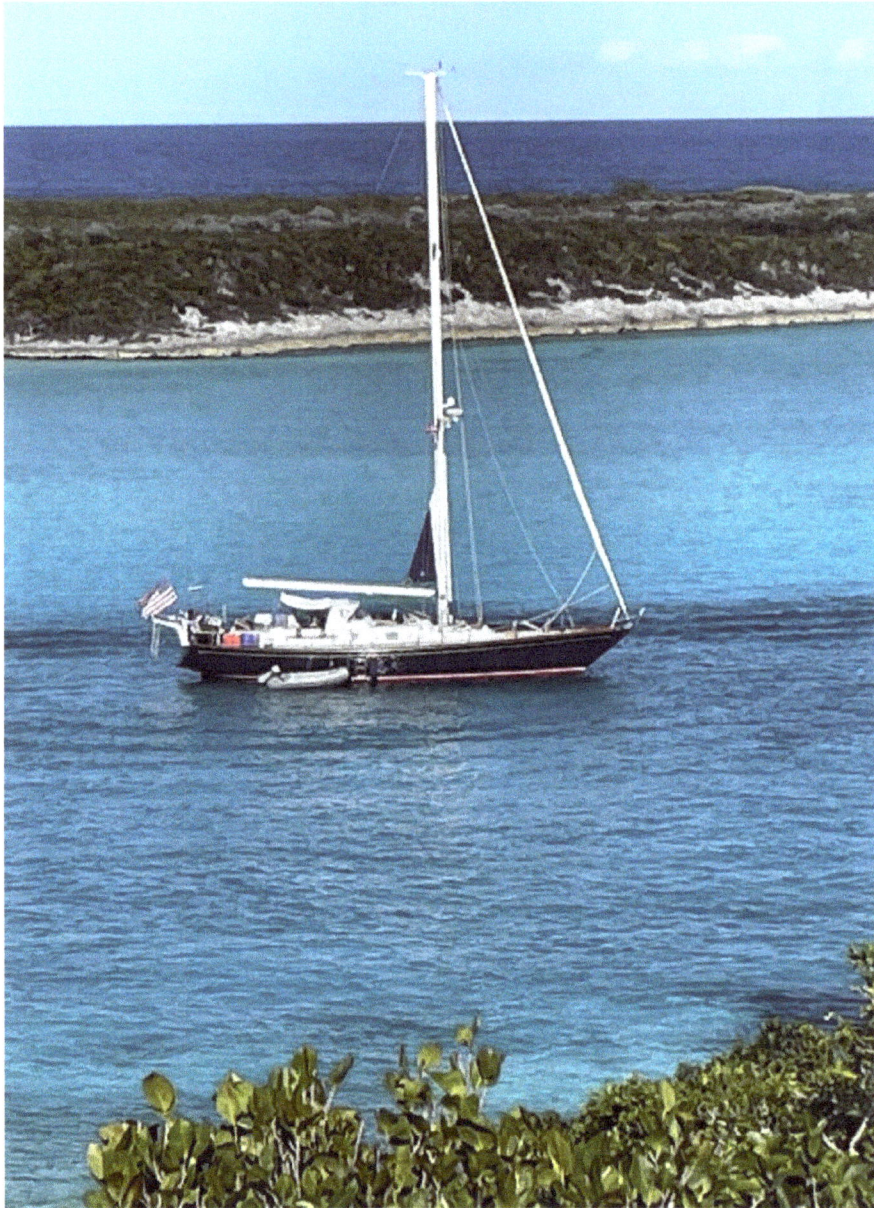

S/Y *Parole*, fka *Carpe Mañana*, fka *Mary Sunshine*, 59' Hinckley sloop, Howard Story, Jan.-Feb., 2023. On it we found a Hellcat fighter in Moore's Island, a PBM at Royal Island, went after two B-25s in Tarpum Bay and Bannerman Town, Eleuthera, the Norwegian grave in Cross Harbour, Abaco, the 1930 wreck in Exuma, found the PBY Catalina at Ragged Island, and the site of USS *K-74* off Elbow Cay, Cay Sal Bank.

Introduction

At least 170 allied aircraft had accidents on airfields, in the oceans and on the islands of The Bahamas during World War II. Of these, roughly 100 were found or salvaged, and the 70 or so others were not—until 2021. The status of 26 are unknown, lost, or simply missing. Many hundreds of warplanes went missing between Florida and Trinidad; only those confirmed to have crashed in the over 100,000 square miles of The Bahamas are included herein. Out of at least 424 people involved in accidents, there are 131 known fatalities, a number of whom are buried in the Royal Air Force (RAF) or War Cemetery on New Providence. Over 112 survived the accidents, while others succumbed to the propellers or sank with their aircraft. Most of the airplanes were manufactured in the United States and Canada and made their way to the RAF bases on New Providence.

RAF activities were split between a transport group at Windsor Field and a training school at Oakes Field. Windsor Field is presently the Lyndon Pindling International Airport and Oakes Field is closed and has been surrounded by the University of The Bahamas, National Stadium, and defense force and police bases. The vast majority—over 80—of the accidents took place on or near New Providence Island between 1942 and 1946.

A significant portion of aircraft accidents, particularly those far from Nassau, were aboard the USAAF (United States Army Air Force; a precursor to the US Air Force), which included civilian personnel and aircraft, while others were US Navy aviators on amphibious craft and fighters from Florida or attached to the Naval Operating Base (NOB) and Naval Air Station (NAS) in Great Exuma. Many of those aircraft were lost *en route* between Florida and Trinidad via Puerto Rico. It is believed that roughly a dozen water wrecks and perhaps two dozen land wrecks are still discoverable, though neither intact aircraft nor deceased airmen are likely to be found.

The general lack of study or knowledge of this trove of historical material is attributable to the passage of time, censorship, destruction or loss of *RAF Form 412* accident and investigative reports, and the death of almost all eyewitnesses in the intervening 80 years. The availability of new technologies, including online satellite imagery, drones, diving and exploratory equipment makes verifying sites more possible than ever. The potential to reconnect the Bahamian public with WWII artifacts and families of the servicemen and civilians who were in accidents or killed in action who are from Argentina, Australia, New Zealand, the UK, Canada, the US, the Czech Republic, Norway, and many other places, is significant.

The clearest way to outline these events is to share stress-tested data which has been plumbed from archives globally and contributed to by many aviation experts. Though in the chapters ahead, a dozen or so cases will be studied carefully as well as illustrated, it is important to first conceptualize the extent of the accidents, starting by island group.

Abaco and its islands were the site of five WWII aviation accidents, Acklins four, Andros eight, ten simply were lost in the waters of Bahamas, and one in the Berry Islands. Seven planes crashed in Bimini, one to the east of Cat Island, two off Crooked Island, one off Cay Sal Bank, nine at Eleuthera, twelve in the Exumas, eleven off Grand Bahama, four off Inagua, five at Mayaguana, and nearly eighty on New Providence or in the waters of Clifton Pier, Yamacraw, Delaporte, and Athol Island. Oakes Field runways saw ten accidents, and Windsor Field over twenty. Ragged Island had two planes wreck there, and San Salvador one. Some of these were seaplanes which were salvaged.

Seen on a timeline, 1942 saw seven accidents from September, which spiked to eighty-one in 1943 and thirty-seven in 1944. Then in 1945 there were thirty-five and only a fuel hut fire in 1946. Broken down by type of aircraft, using the popular names, there were four Kingfishers, twenty-four Havoc or Boston smaller bombers, only a single B-17, a pair of B-18 Bolo bombers, and thirteen larger B-24 Liberators. The most popular training aircraft, B-25 Mitchells, experienced twenty-eight accidents in The Bahamas, with seven B-26 Marauders, and one B-29.

There were other aircraft, including a US Navy blimp or dirigible airship, three Curtiss C-46 Commandos, seven Douglas C-47 Dakotas, three F-6 Hellcat fighters, a Dauntless, several Hudson and FM-2 (also F4-F) Wildcats, and seven de Havilland DH.98 Mosquitoes fighter-bombers. On the amphibious side, there were eight large PBM Catalina planes, fourteen PBY types, and several types unknown, including the same type given several different names; for example, Cansos were Catalinas, and the Douglas A-20 was known as the Havoc in the US, Douglas Boston in the UK, and Douglas DB-7 in France. Eighty of the aircraft were under the ownership and control of the RAF and personnel, including training aircraft and RAF Transport Command planes. The USAAF controlled twenty-seven of the planes, and fifty-nine were part of the US Navy.

The worst losses of life were with B-24 and PBY aircraft, with fourteen lost at a time, or a dozen in large flying boats. Forty-five accidents had fatalities, and sixty-six accidents had survivors, of whom the largest number were thirteen in the PBY which grounded on a reef and beached in Ragged Island. Eight men survived a blimp being shot down off Cay Sal, and eight others from a PBY. Roughly half of the casualties' crews can be named, and those buried at the RAF Cemetery are particularly well documented.

The final losses of the immediate post-war period saw continued training up to and beyond V-J Day, amphibian rescue of personnel hurt in industrial accidents in Abaco, Grand Bahama, and Andros, including the September 1, 1945 loss of a Grumman F6F Hellcat overdue from Vero Beach last seen west of West End. On January 11, 1946, the RAF bases' Fuel Hut 201 caught fire, straining resources to put it out and find alternate fueling in the short term. The bones of that building are still visible near the modern Clifton Pier oil terminal. By 1946, the air bases and all the ancillary supports, from nurses to censors, lawyers, technicians, a rugby team newspaper, choir, hospital, engineers, under-takers, accountants, lorry drivers, base perimeter security, road builders, rescue boat operators, and much more were being wound down and repatriated. Often the relatives of those who perished and went missing are still alive to connect with using online tools, to honor the missing and share their fates with family.

The military also left airfields intact to better enable post-war tourism and the ongoing rediscovery of their comrades. Dozens of World War II sites, docks, facilities, buildings, hospitals, hotels, (and graves) are visible today. While almost all evidence of the 113 German and Italian submarine patrols and attacks on 130 merchant ships were in prohibitively deep water and thus economically undiscoverable, the salient and extraordinary aspect of aviation research is how relatively easy it proved to be for small teams of well-prepared volunteers to work with those on the ground to rediscover the wreckage of so many planes so quickly.

The following pages describe how volunteers found a dozen or so important artifacts of aviation history right beneath our eyes and our feet, often with help from those who rescued them or the family of those who crashed. It is becoming clear that the metal remnants may outlive those who built, delivered, flew, crashed, and salvaged them.

Hand-over of a Martin 187 Baltimore medium bomber from USAAF to RAFTC at Windsor Field, in March 1945, from the British Air Ministry and RAFTC.

B-24 Liberator BZ811 MB and mostly Czech trainees in Crew 30 and Crew 31 on Course 40 (O.T.U. 111) returning safely from a training sortie at Oakes Field between November 1944 and March, 1945. Above the head of the crew at left, outside the engine under the wing is the Leigh Light to stun U-boat gunners at night. Sadly, roughly two months later, on June 2, 1945 this aircraft was lost 8 miles north of Cabbage Beach, Paradise (Hog) Island. Crash boats found and towed a dinghy and wreckage, but had to give up and hand it to the US Navy, who were forced to sink it. Pilot George Robert Allbut and seven other men were all killed, their remains never found. It would appear from Czech records that none of the men in this photo were killed in the aircraft later; rather had been rotated to the front. FCAFA.com, Czechoslovak RAF Airmen in the Caribbean.

Windsor Field with Lake Killarney and Lake Cunningham shows how close Delaporte Point is in the center-left coastal of this image, the peninsula.

Czech aviators confer at Windsor Field as part of 311 Squadron training at No. 111 O.T.U., beneath B-25 Mitchells FF and FK on New Providence during the war. Neither aircraf are believed to have crashed while in Bahamas. From the Jaroslav Popelka collection, fcafa.com

Chapter One:

Wives & Bases

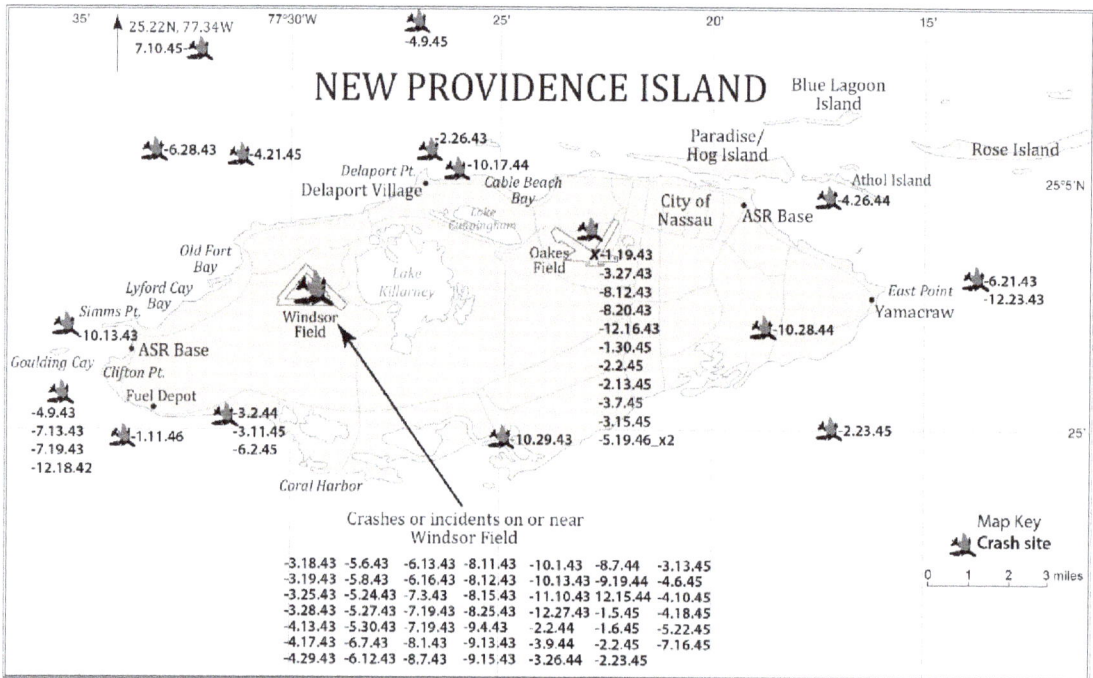

NEW PROVIDENCE ISLAND

Crashes or incidents on or near Windsor Field

Map Key — Crash site

Sylvia Mary Moverley of Argentina and London, Patricia Jana Ashley of Brampton, Ontario, Canada and Jean Isobel Hayes of Preston, Ontario, were living in Nassau with their husbands who were aviators with the Royal Air Force. Their anxieties were realized when nine men perished in a single collision and another husband was taken by a training accident. Cyril Somerville, Allan Hayes, and Deryk Cribbes have never left The Bahamas. Instead of greeting them outside the airfield, their wives interred their remains into the new RAF, or War Cemetery.

The buildup of New Providence into the hub of all South Atlantic air deliveries to the Allies in Africa, the Mediterranean, Middle East, and Far East was not only sudden, it was controversial, and led to deadly riots on Bay Street. As a result, very few people realize that the present-day national air hub was built as Windsor Field for the RAF Ferry Command, the RAF and US Transport Command, the No. 113 Transport Wing, and to also support USAAF. Even fewer were aware that roughly a third of New Providence's population was RAF employed. They took over the Montague and Royal Victoria Hotels, recreated at the Emerald Beach Hotel, sequestered the Bahamian Club, chartered every vehicle the islanders could spare, and built and staffed their own hospitals, barracks, churches, ports, sentry lines, boat basins and fuel depots.

The sailors and soldiers were shot in fights, lost arms to passing lorries, drowned in diving and sailing accidents, and were arrested and imprisoned for the crime of going to the less-prosperous, perhaps more-permissive area known over the hill, and crossing the color bar by fraternizing with Bahamians of color. Usually, dancing was sufficient evidence of this 'crime,' though the targeted behaviors often involved women. They stopped all flying each year on the day of the riots and manned the perimeter in the event of another flare-up; on that day, the supply chain delivering airpower to the front stopped. They had newspapers, rugby teams, bands, orderlies, servants, cooks, butchers, drivers, signalmen, censors, nurses and nuns, padres, journalists and all manner of mechanics, engineers, electricians and tradesmen.

The RAF instructors trained over 7,000 students for the front: pilots and navigators, copilots, and radio operators moved over 9,000 aircraft to Africa. Or that is what they set out to do, at least. Nassau probably hadn't been so saturated with people since the Prohibition, only for a much more serious and deadly reason. It was so difficult to secure experienced pilots that not only civilian airmen from all over (mainly the US and Canada) were brought in, but planes owned by Eastern Airlines and Pan American were put to use for the military.

The men even had Soldier Road laid out for them, with curves often enough that they didn't despair of their long marches into Nassau and back for royal occasions, parades, the funeral of the governor's brother, or to bury comrades. Some of the men were able to go home to their spouses. Most of them were young, from afar, and had recently been wed. Pilot Cyril Somerville's church historian recalls, he "was born in St. Thomas in 1922 and was in his 21st year. He received his earlier education in London and Guelph, and finished his upper-school courses at Brampton High School. He graduated from the Electronics Institute, Toronto, in 1941 and in August of the same year he joined the Merchant Marine as Wireless Operator. Cyril …was married six weeks prior to Patricia Jana Ashley, the ceremony being performed at Grace United Church, and they returned to Nassau to take up residence there.

Cyril stood 5 foot, 10 inches and had a medium complexion with black hair and hazel eyes. A Border Crossing notice shows that he went to the US via the Detroit and

Canada Tunnel and came to Detroit on September 5, 1942. He was being transferred to the RAFTC and was carrying $50 in his pocket. ... in June 1942, he was part of the No. 45 Atlantic Transport Group flying the South Atlantic route to Africa." On May 30, 1942, a Martin 187 Baltimore took off from the Operational Training Unit at Oakes Field with three men aboard for a training mission. For the recruits and trainees to recognize the plane, it had FA227 painted on its tail and fuselage. The twin-engine light attack bomber was 48' 6" long with a 61' 4" wingspan and was powered by two radial engines of 1,700 horsepower and it even tucked machine guns into a powered dorsal turret. It could achieve 305 mph and fly up to 980 miles. On its final day, it didn't fly anywhere close to that distance.

The pilot was Henri Chouteau, from a family considered aristocracy in St. Louis, due to a 1747 French land grant. Test observer J. P. Lynes, by contrast, had his name misconstrued as 'Lyons' even on the national death registry. That is because at 2:31 p.m. that day, their airplane "crashed on fire 2.5 miles southeast of Satellite Aerodrome, Nassau... It took off in a tail-down position, and it is presumed that it stalled and spun inwards." Somewhere between Oakes and Windsor, their plane lost an engine and slammed at high speed into the bush, then burst into flames. The airfield ambulances and fire trucks were not able to save them. The site of their deaths has probably not been disturbed since. Often anything with intelligence value was salvaged, though in this case, probably not much remained of the plane.

Cyril's wife, Patricia would have learned almost instantly; would have heard the siren and sensed the muted terror that such a crash can spread. Her in-laws were Ewart and Dorothy Somerville, of Sudbury. The next day, at 2:50 p.m., marked "extra rush," a telegram arrived in Canada which read: "Your son, Radio Officer Cyril Somerville was fatally injured as the result of an air plane accident yesterday. Further details will be sent... please accept my profound sympathy, Air Officer Commanding, No. 45 Atlantic RAF." These first personnel to perish in a war wreck in The Bahamas were buried in what is now the National War Cemetery, consecrated on October 3, 1943.

The gruesome reality of what happened is inescapable in the coroner's report in the register for Western District that day. After describing Cyril as a 20-year-old male of European descent, he wrote that all the men died of "multiple severe injuries and severe burns as a result of aircraft accident." At 7 p.m. on the day after the crash, the base log recorded that "a full-service funeral was given. Dean [Sheffield] of Nassau conducted the service for C. J. Somerville and the Rev. Father Hagarty, R. C. Father for

H. Chouteau and J. P. Lynes. The commanding officer represented the A.C.C. Mrs. Somerville, wife of C. J. Somerville, was at the funeral." The epitaph which Patricia and his family chose for Cyril was: *There is a link which death cannot sever, love and remembrance last forever.*"

Joseph Paul Lynes was just 19, and his parents, Joseph and Lillian received the telegram in Hampstead, Quebec. Chouteau, age 25, is the only American of 51 servicemen buried there; his parents were Henri and Jane Bagnell Chouteau. Henri left behind two brothers, Rene and Pierre, and a sister, Mrs. Marie Yocum. Jane Lloyd, last president of the Imperial Order of the Daughters of Empire, or IODE, in The Bahamas, says that the Chouteau family have been lively and engaged correspondents regarding Henri over several decades. This crash represented the first on-field fatalities out of many, though it would be seven months until the next. By then there were enough crashes that the trowel used to form the masonry was made of melted aircraft.

Under the headline *Married only Six Weeks Ago to Brampton Girl*, a local news clipping read "Brampton was grieved to learn of the untimely death of Cyril... Mrs. Somerville arrived in Brampton last night. Cyril was a devout member of Grace United Church, and took a great interest in the activities of young people. Besides his wife and his parents, there are left to mourn his loss, a brother, Norman, and sister, Donna, both at home." The article notes that Mrs. Somerville arrived from Nassau less than a week after losing her husband and less than two months after marrying him. She confirmed that the funeral was held "with full military honors" with the dean officiating. The three men were buried with white wooden crosses at first, and now have marble engraved headstones. Cyril is buried beside the two men he died alongside in the plane that day, in East Plot, Row B, grave 7, still tended by volunteers.

Sylvia Mary Moverley married Deryk Cribbes on May 1, 1943, at Clapham Village Church, near Bedford, England. She was born in Lomas de Zamora, Buenos Aires, in 1920. Sylvia and Deryk moved together from Argentina to the UK and Canada for his training and her RAF work, and their ultimate home was in New Providence. Deryk enrolled in the RAFVR as an Argentinean; in fact, his niece still has his uniforms. His parents were George John Cribbes Burnet and Sylvia Aida Jefferies. He and his younger brother Harold seemed to have an enjoyable childhood in their home named Isca, alternating on teams of cricket and tennis, dressing smartly and carrying themselves with confident ease and aplomb.

Sylvia and Deryk's families were both active in the British Community Council (BCC) of Argentina whose *Bulletin* newspaper featured updates about him. In numerous photos of Deryk with his peers, he appears consistently most comfortable in smaller groups, whereas, when surrounded by avuncular barrack-mates, he takes on a more reticent, almost bemused, if not shy, look. He appears to have been a thoughtful person, and was the happiest in Sylvia's company.

On the same island, while she was seeing her man off to a training flight near the close of the war in Europe, there was a performance by a former music sensation from Kitchener, Ontario. Jean Isobel (*nee* Germann) Hayes was "a well-known soprano of this city whom [Allan Hayes] married while home on leave last August. [She] has been in the Bahamas with him." Allan (Al) dabbled in music composition and performance as well.

On Friday, February 23, 1945, Al was flight instructor on a B-24V, tail number LM, with a total crew of nine. They took off from Windsor Field at 8:38 a.m. to perform the local exercise known as "Number 4," in which they would fly in tandem, or dually in pairs, with another aircraft, known by the tail number LA. In the exercise, E. W. Hutchins, and C. Cribbes were the first and second pilots respectively; L. A. Birkett and A. E. Tomlinson were the navigators. Sergeant Birch was aboard with Sergeant Holland as flight engineer, and sergeants Jackson and Richards were air gunners. Ten minutes later, the aircraft collided with one another as they both entered the downwind leg of a circuit around the field. Hayes' aircraft LM plummeted out of control and hit the earth south of Windsor Field aerodrome where it caught fire on the ground. There were no survivors. The LA aircraft managed to land on its belly with one injury. Aviation historian Chris Charland sums up the events thus:

"The crew was in the circuit when for some unknown reason [Hayes' aircraft, BZ746] overtook and then collided with Liberator FL994, which landed safely. Since Allan was a young [age 22] pilot instructor and the overtaking maneuver appears to have been considered by some experts as a proximate or contributory cause of the accident. For Jean and other family [members], the many deaths must have compounded the misery of losing a loved one. Then again, it was just as likely that a trainee was at the helm; we will never know."

Al's parents were Cyril and Frances, of Preston, Ontario. The base diary records, somewhat drily, that the month's casualties included "one officer on the strength of the Permanent Staff (Instructor)," meaning Hayes, was said to have "died as the result of a flying accident." The nine men that made up the aircrew of BZ746 are described by the coroner as all having suffered "multiple injuries [as a] result of aircraft accident." The men's remains would no doubt have been kept out of sight from their wives.

Hayes was classified as a Commonwealth war casualty. His epitaph reads, "*They shall mount up with wings as eagles; they shall run, and not be weary*" at the War Cemetery, West D. 7, close to the graves of the men he died with that day. On her returning to Montreal Jean was met by her sister and Allan's parents. She managed to muster her inner strength: "With remarkable support from sister Louise, she returned home to continue a professional singing career, most notably on the Dominion Network in *Singing Stars of Tomorrow*, and Good Year's *Parade of Stars*."

In 1946, she was the concert soloist at the Banff Springs Hotel and the Chateau Lake Louise, where she married another musician; "her future husband and lifelong accompanist, Dr. Harold Robinson, who was also an accomplished pianist." They remained married for 67 years until Jean was widowed a second time, less than a year before her death at age 94 in 2015 in Surrey, British Columbia.

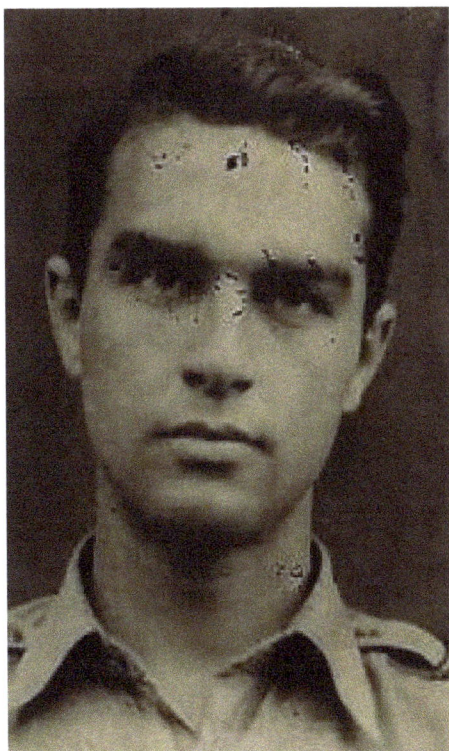

Cyril Somerville

G. Deryk Cribbes

Henri Chouteau

Deryk and Sylvia on the beaches of Argentina.

Newlyweds Deryk and Sylvia Cribbes in Buenos Aires, where they grew up.

Sylvia served in the RAF in the UK as well.

Rare after-accident photographs taken on 23 February 1945 of crash-landed B-24 Liberator III FL884 on Windsor Field following a fatal collsion with GR.V BZ746 in which Alan Hayes and eight others including Deryk Cribbes perished.
Aircrewremembered.com

Wreck of B-24 Liberator FL884 on Windsor Field following a fatal collsion with GR.V BZ746 at Windsor Field when taking off. This aircraft and its crew suvived.
Aircrewremembered.com

The funeral for nine men concurrently was the largest since six Czech and one British aviator crashed and all perished six months earlier. The left of this images shows three young women, one appearing to comfort the other in the middle, during the carrying of caskets into the cemetery. Two of these women were likely Sylvia Mary Moverley and Jean Isobel Hayes, having been widowed the day before.

Left: Jean Isobel Germann Hayes (later Robinson) was born in Waterloo, Ontario, and was always an avid musician. "She grew up in a household full of music; Jean and sister Louise inherited their father's wonderful musicality. She married her high school sweetheart, Allan Hayes in 1944 and moved to Nassau where he was based...." Right: Her husband Allan Hayes, from Aircrewremembered.com, Operation Picture Me.

Chapter Two:

New Providence; Sixty Land Accidents

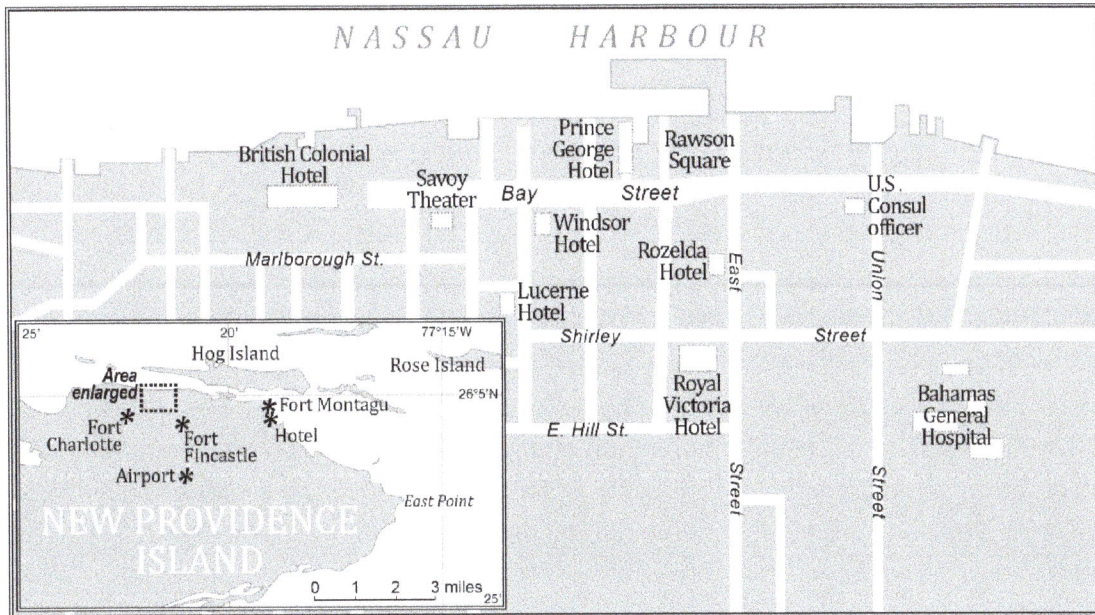

Nassau, New Providence, in World War II. Oakes Field is just south of the hospital.

Out of over sixty accidents on land in New Providence, over 15 were fatal, in which over 50 persons, including a young family asleep at home in Delaporte Village, perished. Most of them were around the training base at Oakes Field and the transport wing base at Windsor Field, with others crashing into Yamacraw Hill, near Soldier Road and Fox Hill Road, and Lake Killarney. The causes included aircraft collisions, abandoned planes crashing into a residence, takeoff and landing mishaps, and equipment failure. The remnants of many of these crashes still litter the bush as well as populated areas of New Providence. The remains of most of those killed are interred at the War Cemetery, which volunteers have maintained since.

Whether planes touched wingtips, men walked into propellers, bombers collided, planes were lost in microbursts, or had training gunnery mishaps; the brush, air fields, and adjacent waters claimed many lives during World War II. More than half of all accidents in the colony—80 of 150—took place on and around the capital island. Fifty-five of them ended up on land. In the three years from January 1943, 131 aviators and a Bahamian family of three were killed. Eighty-three were successfully rescued . Oakes Field was the site of an estimated 30 mishaps or crashes, and Windsor Field was the site of 21 accidents.

Some accidents resulted from blown tires, heavy bounces, uncontrolled loop-arounds, mid-air collisions, and machine guns accidentally shooting at aircraft. Sixteen of the planes burnt out, one hit the control tower, and 40 were at least partially salvaged and removed at the time. Photos show masses of gnarled metal from collisions and crashes in the pine barrens just off the fields. Aside from RAF aircraft including B-25, B-24, B-26, A-20, A-30, B-18, C-47, Mosquitos, damaged on New Providence, other aircraft were mostly in transit to the south for the USAAF. Some aircraft were seen by the tower and residents crashing into Yamacraw Hill, Soldier Road, Fox Hill Road, and Lake Killarney.

Exactly five weeks after she was married to Charles Bullard, a laborer aged 24, Louise Marguerite Newbold, a 19-year-old seamstress, tucked in their newborn infant, Philip, and went to bed in Delaporte Village. Hours later, at 3:36 a.m. on Friday, February 26, 1943, a 68' wide, 53' long, and 16' tall B-25 Mitchell bomber which had recently been abandoned by its crew of three British aviators in parachutes, hurtled into their dwelling at over 200 miles per hour. The coroner's report described how the child's skull was fractured, his mother Louise died of asphyxia, and the child's father Charles died of "fractured ribs and internal hemorrhage result of RAF airplane crash at Delaporte." Amazingly, Louise's uncle managed to escape the inferno alive.

Thes 60 accidents were spread over 40 months; more than half—37 in 1943 alone, six in 1944, and 15 in 1945, the last being an unknown lorry driver who struck an aircraft meant to carry VIPs to Canada. The primary causes were damages to undercarriages due to faulty landings or takeoffs, with aircraft salvaged, or catastrophic pilot error or equipment failure resulting in nose-dive crashes into the bush from which no one survived.

Among the fatalities, Ian Simpson Glen was thrown through his cockpit cover, and Daiken and Zdan were trapped in a burning B-25. Houlding, Downey, and Anderson survived over-shooting the runway in an A-30, while their colleagues Harris, Anderson, and Thompson hit earth when the plane veered uncontrollably after takeoff. Likewise, Parson, Gedye, and Hunt had dangerous undercarriage failures yet jettisoned the tanks and survived a belly landing. Amazingly, B. L. Dawson was under an aircraft when the crew dropped the Dakota airplane on top of him, yet he survived. In one case, a plane lost its entire tail and wheel assembly whilst testing fuel consumption. Tragically, John Francis Hole and Edred Day were both killed while repairing an aircraft at night—the eruption of a carburetor fire drove them instinctively backwards but into an active propeller.

August 7, 1943, witnessed one of the greatest losses of life in a single day when a B-25 piloted by Free Czech airmen crashed and burned two miles east of Windsor, at Soldier Road area, after reaching 1,000 feet of altitude. Two minutes into the flight, the nose rose sharply and it then nose-dived, burst into flames, and crashed to earth within sight of the airfield hangars. Lost were Briza, Hadravek, Mares, Salz, Turna, and Satola. Another pilot, J. H. West, landed without deploying wheels and Learmont, Cunliffe, and Aitken in an A-30 over-ran the runway without a port engine.

Three men survived the initial airfield crash of a B-25 on September 13, 1943, that took off from Oakes Field, when the aircraft swung wildly, crashed into trees, and burst into fire. The aircraft was destroyed and Rafuse was taken alive to RAF hospital where he died at 4:30 p.m. Days later, his copilot mistook the signal from his captain and raised the undercarriage at takeoff, causing the engine of the B-26 Marauder to burn out. Ross, Merckercher and Fisher must have remained in Nassau a few days following a B-24 Liberator which lost its brakes and nose wheel, veered off the runway with the pump not activated, and was damaged beyond repair.

Pilots Grant and Pynn suffered ignominy after landing at Windsor and taxiing the aircraft when the copilot accidentally raised the landing gear, buckling the lower frames and port propellers. They were more fortunate than Bartlett, Carberry, Foreman, Lewis, Woodeson, and Bentick. Those men perished when their B-25 lost height after a bombing run and flew into trees at Yamacraw Hill, with smoke seen by civilians. Other planes observed and reported that an aircraft was on fire in swampy bush and disintegrated, yet they had difficulty identifying the aircraft type. The base reported that "ambulance and fire tender were sent and found it was the B-25, which had commenced bombing practice but banked steeply, crashed, and only after hitting the earth caught fire."

Just before V-E Day on April 10, 1945, a pilot named Creed found that the nose-wheel was jammed and would not extend on landing, thereby damaging the front of the plane. As an incubator for pilots who left The Bahamas directly for the front lines against German and Japanese aces, it was part of the tragic math that aircraft and pilots, and sometimes both at the same time, might fail.

B-25's lined up for training at the O.T.U. 111 at Oakes, or Main Field, Nassau, in World War II, from the Australian War Museum.

Senior administrative officers of the RAFTC Base at Windsor Field.

A young person looks out from their home in Delaporte Village in the 1940s (Sands)

Yellow: FK176 killed the Bullard family in Delaport (ages 1, 19, 24), 25/26 Feb. 1943

Where the abandoned RAF aircraft slammed into the Bullard home in Delaporte, killing all except an uncle.

DELAPORTE, BAHAMAS

Photo by Sands

Delaporte, as it looked in the 1940s (photo by Sands).

Oakes Field during World War II; planes lined up on the tarmac.
VintageBahamas.com, Iain Crump, 2020.

The only Bahamian WWII air crash from which contemporary photographs remain.

From expert Bob Livingstone, an Australian pilot whose father served on B-24's in Bahamas: "It appears to be a wooded area, just back from the water, which suggests to me a takeoff accident from Runway 32. Furthermore, most accident's locations are found in the splay areas from the upwind threshold—left or right depending on circumstances. If the B-25 lost an engine immediately after takeoff it would tend to skid off whole plane towards that engine...." Aircrewremembered.com

Chapter Three:

New Providence; Twenty Sea Accidents

New Providence saw over twenty World War II aircraft crash and explode into its adjacent waters. Most of these were to the south, east, and north of the island, depending on the direction of the winds, which airfield was used, complexity of the night-time exercises using extremely bright Leigh Lights, and flight formation. Mechanical failures from aircraft freshly delivered from American factories played a role as well. Seventy-nine persons were killed in the waters, with five known survivors. The majority of water-borne accidents involved Royal Air Force training and transport bombers, like the B-25 Mitchells, B-24 Liberators, B-26 Marauders, and A-20 or A-30 Baltimore's. Five were operated by the US Army Air Force—one was consumed by a microburst on final approach to Windsor. Five airplanes were amphibious: PBY Catalina, Grumman Goose, PBM Mariner, and a Kingfisher. Seven were with the USN, particularly at the Nassau Harbour ramp, which became Pan Am and is now the RBDF and BASRA base downtown.

Six of the aircraft crashed to the west in Lake Killarney, Clifton Bay, or Delaporte Bay. Ten of them either got wrecked near, or had pieces drift up in Montague Bay, Eastern Foreshore, and Athol Island. Three sank to the north so deeply as to be economically unsalvageable, and the others crashed south of the capital island between Yamacraw and Green Cay. Nine, or about half, of the accidents occurred in 1943, while the others were split between 1944 and 1945. Survivors include Baxter and David, whose seaplane hit the hangar at the harbor ramp, followed by Robert Allen of the USAAF who swam away from a plane which he was forced to ditch on delivery on March 2, 1944. On June 21 of that year, James McLean, John Tickler, and John Vallance went missing when their RAF B-25 was lost 10 miles east of Nassau.

Then, the following week, more staggering losses of life occurred when another B-25 bomber took off for training at 2:45 p.m. Radio communications were lost at 3:15 p.m. and later, rescuers found an empty dinghy and oleo leg just 3.5 miles north-northwest of Old Fort Bay. No trace of survivors was found, and Beaulieu, Keayes, Ogren, Smart, Stinson, Torrens, and Wallace were all lost. On the 9th of April, 1943, an aircraft ditched at sea, crashed 15 miles southwest of Clifton Bay. A yellow-orange light was found by Lyford Air Sea Rescue. A Windsor Field aircraft on exercise sighted a dinghy which, when retrieved by the surface craft, was found to be empty and damaged. Twelve days later, an ASR boat found an empty aircraft dinghy. No trace of the men was found. Schafer, Waton, Goodman, Fenton, Farnsworth, Tomkins, and Burchell are still missing and presumed dead.

More troubling and unresolved is a case of a B-24 on October 29, 1943, which went missing between Florida and Puerto Rico. Though a life raft signal was seen, it was not confirmed. Amongst the aircraft wreckage, a tobacco pouch and a shattered airplane piece were found; mysteriously, at about the same time, four explosions were heard northeast of Green Cay. The December 23, 1943 crash, which claimed the lives of Frye, McLean, Wilcox, Petersen, Swire and Craig, was both tragic and frustrating, with the RAF crash boats noting that it ditched in the sea 6.5 miles from the New Providence airfield. The plane was discovered three weeks later, in just 10 feet of water riddled with strong tides. There was no trace of the crew. A resident on Athol Island confirmed the crash, and showed them parts of the disintegrated fuselage.

Later, on November 24, 1944, two bombers practicing the blinding Leigh Lights against German U-Boats, collided with each other in a dive—they essentially followed the light beams into the sea. This tragic error cost the lives of John Scammell, George Gamble, and David Strachan. Gamble was highly decorated, having sunk the German submarine U-964 the year before. On the other aircraft involved, tail number BM, Captain Allbut with seven other trainees crashed deep into the ocean about 3.5 miles north of Cabbage Beach, Paradise Beach.

Several other planes were ordered airborne to search for and locate wreckage. Then ASR launched HMS *P-89* and HMS *P-181* to the scene, and men on those vessels found a dinghy matched to the wreck. They tried to tow a portion of the fuselage three miles or so to shore, yet were unable to do so. Prior to departing the wreck site, the ASR officers requested that a USN vessel destroy the remainder of the fuselage so as to avoid a hazard to navigation. No bodies were recovered.

Though without casualties, a PBY Mariner broke free of its mooring in a storm and had to be corralled back to base by boat on December 11, 1944. On April 9, 1945, Acton, Dumble, Hallett, Hutchinson, Moule, Scott, and Wild were killed when their B-25 ditched in a trail of smoke and crashed to the sea south of East Point. RAF ASR boat HMS *P-2779* from Montague and the plane B-25 FY, airborne at 8:30 p.m., were sent to search for the wreckage. Two parachutes were found and later identified as those issued to the crew of the missing aircraft.

Similarly, on April 21, a B-25 with Beyon, Hamlin, Hanney, Lunam, McLean, and Smith crashed into the sea while performing exercises five miles north of New Providence. ASR boats HMS *P-170* and HMS *P-191* found an oil patch and an airplane dinghy which helped them trace the oil to the plane with the same tail number, however they were unable to find survivors. On July 10, 1945, a USN PBM-3 was lost with a crew of 12 when on a flight to Exuma over Nassau. They flew from Florida to Windsor *en route* Exuma, but were overwhelmed by a severe storm 10 miles north of the island and were last reported eight miles north of Cabbage Beach. The official summary simply concluded that the aircraft and all the men in it "flew into a severe storm in that area, and… went missing."

Overall, the waters around New Providence have everything researchers would want; the busiest airport in the country, the most SCUBA infrastructure, and fairly shallow waters, primarily to the south and east. In fact, two B-26 bombers have been found in these waters in less than a year; one has been salvaged post-war from Lake Killarney, and no doubt, more discoveries will follow. Also, the graves where the men were buried and dozens of sites relevant to WWII are still there.

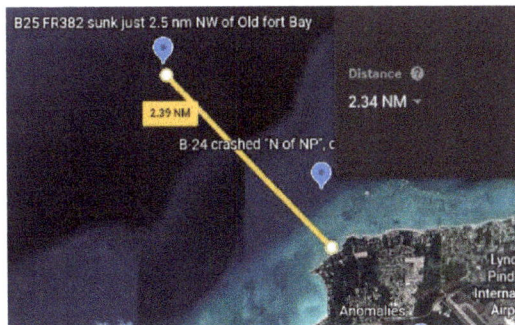

Part of the grim calculus of diving from official reports, and parts found drifting, where men died.

Soldiers marching down Soldier Road from the barracks to the town to the RAF Cemetery. Note the black arm bands on the arms of the officers; they are either going to or coming back from a funeral.

Oakes Field under construction during the war, with two Martin 187 Baltimore planes in the near-distance, to the left.

The B-24 Liberator KH252NH, which appears to have survived its duties in the Bahamas. For persons seeking clues of such an aircraf in items found, the number or propellers, engines, type of nose, and side-locking wheels (open at one end) are all distinctive features. Note also the plexiglass nose, often with machine guns, and a hatch atop the cockpit. The most durable parts seem to be the wheel struts (oleos) and the heaviest and therefore the least likely to be moved by hurricanes – the engines. From the Jaroslav Popelka collection, fcafa.com

Chapter Four:

Marley Resort, Delaporte, B-26 Marauder

On October 17, 1944, five years into World War II, a B-26 Marauder aircraft assigned to the RAFTC took off from the Windsor Field. Two young Canadians were training at takeoffs and landings and were on their seventh such touch-and-go when their starboard engine caught fire. The pilots, Jack Wood of Toronto and Maurice O'Neill of Halifax, struggled to cross Prospect Ridge for three minutes. One of only two engines, the starboard one, caught fire and lost power causing the pilots to feather it or crash the plane at low altitude. With eight propellers, that was a dicey operation at best. The pilots banked left from Windsor Field heading northeast, crossed Lake Killarney and Lake Cunningham, and struggled to cross Skyline Heights.

The young men's takeoff at 10:21 a.m. and death were separated by only a few precious, terrifying minutes. Clearing the last ridge by a hair, they roared over what is now Super Value at over 100 mph, with the starboard engine useless, smoking, and possibly the four large propeller blades un-feathered. A pilot said "loss of an engine on takeoff is the most critical thing in flying, and if you can't get the prop on the failed engine feathered quickly, the drag will stall you, and in you go."

The aircraft skimmed over the roof of the present-day Marley Resort, at the time the home of realtor Frank Christie, and crashed in shallow waters just 400 yards off the coast, in sight of both a nurse and doctor. On a calm day they would likely have survived, but a building hurricane made for a large chop which caused the plane to disintegrate. When the plane tried to belly-land on smooth seas, instead it hit sizeable cross-seas on the starboard side. This caused the bomber to dig the wing in the seas, and had a catastrophic, wrenching crash which would have killed both men instantly. Since then, we have found the seat they were in, the seat belt buckle, instrument dials, and the escape hatch above the pilot's seat that Wood and O'Neill must have struggled to open as they perished in the murky waves.

Dr. H. A. Quackenbush was at Aquamarine, then occupied by a Nepalese prince. A military nurse named D. A. Rodwell lived along Cable Beach in one of the last homes to the west at the time, and described what she saw:

"I was in the lounge of my house on Cable Beach, when an aircraft flying very low passed overhead out to sea. I dashed out onto the beach. It was losing altitude and obviously could not pull out, and within 1 to 2 seconds hit the water, not in a nose dive, but at such an angle to cut the waves… After the crash, when the initial wave of water had subsided, two objects were visible on top of the starboard wing, but they could not be identified. The [plane's] dinghy appeared on the left, but no effort was made to occupy it."

Though fishermen from Delaporte were seen, oxygen bottles and a life raft floated free, and an RAF rescue boat made it from Montague Bay to Cable Beach and saw the plane under the sea, no trace of either Jack Wood or Maurice O'Neill have ever been found. Nurse Rodwell said she thought she saw men scrambling along one of the wings, but could not be sure. The seat and hatch were recovered 78 years later, along with a surveillance camera. Fishermen from nearby Delaporte village were seen over the wreck, but nothing was recovered. Three weeks later, navy divers went to the crash site and reported "no traces of bodies—aircraft completely wrecked and now disintegrated."

The B-26 was known as a Flying Prostitute because of its graceful lines yet small wing area, giving it no visible means of support, and was a handful on one engine. One historian shared that "Among those who hated the airplane were the crews of the Air Transport Command's Ferrying Division who picked the Marauders up at the factory and delivered them to combat units. Those who loved it included Lt. Gen. James H. 'Jimmy' Doolittle, who used a B-26 Marauder as his personal airplane, and most of the pilots and crew members who flew the airplane in combat."

I felt it a duty to find this wreck. And the niece of Pilot Jack Wood told me to be safe and smart, not to end up dead as well. My godson was working in a SCUBA company and I had planned to give him this location to dive, but he passed away in June 2021, and I was determined to find it for his memory. In November 2021, as our mother fought for the last weeks of her life, I found it. The moment that I knew I'd found the aircraft with two men entombed with the distinctive military four-bladed engine on the seafloor, with cowlings, radio, seats, and unopened bottle, I logged the day thus:

"Swim Day Six: heavy round steel or iron objects, with an aluminum find or skeg of some type, pieces of aluminum, chair seat (actually escape hatch) found but left, as was the engine with four propellers—found twice never logged, never photographed)."

RAF Transport Wing No. 113's war diary relates: "crashed into sea 500 yards off north shore… aircraft entirely submerged; no survivors recovered from aircraft."

It lay wrecked in just 12 feet of water. Jack Wood was 28 years old, 5' 9" and of medium build, with grey eyes, brown hair, and a mustache. His wife was Grace Edwina Ruth and parents, Walter and Elsie, were both born in Putney and Yorkshire, in the UK. Jack's niece shared that he was an assistant dress buyer for Robert Simpson Eastern. From 1932-33 he was a Cadet in Hamilton, Ontario. He played rugby, swam, and did track and field.

Jack Wood had many items to list, from socks to batteries, shorts, kid gloves, shoulder straps, films, pocket knife, shoe trees, fountain pens, torch, hair brush, letters and papers, overshoes, white towel, chamois vest, blue tunic, gaberdine windbreaker, pipe, pilot's brevet, propelling pencils, cribbage board, leather writing folder, leather cigarette case, book *'Life with Father'*, packet of golf tees, book of four photographs... swimming trunks...". I think of his poor dad, Walter, and as a father, how moved he must have been to learn his son's last reading was a book named *Life with Father*. Jack's niece, Joanne Green, said her mother was crushed to have lost her brother, and that she, too, wishes she knew her charismatic Uncle Jack.

Copilot Maurice Francis O'Neill was 27 years old and unmarried; his parents were Francis Maurice and Rose O'Neill. He attended St. Mary's University, Halifax, and his kid brother, Neville J., was also in the service. Maurice was a retail clerk whose father was from Ketch Harbour, Nova Scotia and owned a stationery business. Maurice joined the 1st Artillery Battery as a gunner. They enlisted and trained in very close proximity to one another and are remembered in the Ottawa Memorial, though neither appears in the Bahamian cathedral or cemetery lists. They are in the War Cemetery among the names, and a piece of the plane and poppy were laid at their memorial on the anniversary of the day when they died suddenly together.

Inventoried after his death, Maurice O'Neill's personal effects included: "blue side bag, key, hat, religious pendant, small notebook, lot of papers, socks, handkerchiefs, swimming trunks, playing cards, padlocks, pencil refills, prayer beads, filigree silver cigarette case, 6 foreign coins in an envelope, diary, perfume, bracelet, money belt, leopard skin ladies' handbag, leather bag fancy, book, radio replies, foreign notes, prayer book, brushes, broken torch, razor, scissors... mirror. "

Just over a month after the fatal crash, Reverend Flint joined Wing Commander Blaskett, DFC, Commanding Officer, and six other RAF VIPs aboard an air search and rescue vessel to perform a solemn wreath-laying ceremony with photographs and flowers on the sea above the site. After the war, the B-26 bombers used to bomb

Japanese targets and incapacitate Axis Europe's munitions strength were themselves destroyed and dismantled to rebuild Germany; 2,000 were scrapped.

Each site yields its own unique and unexpected stories. On Veterans Day 2021, I found an unopened bottle of scotch for sale to Ascension, along with a junction box. Later I found the plane camera (did they film their crash?), the escape hatch, their seat, panel dial, and bomb rack. But why was the bottle still sealed? The answer lay far away, on an island in the middle of the South Atlantic. A man was waiting on the desolate airstrip for the Bahamas bombers with a pouch full of cash. He was the club manager responsible for selling hundreds of servicemen liquor on a barren windswept pinnacle. Captain Henry Flory, who delivered B-24s from the US via Bahamas to West Africa, always stopped on Ascension Island. During World War II there was an important air base there, on what was then a Dependency of St. Helena about 1,000 miles from Africa and 1,400 miles from Brazil. These terrestrial aircraft carriers were known as "stone frigates," as though they were in the Royal Navy and the men on them could grow to feel desperately isolated manning what was nicknamed *WideAwake Airfield*, like its Icelandic counterpart, *Camp Kwitchyerbitchen*.

Captain Flory and his colleagues confirm that on first arriving on Ascension they were offered "any price at all" for bottles of whiskey. Pretty soon, more than a dozen cases of booze were being stowed in the nose, nacelles, and where the main landing gear and gunner nests were. Pilot 'Red' Syrett says that from mid-1943 "we kept the Officer's Club in Ascension Island [stocked] in booze that we purchased duty-free in Nassau and… were heartily greeted by the base entertainment officer and his cheque book… We were popular." Flory confirmed that they "collected ample loose cash to lose in the numerous poker games…".

"Each time we flew a Liberator from Nassau to Miami to take on a load… the plane was completely empty except for whiskey loaded right up in the nose. This put us completely out of balance so that pilots would have to send the rest of the crew back to the toilet. Otherwise, the plane would keep trying to dive into the ground." Does this help explain at least one of the hundreds of aircraft accidents which befell planes taking off for Trinidad, Guyana, Brazil, and points to the south? We may never know. We do know that this aircraft, at the time of the crash, was only doing training and not transport. Yet we also know that on the site of this crash there were many bottles, and one of them was Scots whiskey readily available in Nassau and it was unopened.

Although this might give rise to a supposition that the bottle was being carried aboard the B-26 Marauder destined for Ascension, it was clearly the flame-out in the starboard engine after numerous takeoffs which brought down the plane, and not being unbalanced. Out of 45 artifacts found, preserved, and given to the AMMC at the end of 2021, at least eight of them were bottles, many from 200–400 years ago.

The day I found the bottle, I excitedly wrote to two helpful volunteer colleagues, Denis Galipeau and Henrik Gedde Moos, to say "I found an intact cork in the Bloch, Glasgow Ambassador-brand whiskey bottle. I personally believe, though it's impossible to tell, that the men brought this whiskey for the long trip to Africa and Europe and back. How it survived the crash I have no idea, but who would possibly throw a full sealed whiskey bottle in the sea 75 years ago otherwise? One thing is for sure: Bahamians are not known to habitually throw full bottles of liquor into the ocean."

If anyone deserved a swig of that whiskey it was Maurice and Jack, their lives cut short navigating that plane over nurse Rodwell and Dr. Quackenbush's heads to avoid the calamity which befell the Bullard family, all of them killed in Delaporte nearby when three members of the crew from a B-25 Mitchell bomber bailed out during night exercises only to have the plane hit their home. Were it not for Jack and Maurice's determination to keep their aircraft in the air until it hit the seas, it is likely that several more people would have been killed or injured.

Log of swims and finds—solo—during November and December, 2021:

Swim Day 1: Junction box, wires, aluminum hydraulic fuel lines recovered. Eric in Nassau photographs the ridge the B-26 was clearing before crash—Prospect Ridge/ Oakes Ridge—Cleaned Junction box, looked for numbers, bought and studied charts, toured and photographed the last RAF buildings extant at Pindling Intl. Airport, research day, Nassau.

Swim Day 2: Pilot seat, bomb cradle with hinge, aluminum strip, misc. modern PVC tubing.

Swim Day 3: Bomb fuse in rectangular case, round instrument panel disc with wire, padding, both taken apart, the latter brittle and damaged. Cold front prevented swimming safely.

Swim Day 4: Just ginger bottle, items not taken this day, too heavy and considered unwise to damage them, and not sufficient carriage capability with *Clemmie*, inflatable pool raft.

Swim Day 5: Early swim, cold, cold front, found historic bottles, not much else.

Swim Day 6: Heavy round steel or iron objects, with an aluminum find or skeg of some type, pieces of aluminum, chair seat (escape hatch) found but left, as was the engine with 4 propellers. Contacted members of the Bahamas' historical community. Cold front prevented swimming safely, or boating. Developed film from underwater with Jordan.

Swim Day 7: Unable to find/relocate escape hatch or engine, however, the pilot seat's back-rest, turned out to be pilot's escape hatch.

Swim Day 8: Found more aluminum pieces, parts of boxes, clasps, another stainless-steel bracket for raising and lowering bombs, steel braces, brackets for pumps, misc., some debris found much closer to shore than usual. Smaller aluminum fuselage pieces.

Swim Day 9: Cowling retrieved: the culmination of trip, c.350 lbs. large cowling of port engine, undamaged, moved from sand to Ulric Williams' boat *Yisel*. Other items like a metal belaying pin, but the cowling was the largest and most B-26-centric artifact of this trip. Reached out to Bahamian & other WWII filmmakers, documentarians. On a rare day off from swimming. By then I was making three solo trips a day in rough water, 3-5 hours, 2-3 miles, halfway to Balmoral Island.

Swim Day 10: Found a large 5' X 6' fuselage piece probably from the tail, with three large, dark brown, operable pulleys. Dr. Grace Turner, archaeologist with AMMC, National Museum calls back.

Swim Day 11: Short exploratory swim along shore to ensure I didn't miss obvious pieces. The next step was to donate all the 45 or so finds to the National Museum of The Bahamas. Senior leadership and a support team procured a large vehicle and drove to our parents' house and retrieved it. They also inventoried the items and had me comment on their provenance by making short videos and taking hundreds of photos.

Our Dad allowed me to keep these parts at home and loaned a car for daily exploratory trips. A former officer in the Royal Swedish Army, he inspected and oversaw the items. Former Royal Danish Navy navigating officer Henrik Gedde Moos assisted in putting items in the car as did neighbor, Jean Cote. Then I flew back to Boston and prepared a 100-page report on the 35-year recovery efforts.

A WWII bomber lands on remote Ascension Island, in the middle of the South Atlantic, possibly from Bahamas via Trinidad and Brazil on the way to West Africa.

This whiskey bottle, with the cork intact in the plastic wrapping, was one of the first items found on the B-26 site and seemed at the time of little consequence as it was of fairly modern manufacturer. However, the cork was still in it, suggesting a larger story, which indeed it is part of. Also, half a dozen other bottles were found which the archaeologists Dr. Curry and Dr. Turner took great interest in.

Pilot F/O John Walter Wood RCAF, 28 years.

Left: Pilot F/O Maurice Francis O'Neill of Halifax, 27 years. Since their ID's are just three digits apart, he and Jack Wood enlisted very close in time to one another.

WW2 B-26 Propellers and Hub, Delaporte Bay, Nassau, Bahamas, by Rich Ashman.

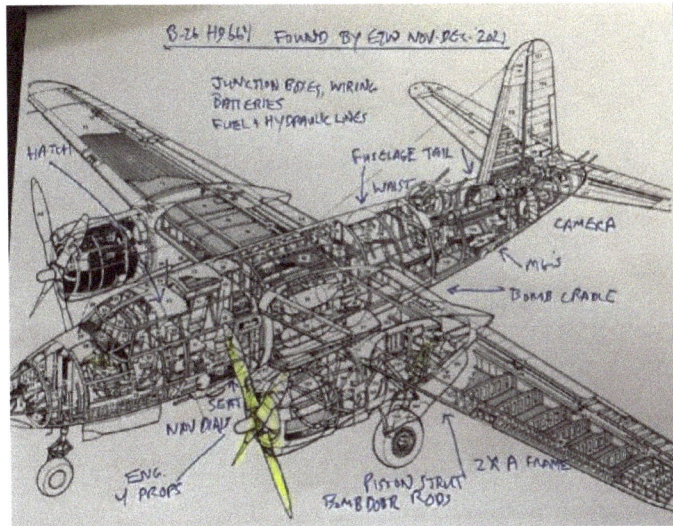

Diagram showing the myriad of systems and components of a B-26 Marauder.

Cowling, or cover to one of the B-26's engines, probably port as this one is not burnt out.

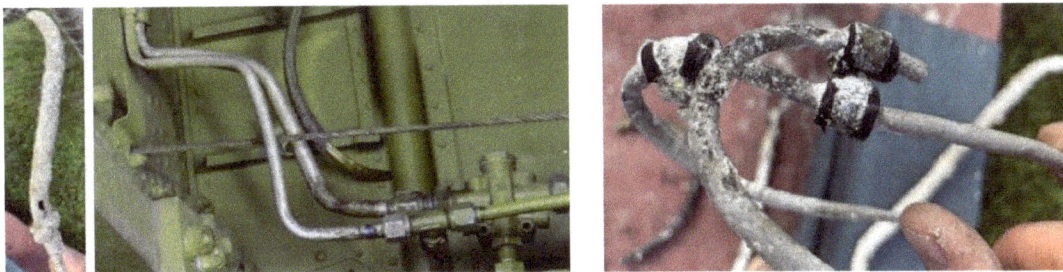

Hydraulic lines similar to those needed to turn flaps, open hatches, and bomb doors.

Camera from the B-26 Marauder, Delaporte Bay.

Details of camera, showing wiring and that, when found, it was in the "off" position.

The escape hatch above the pilots' seats in the cockpit of a B-26 Marauder.

Machine guns for B-26, on the aircraft and on the seafloor of Delaporte Bay.

Jack Wood and Maurice O'Neill's aircraft was found in November, so the first piece of their aircraft fuselage and memorial poppy for Remembrance Day were brought to the RAF Cemetery nearby to commemorate them.

The only reason I took this photo was because I was alone, over half a mile from land, and surrounded by a severe lightning, rain, and thunder storm. Since I had a waterproof camera and was completely helpless in the event that lightning struck, I took this single image, showing hydraulic rams and bits of the fuselage on a flimsy surfboard, as evidence to enable search and rescue persons to figure out what happened, and primarily for our son Felix, then 13, who I had not seen in a month.

Chapter Five:

Acklins, B-18 Bolo Water Landing

Three US warplanes crash-landed on or near Castle Island, Acklins in World War II. To the aviators, the large lighthouse was an uncomfortable halfway point-of-no-return. Faced with mostly open ocean ahead, if in trouble they had to make the decision to ditch, and if so, where to crash-land. If they survived the landing, Castle Island Light was a good place to be found and rescued. On September 4, 1942, a USAAF crew under Pilot Richard Ginther, supported by Arthur Hammer, John Smith, Charles Perkins, George Oakes, John Boener, and John Soar, were patrolling from Cuba to The Bahamas against German and Italian submarines in a new Douglas B-18A Bolo heavy bomber.

At 6:30 p.m. Ginther logged that the aircraft's right engine began "getting rough," understatement for failing. It sputtered and vibrated badly. At 900 feet, the commander abandoned the patrol and turned towards Cuba. When the engine began vibrating more, he headed for the nearest land: Acklins. As the aircraft's engines both lost oil pressure and began overheating, the crew were ordered to prepare for a forced landing. As a precaution, they dropped the depth charges while still in armed status.

Feathering the three propellers on the starboard engine at 500 feet, Ginther ordered three of the men into the back of the plane and headed northeast, paralleling the coast of Castle Island about two miles to the west of it. Unable to find a landing spot on shore, he shouted to prepare for a water landing. At that point, the plane was only 200 feet high and making over 100 knots. Ginther then put the port engine into full RPM. Navigator Smith said, "When we turned back to Acklins Island [it] was just visible about 10 miles NE of us. At 6:35 p.m. I told Oakes [Radio Operator] to get out a forced landing message. As we turned to make a landing on the beach, the right engine failed completely, so we turned towards open water to the west. The landing was very smooth."

After passing Castle Island Light Ginther shut off then feathered the port engine, and the plane "hit the water easily at a nose-high attitude. The nose plowed under the water, but recovered." Soar relates that the three men in the back of the plane used parachutes "to cushion their shock as we landed. When we hit the water, I slid forward. Then all of a sudden, we were in the water. We were about one mile from shore. Darkness had begun to approach." Oakes wrote that, "first I got out of the plane onto the raft. Then, seeing that the plane was floating, I re-entered it."

With some help, the doors released the inflatable rafts in less than a minute. Then Perkins noted that "... we tried to detonate [sensitive technology] without success. It was under water at the time. Hammer, Ginther, Oakes, and myself went out through the pilot's escape hatch and sat on the fuselage, loading the life rafts. A strong east wind was blowing [to the west], and the airplane was drifting away from the land, so we decided to go ashore at once."

A raft was loaded with safety supplies and sent to shore. Once it returned, all the men boarded the two rafts and rowed to Acklins. At dusk and in pouring rain "while rowing ashore, a British constable and his son rowed alongside, and accompanied us ashore. They offered any help they could give. They left after about 15 minutes." After 8 p.m., to their relief, a Consolidated PBY Catalina approached and they fired flares with the signal "OK." They said help was on the way. All seven of the aircrew were seen on the beach.

Smith continues: "We tried to sleep, but bugs and continued rain showers prevented it." Oakes said "... after we first landed, a native of the island came out and asked us if we needed any help." Soar said that "about halfway to the shore, two natives who live on the island came up and offered us assistance. They came onto shore with us. They departed and said that they would come back the next morning, which they did. We built a fire and dried our clothes... We slept as best we could, although it rained five or six times during the night." The men offering assistance are believed to be members of the Forbes family of Salina Point, who have served for generations as lighthouse keepers, commissioners, and constables.

The next day at 4:45 a.m., rescuers left Cuba in a Catalina designated PBY6 and arrived at the small camp at 6:27 a.m. At 7 a.m. the rescuers made a water landing a mile from Acklins, and the survivors paddled out to the rescue plane in rafts. The officer in charge conveyed his orders from Guantanamo to the destroyer USS *Borie* (DD-215), which sent a boat over, that if the plane could not be salvaged it was to be stripped of sensitive items and destroyed. By 7:50 a.m. all the crew from the B-18 were aboard the PBY, which took off, leaving the crew's rafts to be retrieved by USS *Borie*.

USS *Borie* had first sighted the abandoned plane at 6:35 that morning. After 7 a.m., they made haste for Jamaica Bay, southwest Acklins to pick up survivors. Before 8 a.m. USS *Borie* "hove to alongside the plane while the party led by Lt. (j.g.) Arnold set out to salvage all equipment possible." At 8:05 a.m. the ship sighted patrol craft USS *PC-465*, and later the destroyer USS *J. Fred Talbot*. At 9:43 a.m. Lt. Arnold's salvage party returned, and by 9:56 a.m. the *Borie* sailors "commenced firing at plane in order to sink it." Less than half an hour later, at 10:22 the men logged: "Plane sank. Ceased firing." They had expended 156 cartridges, most of them the 4" and 50-caliber, some with tracers. Six hours after arriving, at 10:35 a.m., USS *Borie* sped away from Castle Island and Acklins headed for Guantanamo, her mission complete.

At 8:10 a.m., before the men of USS *Borie* went to work, another PBY sighted the stricken B-18 Bolo appearing to be floating on the water. By 8:50 a.m. all of Lt. Ginther's B-18 crew landed safely at Guantanamo, were checked for shock and exposure, and found to be fit. The commander noted, "Airplane finally destroyed by the destroyer." Ginther commended his crew highly: "The emergency equipment functioned perfectly. Mosquito bars are recommended as an addition to the drop kit, as well as a carton of cigarettes. The action of the Navy in effecting our rescue shows a well-trained and efficient organization."

USS *Borie*, built in 1920, was damaged beyond repair during a dramatic ramming, strafing, and sinking attack on the German supply submarine U-405 under *Fregattenkapitän* Rolf-Heinrich Hopmann. Left in a sinking state, she had to be scuttled away by an Avenger fighter plane with her crew rescued by the aircraft carrier USS *Card* (ACV-11). They earned three Navy Cross medals: two Silver Star medals and one Legion of Merit medal. Just two months before her exploits in The Bahamas, *Borie* had rescued the crew of the transport USS USAT *Merrimack*, which had been torpedoed by German U-107 in the Yucatan Channel.

Rescue plane PYP 6 was a patrol seaplane from Squadron VP-34, based in Georgetown, Exuma and looked like this.

| 9-4-42 DATE | Mitchel Field STATION | 13th Bomb (M) GROUP NO. AND TYPE | B-18B AIRPLANE MODEL |
| T/Sgt. Cheever CREW CHIEF OR AERIAL ENGINEER | | 40th Bomb (M) SQUADRON NO. AND TYPE | 37-539 AIRPLANE SERIAL NO. |

PERS CLASS	— PRINT PLAINLY — NAME — RANK — ORGANIZATION	USE AS DIRECTED LOCALLY	DUTY	N OR I	DUTY	N OR I	DUTY	N OR I	DUTY	N OR I	TERMINALS AND MISSION	
2C-1	GINTHER, Richard F., 1st Lt.		P 2:55								FROM: Guantanamo Bay	16 05
2C-1	HAMMER, Arthur J., 2nd Lt.		OP 2:55								TO: Patrol	19'00
2C-1	SMITH, John W., 2nd Lt.		N 2 55								MISSION C NO. OF LANDINGS 1	2'55
1E-1	PERKINS, Charles V., Cpl.		B 2 55								FROM:	
1E-1	OAKES, George W., Cpl.		R 2:55								TO:	
1E-1	BOENER, John F., S/Sgt.		EG 2:55								MISSION NO. OF LANDINGS	
1E-1	SOAR, John S., Pvt.		RAD 2 55								FROM: TO:	

The USAAF aircraft loss report for the B-18 Bolo under Lt. Richard Ginther.

Rev. Felton Rolle and the author passing through Portland, Acklins in search of aircraft remnants and witnesses to guide us to them.

Chapter Six:

Castle Island, A-20 Pilot Libby on Lake

The 112-foot Castle Island Light, which has guarded the Crooked Island Channel for 200 years, is a critically important beacon. It is the only lighthouse chosen by three World War II bomber pilots to crash-land near to facilitate rescue. This is the story of the first wreck there, described as sitting atop a hard-packed lake on all its wheels by other pilots in distress who scouted the spot. Once the small lake was 'occupied' by a wrecked airplane, other pilots hoping to ditch there were forced to belly-land in the sea or the bush, as though it were a cruel game of musical chairs.

On February 19, 1943, Captain D. A. Libby of the USAAF was piloting a Douglas A-20B Havoc medium bomber on its journey from Memphis to the Soviet Air Force via Florida and Puerto Rico. His copilot was Murray White and navigator J. S. Veronko. Theirs was the lead plane out of seven that day, flying from Homestead Air Force Base. Over the Crooked Island Channel, Libby, who had 60 hours of pilot time on this aircraft and 1,865 total pilot hours overall, was told by the other pilots that their right engine was smoking.

Maintaining discretion, Libby later described how they were "on a foreign mission, destination and purpose secret… the right motor started to cut in and out intermittently and smoke. I discovered an island [Castle] approximately two miles to the left, and proceeded to circle it five times, awaiting developments in engine trouble. While circling, I tried single-engine procedure, and found that I could not keep altitude, so I decided to land." Before crash-landing, Libby turned and "asked the navigator, Murray White, to jump [by parachute]. He stated that he would prefer to stay with the ship. I warned him that in previous crack-ups of A-20's the navigator had been dangerously injured because of his exposed position. Lt. White still preferred to stay with the ship."

Twenty minutes after noon, Libby says he "made a normal approach, wheels down, and landed on a dry lake bed. I cut all electric switches, and proceeded to try to bring the ship to a stop. After running approximately 500 feet over the lake bed, the main [landing] gear suddenly dropped into the mud hole and set the nose wheel into the mud, throwing Lt. White through the front of the ship."

"As soon as the ship stopped completely, I opened my hatch and jumped down into the mud to extract Lt. White from the wreckage. His right leg was caught under a piece of the nose section." Showing extraordinary strength, Libby and Veronko were able to lift the nose of the aircraft off their colleague's injured leg and free him, sparing him from further injury or drowning. The men must have crawled to the edge of the small lake (400 by 225 yards), and spent the night there or along the sea shore which lay just over the berm, the surf audible from the crash site.

The six other planes vectored the US Navy, which sent a patrol craft to the rescue, then returned to Florida. The submarine chaser USS *SC-696* set off from Guantanamo at about midnight. Her handwritten Deck Log for February 20, 1943, records that at 11:00 a.m. they sighted an Allied airplane which signaled course to Castle Island, which was sighted half an hour later. At 12:45 p.m. they stopped, and hoisted their wherry; light rowboat for carrying passengers, over the side. Then a crewman named A. Kravitz and a helmsman named B. Noble rowed the wherry ashore, intending to bring survivors of the wrecked plane back to the sub-chaser.

An hour later, at 1:50 p.m., Noble returned on board with the injured survivor, Murray White, who was "hoisted aboard and tended to by Doctor." Just 10 minutes later, Noble was heading back ashore, and returned to the ship at 2:45 p.m. with Pilot Libby and Engineer Veronko. Finally, at 3:15 p.m. Noble returned ashore to pick up his shipmate Kravitz and the survivor's baggage and papers. At 4 p.m. both men returned aboard with the items, and the wherry was hoisted aboard. By 4:20 p.m., less than five hours after arriving, USS *SC-696* was under way. She docked at Pier A in Guantanamo at 10:26 a.m. the following day, and Murray White was promptly taken ashore on a stretcher. The aviators were found less than 24 hours after crashing and delivered safely ashore less than 24 hours after that.

The aircraft remained visible for many years, and traces of it can be seen from space today. On September 20 that year, Captain O'Neil reported in Miami that a "plane had landed on Castle Island in a marshy spot, with its wheels down. All hatches were open, and there were no signs of life about." For years, Bahamian telephone services also received messages from passing ships such as this one: "... a signal was intercepted from a ship off Inagua reporting that a crashed aircraft had been sighted on Castle Island."

Soon thereafter, First Lt. James F. Hunt had to crash his B-26C Marauder bomber in the bush of the Acklins mainland on April 7, 1943, because (as he told investigators), having run out of fuel "we saw that it would be practically impossible to set the airplane down on the beach, and we saw an A-20 on Castle Island, so we decided the safest thing to do would be to abandon ship." The startled investigation board asked, "You saw an A-20 on Castle Island? How could you tell the type of [air]ship?" To which Hunt replied, "Yes sir. I figured that is what it was." It is still there, with periodic sightings by yachtsmen passing through as well.

The board of inquiry summarized the incident thus: "Forced landing on a small island off the coast of Acklins Island. Nose section buckled; fuselage wrinkled. Cause of accident: power plant failure." Libby suffered only minor injuries, White's were deemed major, and Veronko's classed simply as 'none.' The panel concluded that "Lt. Libby handled his plane and crew in a highly satisfactory manner."

Then, soon after dawn on the rainy morning of August 5, 2022, Captain Kendres Williams and I disembarked onto Castle Island with supplies for three days. We left Salina Bonefish Lodge at dawn, and Ken pushed his Boston Whaler into rainstorms, and over water so deep that bluewater flying fish leapt. With precision we nudged into rocky Mundian Harbour (lighthouse keeper Jeffrey Forbes pronounces it *moojian*), and offloaded a kayak, hundreds of feet of line, a cooler of food, mask and fins, and enough supplies to last three days.

As the one tasked with knowing what to look for, I had been up much of the night before confirming my hunch that the plane piloted by young Lt. Libby, which was never salvaged from Castle Island and not been found since, must have sunk into the biggest lake on the island, which is uninhabited and the light inoperative. The island is two miles long and half a mile wide.

Ken and I felt our way from the bay over the berm on foot into a small valley, trying to find the lake. After less than five minutes, I suggested we take a right turn to hit the east end of the lake, and when I looked up, the quiet captain was already walking on—yes *on*—the 'lake,' which turned out to be a salt flat just an inch deep. There, in the middle, was the engine of the Douglas Havoc which had landed audaciously when his engine flamed and Libby circled Castle Island five times, the front landing gear collapsed, ejecting and trapping Murray White

Over the years until the plane gradually sank into the salt brine, essentially pickled. What lies beneath, out of sight? Is it really an intact relic from yesteryear, when the USA and USSR were comrades? Flamingos use the protruding radial engine to nest on. There is no doubt this is precisely that aircraft which was bound for Stalin and the USSR.

When Kendres and I discovered and photographed the large engine sitting atop a pink saline lake, with smaller bits embedded in the salt, which had set like concrete, and fringing the little lake, the moonscape-like images peeled back some 80 years of mystery surrounding this crash. Hundreds of pilots and yachtsmen had seen it, yet the lighthouse keeper who spent a decade on the island didn't recall it. Other aircraft had wrecked since, leaving behind their dead, causing fears of mix-ups. Now, thanks to input from Appalachia to Acklins, the plane has been found.

Submarine chaser USS *SC-696* (ex-*PC-696*) which rescued the A-20 crew using a little wherry rowed by USN sailors Kravitz and Noble.

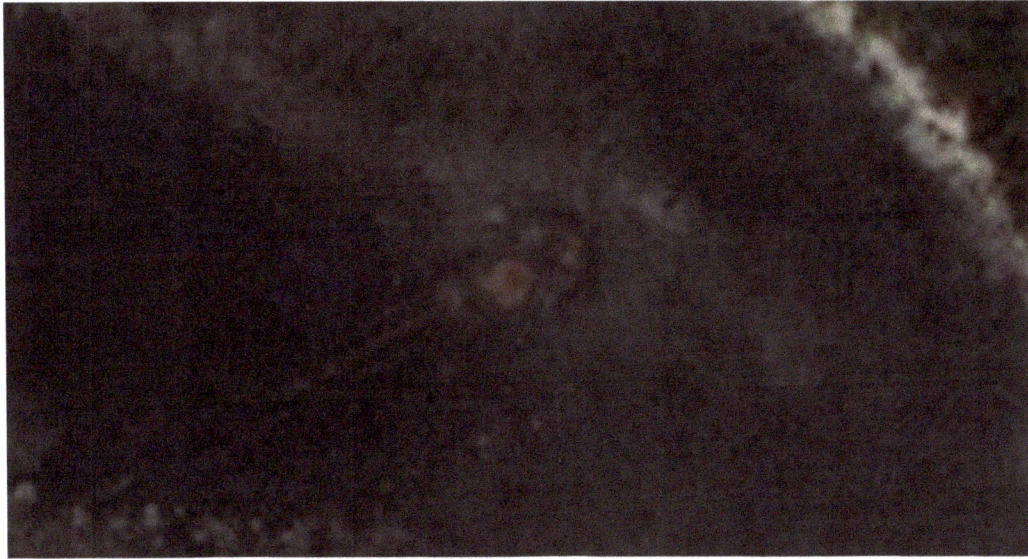

The track in the marsh of the probable crash site of the US bomber, as seen today. This kind of technology is hugely helpful to researchers covering large swathes.

Captain Kendres Williams walks past the engine of Lt. Libby's A-20 Havoc on the lake beneath Castle Island Light, August 5, 2022, moments after the aircraft were rediscovered 80 years after it crash-landed there, crushing Murray White's leg.

Southern Acklins Island with Castle Island at bottom, Jamaica Bay at middle-left, and Pompey Bay out of frame to the top/northeast. Salina Point is center-right bottom.

Castle Island Light, built over 150 years ago, is visually romantic, with ship and plane wrecks, lighthouse, outbuildings, beaches, reefs, ship traffic, and lakes.

Our first toehold on Castle Island, intending to stay for days. And the sandy inlet at the base of the lighthouse.

Chapter Seven:

B-26, Parachutes, at Portland Plantation, Acklins

Women who donated their nylon stockings to the US war effort might not know they often became parachutes, four of which floated down to earth and sea over Acklins, in the southern Bahamas during the war. After Ralph Stevens rolled out of a doomed bomber, spraining his ankle and knee, his parachute was given by the resident commissioner, Chauncy Tynes, to a family of six children in Pompey Bay. As the children grew, their mother sewed the precious nylon into four dresses for three sisters: for christening, church, confirmation, and finally a wedding dress!

When did this unusual textile odyssey begin? As a consequence of the attack on Pearl Harbor, the US military switched from Japanese silk to nylon to make "glider tow ropes, aircraft fuel tanks, flak jackets, shoelaces, mosquito netting, hammocks, and, yes, parachutes." So valuable were these that a B-26 Marauder from the 453rd Bomb Squadron out of Myrtle Beach, South Carolina kept three aircraft circling over the Gulf Stream while they landed back at base to retrieve a forgotten parachute.

The plane's pilot was James Franklin Hunt, and he was not having a good week. To start, he was hospitalized in Indiana, where the crew were to pick up the new aircraft at a factory and fly it to Africa. Every time the pneumonia would abate, the Army Air Force would yank him out of the hospital bed to fly planes. His backup pilot, Arnold Stern, grew up in Manhattan and married his Cornell sweetheart, Stella Newman, at age 21. Every month he sent her a purple orchid on the day of their wedding. Stern admitted he thought his role on the flight was passenger, not as a backup pilot. Radio operator Ralph E. Stevens was 33 years old and enlisted in Indiana with fourth crew member, Flight Sergeant Billy R. Williams. The plane leaked 35 gallons of gasoline on the flight from the Mid-West to Florida.

They took off from Morrison Field (now Palm Beach International Airport), bound for Puerto Rico at 7:30 a.m. the next day with four other planes. However, after just 10 minutes, Stevens noticed his parachute was missing. They re-landed, he got out and found it, and they took off 15 minutes later. Over Acklins Island, near the point -of-no-return, the men were trying to transfer fuel from the wing to the main tanks and failed. B-26's were rushed into service; two days later another B-26 crashed off

Lyford Cay with seven killed; another ran out of fuel and ditched off Abaco, and a fourth crashed into Delaporte Bay, killing two Canadians. They were sent to the front before prototypes could be tested, with generals adding heavy armor and guns in the interim.

Hunt was calm, decisive, and selfless. He swung north to Acklins and informed the other pilots that he would ditch, presciently ordering everyone to drink lots of water. He opened the bomb bay doors and told the two junior crew to jump. Billy Williams was supposed to jump out head-first, but "rolled out," made a complete turn, and said, "as I landed, the chute spread out in front of me." Stevens said he "landed in the middle of the island, in about 10 inches of dirt and almost got dragged away [when the parachute] picked me up [so I] held it down." Injuries included multiple abrasions and some sprains. He and Williams met up, then were found by locals.

Hunt and Stern intended to bail out together, but with no-one at the controls, the plane was erratic. While Hunt stabilized it, Stern hurriedly leapt, ending in the ocean two miles east of Acklins. He wriggled out of the parachute and swam to shore, where fishermen were waiting for him. A weakened Hunt had to fly the 25,000-pound, 71-foot-long plane over the mainland across large salina lakes and the old Hanna slave plantation.

As the plane leaned towards the earth, Hunt ran aft and bailed, then pulled the chord 500 feet beneath the plane. After landing in thick bush, Hunt says, "I ran into two natives on the beach picking fruit [cascarilla], who took me to a settlement." As the locals tell it, a woman ran into the village screaming that she had seen a ghost covered in white silk, emerging bloodied from the bush. Hunt stayed over in Pompey Bay. The others drank coconut juice and "went up to [Commissioner Chauncy Tynes'] house on top of a hill and stayed there that night." A B-25 Liberator circled the school house in Pompey that afternoon and later at night, looking for the pilot. This caused the teacher to send pupils scattering, on account that not all of them would be killed if the plane crashed into the school.

The following morning, the men were rescued by amphibious airplanes and taken to Exuma, and then Cuba. The B-26 was written off as "completely demolished by fire" by the military planes flying over it. Stevens blew up the radio set before jumping. The plane remained largely forgotten, though residents managed to hand-carry some metal to a barge, ship it to Nassau, and sell it. Most of the important heavy equipment was left largely intact because the military must have considered it both far too good, but also too far away—difficult to get to before helicopters were in common military use in The Bahamas.

A teenage bride from Pompey Bay whose mother was given a parachute, and then wore parts of it woven into her wedding dress. She was as not the only one: since "as early as 1943… dedicated and fierce young women were not letting anything go to waste, including the parachutes their husbands jumped from planes in!" A silk parachute wedding dress "became an act to honor the service of these men." Stern would have appreciated this, since he died within the year in another air crash. His bride Stella went back to Cornell and volunteered for the Red Cross. Her anniversary purple orchid arrived by mail several days after Arnold died.

The dress made in The Bahamas of parachute fabric is an artifact, like a small glass vase found at the beachside grave of a Norwegian sailor buried in Abaco, or the silk pajamas given by the Duke of Windsor to a young cadet rescued in Acklins after a U-boat attack. Reports suggested the B-26 may have been broken into at Florida, tampered with, and possibly even had fuel stolen. Thus, the plane's lock, fuel tanks, and fuel transfer pumps were discovered in the bush last year and left intact; these items are significant artifacts which can provide answers. Artifacts tell stories. We need to listen to them and those who care for them.

Nylon stockings are the main reason my family moved to The Bahamas from Sweden starting in 1952. Our grandfather's company, *Malmö Strumpfabrik* ('hosiery fabricator'), was successful enough that relocation to more tax-amenable climes was beneficial. Hence, our father's 1960s purchase of what had been an RAF officer's quarters: Cable Beach Manor.

Though it seemed surprisingly easy to find the Havoc bomber on the lake on Castle Island, I am certain I would never have had the time, funds, and opportunity to go after the B-26 in the bush on land. It was a largely unknown wreck which was believed to have gone down in the water like many others. But, chance had it that my guide insisted I find more work for him with the remaining days before the next biweekly flight to Nassau. So, I found an internet signal and emailed Mike Stowe, an aircraft accident report expert in the Virginia area, and asked him for details. To my surprise, he told me that the remains of a B-26 like the one I had already found near Nassau was lying in the bush just a few miles from the bonefish lodge where I was a guest of Rev. Felton Rolle.

During this frenetic trip, at the encouragement of the editor-in-chief of the *Nassau Tribune*, Eugene Duffy, I penned an account of the journey which runs much like this:

"Found them. As extraordinary as it is, it's really that simple. The first World War II airplane I found at home in Cable Beach took me 35 years. I gave the parts to the AMMC and National Museum, and arranged a reunion for families of the deceased pilots on the site this October. In July, I vaguely planned to follow up on trying to find these planes as a scout for filming a documentary or TV show. Then the list of accidents ballooned to 165, and the project became, to my mind at least, too much to digest and afford."

However, the fever to search struck again, and coincided with my having to find an aircraft before taking the weekly aircraft off the island. In August, I boarded a Bahamas Air flight to Spring Point, Acklins for the first time in 22 years. Why? Well, Rev. Newton Williamson is one of the last first-hand witnesses to WWII U-boat torpedo survivors, and a historian always prefers original sources willing to speak on the record and be photographed. Also, since 1995 I have always enjoyed visiting Acklins. I had three Acklins-related historical loose ends to tie.

In 2012, Reverend Williamson told my colleagues about an American widow staring out to sea in tears. I wanted to learn about the aviator husband she was mourning. Then, I should shift south from Pinefield to try to find the plane said to have crashed on Castle Island. Finally, on a highly aspirational wish-list, I wanted to ask locals what happened to the plane under Lt. Hunt from which four officers of the USAAF crew parachuted weeks after the Libby crash.

I wanted to interview Rev. Williamson, photograph the places where shipwrecked sailors from the 1942 torpedoed American freighter named SS *Potlatch* ate, rested, and were buried. I figured I would be able to enjoy going back to Acklins, home of the hardiest folks I know, taking sailboats, mailboats, and planes, and staying in tents, inns, and bonefish lodges. On the flight, I met my indefatigable host, Rev. Felton Rolle, owner of Salina Point Bonefish Lodge, where, due to his dexterity, I was to double the length of my stay. I relied upon him for everything: transport, guides, logistics, internet, emergency contact when my girlfriend called after me, and food, not to mention a well air-conditioned, safe, and comfortable beachfront room.

I believe that the journeys and voyages which ensued during those few days were extraordinary, even by backpacker standards. With steadfast support, I covered some 1,000 miles—by plane (600 miles), by car (300 miles on Acklins, 50 on New Providence), by foot in 'the bush' (35 miles: 15 solo and 20 with guides), by boat (30 miles to Castle Island and back to Acklins), and two miles swimming. The 17 hours on a mailboat don't count since the thing didn't move an inch the entire time! After finding the Havoc, all plans were put on hold when researcher Mike Stowe emailed confirming a bomber crashed nearby. Like an amphibian switching from sea to land, Rev. Felton, without missing a beat, made urgent calls and we visited elderly locals in Pompey Bay and bush tracking experts in Delectable Bay. The next three days were a blur of 35 miles of walking:

Day 1: Stanford Tynes, Iris Tynes, and Loftus A. Roker all confirmed the details, as did Rev. Rufus Forbes, and guides Charles Williams and George. An Air Traffic Controller at Windsor Field said a white man emerged from the bush with a parachute and scared local women. Iris said headmistress Hester Tynes was so alarmed by a B-25 bomber circling the school erratically looking for the four lost airmen that she told the children to run for their lives, and when smoke was seen towards Portland, the children thought their parents had been killed in the fields. I walked six miles alone in the bush and Salinas of Portland—six hours and nothing.

Day 2: Eight hours with Charles guiding, again nothing, I fell asleep in the forest watching a hummingbird and a gecko and he had to come get me. Resigned, I gave up, and boarded the mailboat in Spring Point at 9 a.m.

Day 3: At 2:30 a.m., my captain's instincts cut in when I realized the engine had finally started. Without much thought, I grabbed my backpack and a little roller duffle with my monogram on it, and marched off the boat as the ramp was being raised. Without pausing to reflect that there was not a soul about, I then walked about 8 miles nonstop and saw that Charles' window light was on, so I called him to ask for drinking water, which he shared with me.

By 5:30 a.m., the sun was rising and I arrived at Portland where the plane was said to have crashed. All the men were rescued, first by a seaplane in Pompey Bay, which then took Hunt to the place where Commissioner Chancy Tynes, supported by a Constable Forbes and others, mustered the three other men. They were whisked to Exuma and then to Guantanamo.

End of story? Hardly! I was so fixated on finding my first WWII land crash site that I was determined to find the plane by breakfast time, emerge from the bush, and teach an online course—in the liquor store at Delectable Bay—at 10 a.m. And I did so, thanks to the divine intervention of Rev. Rufus Forbes. He happened to be up early and, for the first time in months, set out alone to cut cascarilla bark for soaking, beating, and selling for Campari.

I happened to be stowing my gear in the bush and getting outfitted for an exhausting day in the bush alone when he walked past on the trail, whistling in the darkness of the dawn. Hark! I begged him to show me the plane; with grace and ease he did, and I thanked him by carrying two loads of his cascarilla branches out of the forest to the road, where Felton was waiting.

What was at the site? As Mike had optimistically predicted, there is a tremendous amount still there: engines, camera, wheels, machine guns, pumps, valves, some fuselage, bomb racks and bullets... two Pratt & Whitney radial engines (1,200-hp each), at least three machine guns, ammunition (which went off when the plane burnt), bombsights, throttle, wheel assemblies, large camera, fuel transfer pump, bits of fuselage, tanks, and much more—even the pilot's seat. I know as I had found over 40 pieces of another B-26 in Cable Beach. Locals were excited by all these finds and I begged them to preserve the wreck as it is so that we can all visit it, and of course I immediately informed the AMMC.

Tying up loose ends, I studied Rev Williamson's report of a widow mourning her American husband at Pinefield in the 1960s. Since no servicemen died in the three military crashes on Acklins in WWII, I found the likely crash, "the 1965 crash of a United States Air Force Fairchild C-119G Flying Boxcar [with] parts washed up on the northeast shore of Acklins." I was left to ponder how I had the good fortune as a self-funded person to rediscover two World War II wrecks in four days and even help open and solve others. After all, I went to Acklins to find planes and ended up trying to emulate the Acklins Islanders' indubitable toughness, skill, self-reliance, and community spirit. Whether sandy soil, rich reefs, ambergris, boats washed up from West Africa, historic planes, bark, or bush medicine, they will make the most of it. And so did I. Thank you, Acklins.

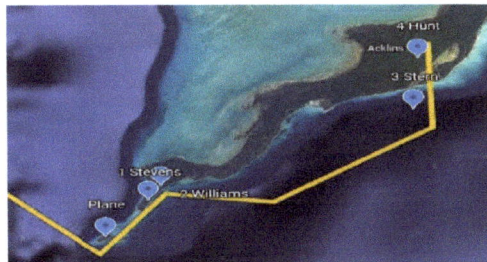

Final route of the B-26 that crashed in the Acklins bush near Pompey Bay and Portland Plantation, April 7, 1943, showing where four men parachuted.

Lieutenant Arnold Stern, Copilot of the B-26 who bailed into the ocean and swam hours and miles to Acklins. He perished when his aircraft ran into Bury St. Edmunds, England, a few months later.

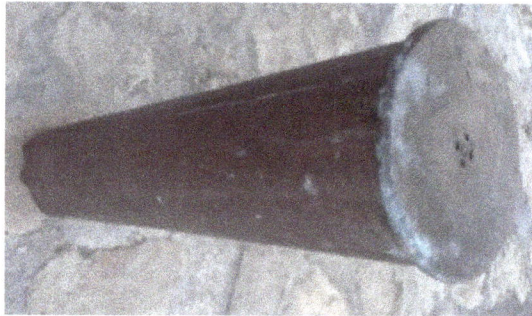

A USN 5-inch-wide Mk5 shell's spent casing as found on Acklins and preserved by the Collie family of Hard Hill. From Mr. Kenwood Collie

One of at least three (of a total of eight) machine guns still on the plane wreck.

Port engine, landing gear, struts and other equipment of the B-26 bomber in Acklins.

Part of the B-26 wing with fuel tanks visible.

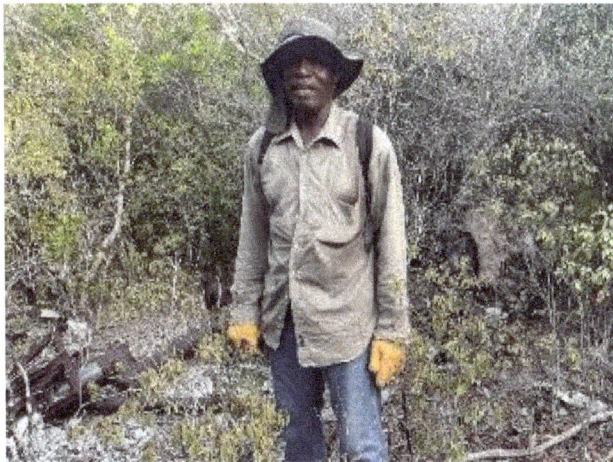

Rev. Rufus Forbes, who showed author the plane last month.

The valve knob on the fuel transfer pump which all the men struggled to fix prior to ditching the aircraft.

Lock mechanism for the B-26 at the crash site in Acklins. Was this used to access the aircraft in Morrison Field, Florida while the crew slept, resulting in loss of fuel and misplacement of the parachute? Very possibly: the evidence suggests that it was.

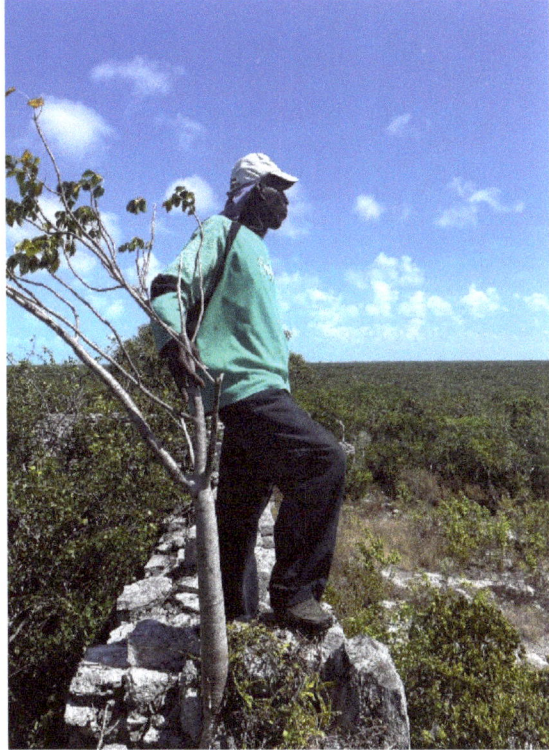

Two helpful resources; top is Mr. Chauncey Tynes, retired air traffic controller, in Pompey Bay, south Acklins, and his northern neighbor Mr. Mackintire, who is well known as a guide over difficult terrain. Here he is atop the breezy ruins of the Hanna Plantation, carefully preserved in Portland, on the way to Salina, Acklins. Mr. Tynes is a friend of both Rev. Felton Rolle and Capt. Paul Aranha and he and relatives including the school mistress at the time vividly recall the sudden arrival of parachuted American aviators including Pilot Hunt, and the exchanges which took place during World War II.

Throttle controls of the B-26 in the bush in Acklins. Poor Lt. Hunt was running
back and forth to these solo, as his copilot thought he was just a passenger.

Chapter Eight:

Moore's Island, Abaco: FM-2 Wildcat Fighter

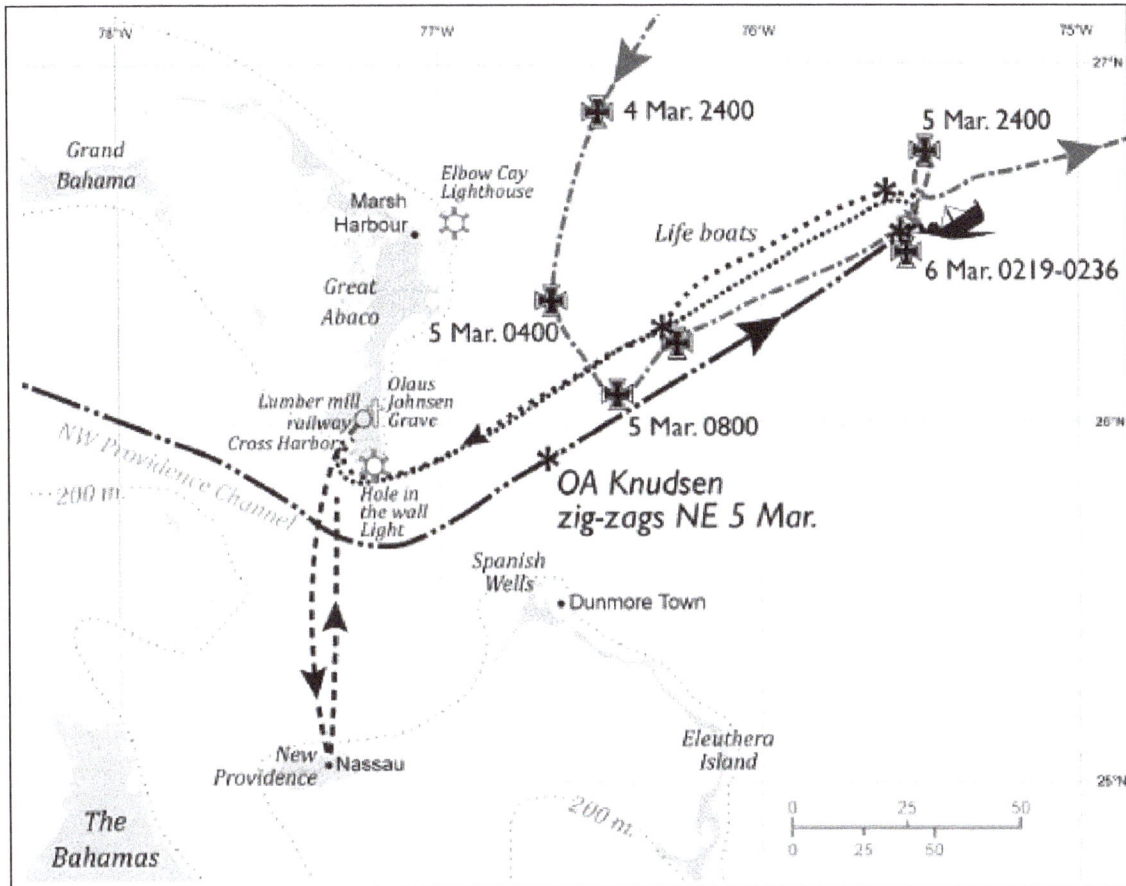

Mere months before V-E Day, an Allied fighter plane crash-landed at the remote Moore's Island, a seven-by-four-mile cay in the Bight of Abaco. The communities of Hard Bargain and The Bight house 950 people, mostly fishermen and government hires. The cay lies between Sandy Point, Abaco and Sweeting's Cay, Grand Bahama. USN Pilot Herbert Stanley Fyfield was born in Manhattan in August 1922, and moved to more bucolic northwestern Connecticut, dying in Roxbury, population 2,260, in March of 1989. Fyfield was an ensign in the US Navy, aged 23. He flew with Squadron VF6 Operational Training Unit out of NAS Sanford, near Daytona.

The Grumman FM-2 Wildcat could accommodate only one pilot, as it was 29' long with a wingspan of 28' and only a single engine. The plane boasted an "improved power plant, increased ammunition capacity, and improved directional stability with a modified fin. It was the first line fighter for the Navy and Marine Corps at the outbreak of World War II [with] more than 35,000 aircraft" produced, and a kill ratio of 7 to 1. Fyfield had 290.4 flying hours, 19.6 of them in this aircraft.

The crash in Bahamas happened on a Thursday at 10:40 a.m., when classes for Jonathan Dean, aged seven, were still in session on the coast south of Hard Bargain. Visibility was 10 miles, wind was from the west-northwest, and Fyfield had been airborne for just 1 hour and 30 minutes. Investigators describe a "deferred emergency landing," explaining that:

"After gunnery run, this pilot became separated from the flight and proceeded to get lost when his compass went out. Pilot became confused and flew around for approximately an hour, when he sighted land. Having only 10 gallons of fuel, and no suitable airstrip available, he made a wheels-up landing in a clear area which turned out to be Mores [sic] Island in the Bahama Group. Had the pilot flown with the sun at his back during morning flight, he would have hit the state of Florida at some familiar section."

In January of 2023, our expedition's *modus operandi* was simple: sail into an anchorage for a few days, go ashore, and have our eldest sailors—in their seventies—inquire after the eldest residents. We took the dinghy in on the evening of arrival and circulated not only books about mailboats, but photos of islanders taken on my previous visit to the island in 1991. Fortunately, these included parents of persons living there now. This effort connected us with folks our age and broadened the base of mutual trust and conviviality considerably. The laptop containing those images was left at a local café for the duration of the second day for anyone to copy from.

As a consequence of this candor, islanders helped us promptly locate, film, and photograph the aircraft's distinctive "uprated R-1820 power plant, [with] water injection for increased power for takeoff from small deck escort carriers." Our chief guide was James 'Modi' Dean, retired fisherman, aged 85, born in 1938, who saw the crash. His son-in-law, Rodney Davis, in his sixties, drove us to Dean's house, where Mrs. Dean recalled speaking to the disoriented young Herbert: "He kept saying he wanted to go home and have lunch with his mother in Fort Lauderdale," she said, smiling broadly on the family porch.

Antoine Davis then took us to the crash site, which was really in the middle of town, between a church and a school, and behind a row of waterfront homes. Almost immediately we found a large engine upright in the mangrove swamp, intractable and wedged in without propellers but clearly a large radial aircraft engine. We also located and photographed a wheel and tire assembly, aluminum framing, and other small metal parts clearly of historic aircraft origin. We eagerly trekked through the bush with AJ Davis, a very helpful guide in his thirties. He is a fisherman and along with his wife, Brenda, is also a restaurateur. Devon Davis is a school teacher and an excellent resource who coordinated communications between various persons and groups after the visit.

Our captain, the yacht owner Howard, spent time speaking with Modi Dean. He learned they were in school when the plane roared overhead and splashed resoundingly into the mud just a few hundred yards inland. They raced to help Herbert Fyfield and took him to the main road. It was important that witnesses make the distinction that this was not the same air crash as the drug-runner whose small plane flipped on the main street in the 1970s and spilled piles of US dollars throughout town!

The disciplinary board recommended "Pilot reprimand. Board action pending, recommended continue training for subject pilot with special emphasis on Navigation and Radio Aids. Assessment: 100% pilot error—gross carelessness. Lost on gunnery exercise. Could have used sun to return to mainland. Compass failed. Poor navigation when compass went out. Lost. Aircraft and engine are strikes," meaning it was stricken from inventory, delisted. The military bulletin reported that a "search was carried out by [Coast Guard] *CG-83497* and *CG-83505*; a Dumbo [air-sea-rescue unit] was sent from Daytona Beach, and four planes from NAS Banana River."

The following day, after six hours, the search was called off by 4:31 p.m. "the FM-2 from NAS Sanford had crash-landed on March 8 in Marsh Harbour at Abaco, and requested RAF Nassau to transfer the pilot by boat to Nassau, where a plane will pick him up. The pilot will be picked up by a JRF [Grumman amphibian] on the morning of March 10 and will arrive at Nassau at 3 p.m." This was corrected at 4:50 p.m. to say the RAF made arrangements to safeguard the IFF [identify if friend or foe beacon]. At 5:26 p.m. ComGulf informed RAF Nassau that the plane had actually crash-landed at Moore's Island, and that the pilot was then at Marsh Harbour.

Jonathan Dean corroborates this, as he saw the schooner carrying young Fyfield from Moore's Island to Marsh Harbor. He saw it sail around the northern tip, then northeast to the Marls, a distance of about 35 miles. The flight to Nassau was 90 miles, and some 400 nautical miles for Fyfield to fly back to base and contemplate his future in the navy. He survived, and his children (Joy and Herbert S. Fyfield Jr.) have much to be joyful for that he did.

Back in Hard Bargain, the patrons of the Talk of the Town bar were accommodating, and fortunately for us it was a national holiday to celebrate women's suffrage in The Bahamas. Without a doubt, the rediscovery of the aircraft was, and is, a team effort. Without their assistance on the ground, I am convinced that we would not have found the plane. And no one asked for anything in return—in fact, we were offered fresh fish and lobster brought out to our boat the following sunrise before we sailed.

Given Abaco's position in the northeast Bahamas, forming with Grand Bahama both the first barrier to the islands from the north as well as the backstop to the Northeast and Northwest Providence Channels facilitating ship traffic between the Americas and Europe, there is much more to say about Abaco in World War II. However, no other aircraft wrecks have yet been found - yet. One was salvaged, and the other is probably enveloped in the mud of the Marls.

Comprising nearly 900 square miles, Great and Little Abaco and its many cays were under observation by several German U-boats during World War II, as well as Allies in transit, and was the site of significant rescues of Allied merchant ship crews in Hope Town and the Cornwall lumber camp in Cross Harbour. At least four aircraft were lost there: Moore's Island, in Pelican Bay, possibly near northern Cornwall in the park area to the south, and off Little Abaco, attributed to Grand Bahama as it was in the Paw Congel Rocks vicinity. After the war, a Grumman Goose seaplane rescued the injured from Norman's Castle, within the vicinity of Cherokee Sound. The Duke and Duchess of Windsor's captain cut the southeast corner of Great Abaco too closely and grounded the large motor yacht *Rene*, owned by the head of General Motors, off Hole-in-the-Wall Light during the war. A seaplane base was stationed for a time in Pelican Bay as well as over a dozen German subs and at least one Italian one—the *Enrico Tazzoli*—towards the eastern approach.

"About midday several smoke clouds come in sight. These proved, after a half-hour hunt, to be a smoking chimney on Great Abaco Island. The east entrance of the Providence Channel is unmonitored. Nothing seen up to the entrance to the Florida Straits; no surveillance," so wrote an enemy invader in command of the German undersea or U-boat U-134. He was 29, born in Spandau, and named *Kapitänleutnant*

Rudolf Schendel. The following day was July 17, 1942, and as he passed Moore's Island he observed, "Lighthouse Great Stirrup Cay in sight, bearing 270° True. Lighthouse Great Isaac in sight. Lighthouse Bimini in sight. Lighthouse Cat Cays in sight. All lights burn as in peacetime... [and later] I have just arrived in the Bahama Channel," adding that "I suspect that traffic now passes close to the Great and Little Bahama Banks."

On April 29, 1942, another German submarine, U-506, under Erich Würdemann, was east of The Bahamas and heading for the entry passage between Eleuthera and Abaco which would provide access to the Straits of Florida and the Gulf of Mexico. Then, on May 2, he ran the sub on the surface right past the capital of the Bahamas with both diesel engines engaged and making 14-to-15 knots in the Northeast Providence Channel. The 29-year-old *Kapitänleutnant* Würdemann noted in the war diary: "Abaco Lighthouse is bearing 0° True, 5 nautical miles distant. Ran through the NW Providence Channel. Except for two small sailing vessels, nothing seen. All lighthouses are lit as in peacetime."

Only when they "entered the Florida Straits" above Great Isaac Light did the U-506 submerge, by which point the conditions were calm, "visibility good, clear, bright as day" even during the night. In short, they transited The Bahamas with impunity, since there were so few defenses at the time. The Allies hoped that a strong RAF presence in Nassau might soon change that. The next U-boat, out of 112 patrols, that claimed seeing Abaco on July 15, 1943, was the U-134 under Hans-Günther Brosin, who also motored due west for Hole-in-the-Wall, Abaco, arriving on the 15th. By the following day, U-134 was in the Gulf Stream heading south in the Straits of Florida to sink the only airship sunk by U-boat in WWII.

At dawn of the leap-year February 29, 1944, the skipper of the motor boat *Blue Fish* and four of his crewmates reported seeing two submarines on the surface 18 miles west of Moore's Island, Abaco. However, there were no U-boats in the area at the time, and it was determined they actually saw two small vessels, the Canadian-Bahamian passenger ferry *Jean Brillant* and her escort, the sub chaser USS *SC-1295*, heading west at the time. Of course, not only foes but also friends, they motored through The Bahamas using the lights of Abaco for guidance: on April 23, 1944, the USS *Dynamic* (AM-91's) commanding officer noted in the log that just after sunset his ship was just eight miles from Hole-in-the-Wall Light, Abaco.

Between 1943 and 1945, USS *Christiana*, IX-80, YAG-32, was under the command of Lt. (j.g.) Anthony DeFrances USNR as a seaplane tender in Pelican Bay,

Abaco and Royal Island, Eleuthera for Squadron VB-132. She was built in New York in 1891 as the Lighthouse Tender *Azalea*, and decommissioned in September, 1945. The ship was 393 gross tons, 145' long, 24' wide, and 12'7" deep. From late 1942 to June 1943, the *Christiana* was at Royal Island, then moved to Pelican Bay, then back to the US for overhaul. Unfortunately, there were seaplane accidents at all the islands in The Bahamas that the *Christiana* was based at including later at Walker's Cay.

On September 20, 1943, a Martin PBM-3S Mariner, the large amphibious plane, suffered a water loop while landing, which is like spinning out of control but on the water. The accident took place in proximity to USS *Christiana* in Pelican Bay, Abaco, and as a result the aircraft was struck from active service, though parts of it were probably salvaged and recycled. It was part of Squadron VP-208. By September 21, 1944, USS *Christiana* was based at Walker's Cay, north of Grand Bahama in FairWing-12, and placed on alert due to a suspected submarine in the region.

On July 20, 1943, US Marine Captain Boyd C. Whitney was in command of the PV-1 belonging to Squadron VPB-2. Ventura's was built by Lockheed Corporation for the US Navy as a much-used twin-engine medium range patrol bomber. Whitney and his crew of five included Thomas G. Johnston, Emil L. Mennes, George L. Parrish, and Albert P. Emsley. The plane was on a navigation instructional flight from NAS Stanford in Florida when, in the air above Great Abaco Island, a fire broke out. They were flying east towards land, and the crew were able to relay details of their emergency to land. Captain Whitney smoothly landed the aircraft in the shallow mangroves known as "the Marls" of western Abaco, thus putting out the fire. The men all walked away and were rescued. Three weeks later, however, at 2.45 p.m. on August 12, 1943 the RAF B-25 Mitchell bomber FR375-CL landed in Nassau at 3.17 pm after training exercises over Abaco. Intriguingly, the pilot reported that "at 14.45 in position DDAJ5743 [a coded position] a Ventura-type aircraft appeared to be forced-landed. The turret and engine had been removed, and the tail was observed to be in a lake nearby." That is Major Whitney's PV-1, and it must be close to main road south of Crossing Rocks.

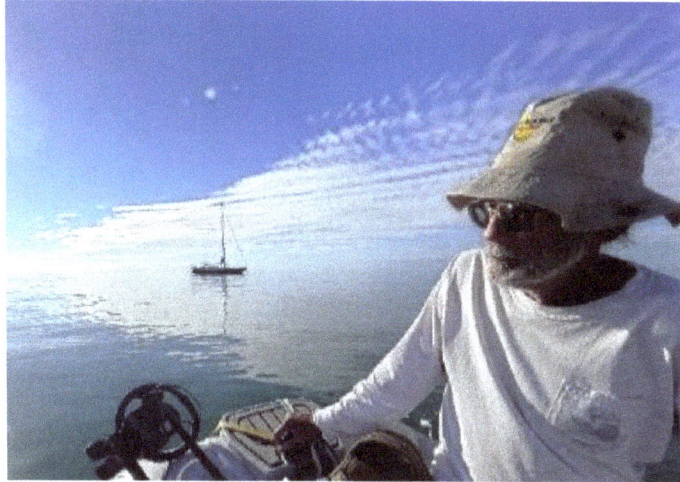

Back to the boat, Hard Bargain. Captain Howard at right with metal detector.

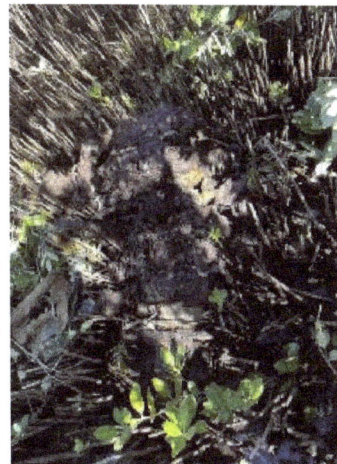

Close-up of the engine we found; on an aircraft and in the mangrove swamp.

Investigating the mangrove swamp for the Wildcat; James, AJ, and Charlie.

Sharing fishing and sea stories shortly after dawn, anchored off Hard Bargain.

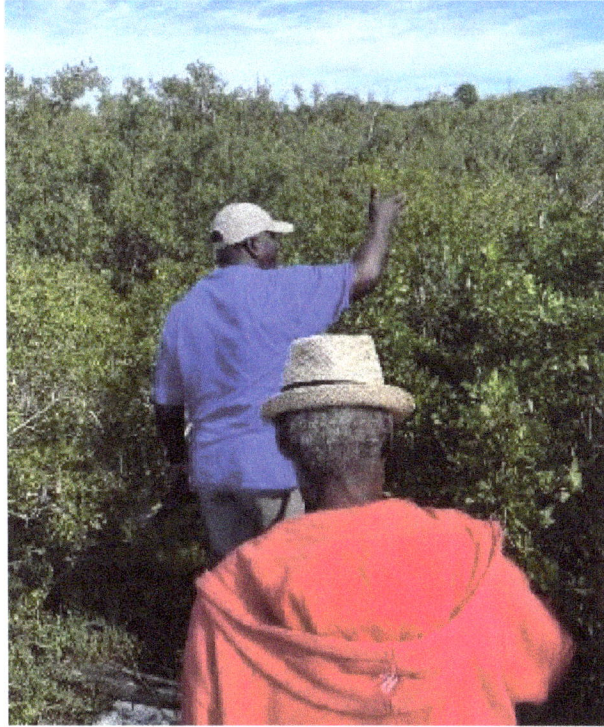

Mr. Modi (Jonathan Dean) and Antoine witnessed the plane crashing and lead us.

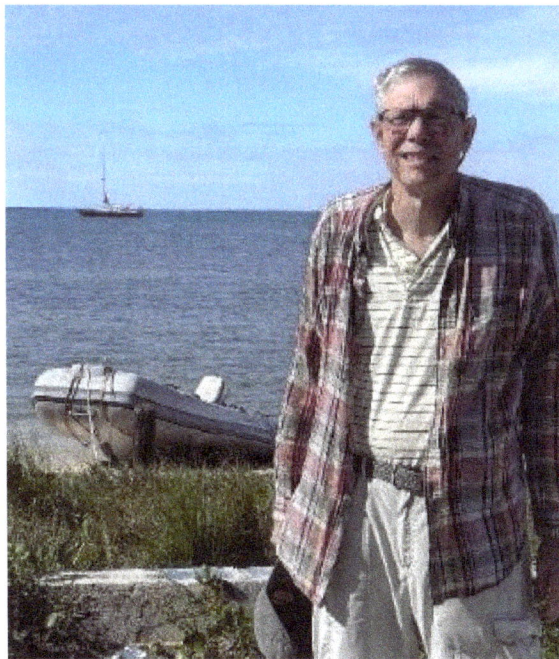

Affable circumnavigator, Boy Scout Troop leader, and adoptive parent, Charlie.

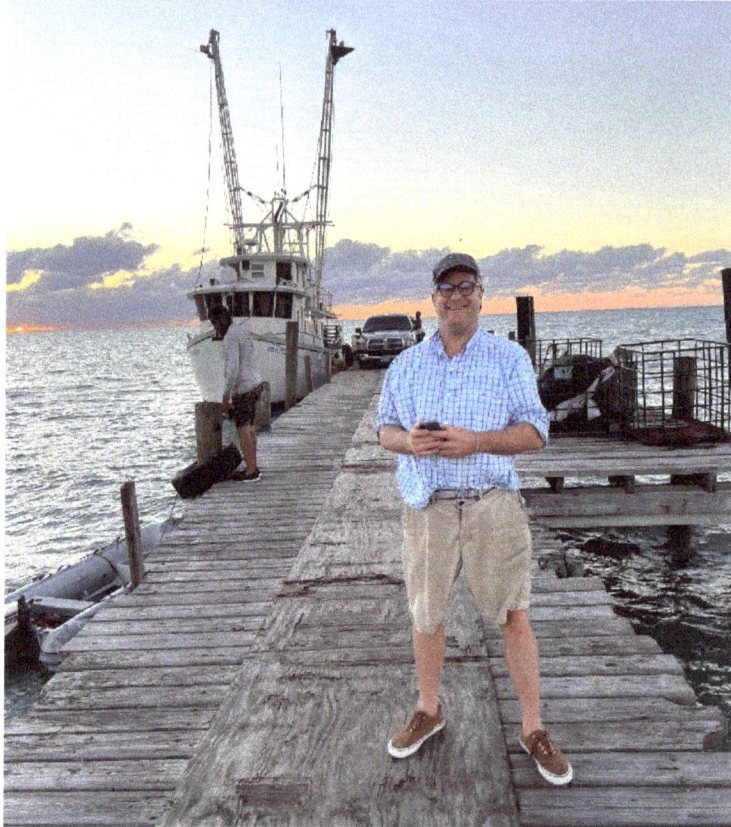

Returning to the public dock at Hard Bargain after 32 years.

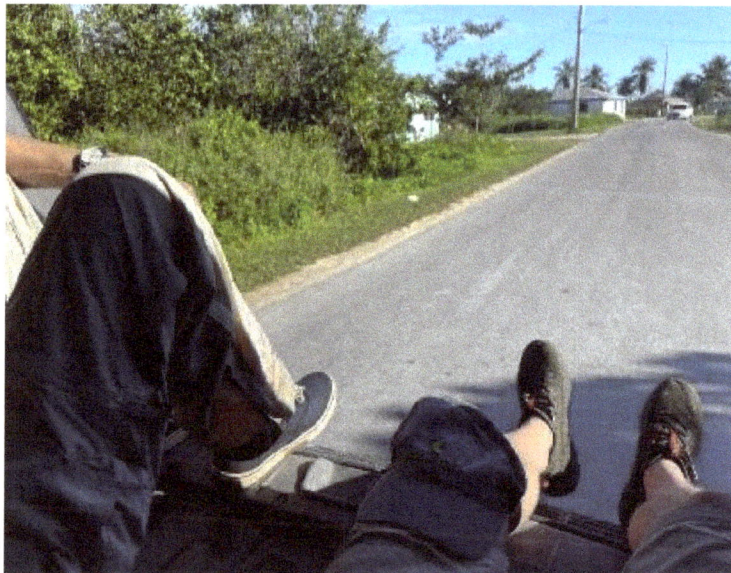

Charlie and I hitch a ride back to the dinghy.

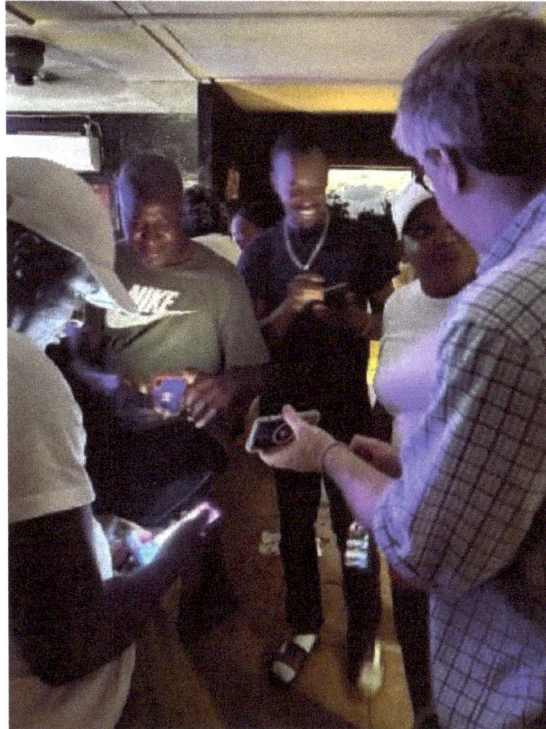

Lighting up the local social hall with smiles over photos from 30 years before;
one man recognized his mother!

View from the roadside store and eatery in Hard Bargain.

Antoine Sr., his son AJ, Jonathan Modi Dean, Capt. Howard, James, our volunteer guide, and Charlie.

A Lockheed Ventura PV-1, like the one lost in Abaco on July 20, 1943. Pilot Major Boyd Whitney, a seasoned US Marine Corps pilot, landed it safely. I've hiked swathes of the Abaco shoreline and pine barrens, looking for a Norwegian sailor in the nebulous "Cornwall" and found ruins of two aircraft. It's not an easy place to find things without precise data, but I reckon that bonefish guides will know.

Ships passing day and night—this tanker *Tokyo Spirit* lay off Freeport waiting to discharge petroleum. It is owned by TeeKay, which stands for Torben Karlshoej, who was based in Nassau in the 1970s; his children went to St. Andrew's.

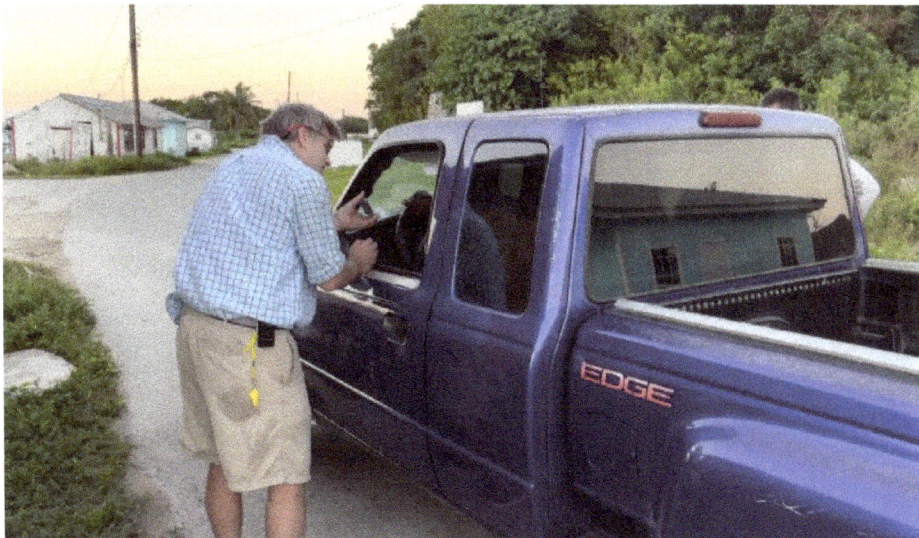

Interviewing Rev. and Mrs. Ishmael Williams in Hard Bargain.

Chapter Nine:

Clifton Bay, Lyford Cay, B-26 All KIA

Four RAF pilots from the UK, Canada, and South Africa, came within 100 feet of a smooth water landing yards off of Lyford Cay one fall evening when things suddenly went horribly wrong. The plane, one of its engines ablaze, smashed into the reef between Goulding Cay and Clifton Bay, Lyford Cay and even though help arrived minutes later, all of them had perished. In November 2022, just under 80 years later, a team of four amateur divers found the distinctive bomb doors with two windows— a circular one inset on a rectangular one—from the B-26 Marauder. It is likely that the two other trainee pilots were not in the cockpit at the time but were anxiously looking through that same belly window at the sea below when they crashed. Two of them were buried in Nassau, the other two were never recovered, and efforts to reach their families have so far not yielded results.

Of the four aviators, Roland Henry Barber, age 21, was the son of Roland Arthur and Gladys Mabel Barber, of Northampton, England. Douglas Waitt Whitehurst Cormack was Canadian, as was Denis Durward. John Griffith Owen was the senior pilot on board, and had earned a Distinguished Flying Cross. Aged 27, Flight Lieutenant Owen was the son of David Griffith and Olive Eveline Owen of Winklespruit, Natal, South Africa. Barber, Durward, and Cormack were student pilots. At 6:30 p.m. the day after the accident, Owen and Barber were buried in the RAF Cemetery in Nassau, with full-service honors, with RAF Chaplain Squadron Leader, the Rev. E. J. Jay, conducting the ceremony.

Douglas Cormack was from Winnipeg, Manitoba and studied at Isaac Brock and Gordon Bell schools. He left a job at the Winnipeg Electrical Company to enlist in the RAF in July of 1941 and earned his wings in Macleod, Alberta. His posting to the RAF Ferry Command took him to Dorval, outside Montreal, and thence to Nassau. At home, Douglas liked to play tennis with the Greenwood Church youth. He left two brothers, Jack and Gordon.

This B-26 was delivered to the RAF from the USAAF just a month before. It took off on Wednesday, October 13, 1943, from Windsor Field on a training flight for No. 113 Transport Wing, RAFTC, heading to the northwest and circling back to practice landings and takeoffs. At 9:20 p.m., it crashed in the sea off Lyford Cay without sending any Mayday message. The RAF relates that "the aircraft was on a routine training flight and had been doing circuits and landings for two hours, when, at about 1,000 feet, the port engine was seen to be on fire. The pilot apparently tried to ditch the aircraft [at sea] but was seen to stall at about 100 feet [altitude], and crashed into the sea." Smoke floats and an oil patch were seen by at least one other aircraft, a B-24 Liberator. A crash, or rescue, boat from the nearby RAF air-sea-rescue base nearby in the original Lyford Cay canal, near the wishing well on Clifton Bay Drive, was quickly on site.

"All of the crew were killed, and only two bodies of F/Lt. J. G. Owen, D.F.C., and F/O R. H. Barber, were recovered." From another observer's perspective, at 9:15 p.m. the "Marauder FB454 dived into the sea one-mile due West of Windsor Field during a training flight. Cause unknown. One engine, believed port, caught fire in air." Durward and Cormack "are missing and in spite of an extensive search being carried out, no trace of the bodies could be found." Since no radio signal was sent, the casualty was not known until other aircraft in training going back and forth to the base noticed it. "First a smoke float and a patch of oil was sighted over Simms Point, Lyford Cay, the very northwest tip of New Providence. Message was intercepted from a Liberator in the vicinity 'Searching for survivors.' An ASR launch was observed to be approaching."

Eyewitnesses included military guards at Clifton Pier who reported that at 9:20 p.m. they saw flames at that location. "At 9:30 p.m. a report was received from D.F.C. 60, Windsor Field, that... a B-26, belonging to the RAFTC... had crashed into flames into the sea, between Lyford Cay and Goulding's Cay. A Liberator on local flying circled the scene of the crash. A.S.R. launch was dispatched... The boat recovered the bodies of two of the occupants. It was thought that there were four occupants of the aircraft. Arrangements were made for a further search to be carried out at dawn."

This crash site is also confused, or conflated, with a B-25 Mitchell due to mis-communications calling the B-26 a B-25, which was a much more common training aircraft in The Bahamas at the time. This in turn led to a belief for over 75 years that there were two different aircraft in Clifton Bay: a B-25, which professional diver Stuart Cove found in 1983, and the B-26, which a team of colleagues and I thought we discovered in November 2022. Stuart personally dived much of this plane wreck going back decades. Our family is fortunate to have a long association with Stuart; when I "ran away from home" to the Caves out West in my early teens, Stuart gave me a lift at dawn, and decades later, he hired my godson.

Unlike many people who find historically significant things, Stuart was very forthright with me about the "B-25" he found in Clifton Bay. Ironically, this stymied any progress until we found aircraft pieces that could only be from a B-26, such as the bomb door with double windows. By that point, I had found two other B-26 Marauders in The Bahamas, both ashore and at sea. Stuart and I had found the same plane, yet we each called it different names.

The volunteers who located pieces of the B-26 in 2022 were led by Rich Ashman of New Orleans aboard his dive support boat *Kimber-L,* and the crew included Lamar Ard, Rusty Schull, and me. Two family members also shared their vessels; my brother John Wiberg and his 23' Mako *Shoal Shaker*, and another relative, Amanda Lindroth, owner of the lobster boat *Schooner Queen*. John towed me behind each boat until I found various pieces of the aircraft on November 13-to-14, 2022. Then from November 15-to-18 I lived aboard Rich's boat, also diving daily, which was an act of faith for all of us, since I had never met Rich or his crew!

My siblings and me often sought shelter in Clifton Bay growing up, and I met Bill Buckley on the bay in the 1990s to discuss my writing. As anyone who has been there can attest, the cove is a very charming and gorgeous place. And it turns out the Cormack and Durward families have others who consider Clifton Bay sacred to the memories of family members; my godson and nephew had his ashes scattered there, and close friends lost their father in a boating accident there.

Douglas Waitt Whitehurst Cormack

The open bomb doors of a B-26 Marauder.

Lifting the bomb door from the sea floor after over 80 years.

Subsea perspective of the Marauder's bomb door.

More images of the bomb door and volunteers from Rich Ashman of *Kimber-L*.

Dinghies at rest, Clifton Bay, looking west to Goulding Cay at sunset.

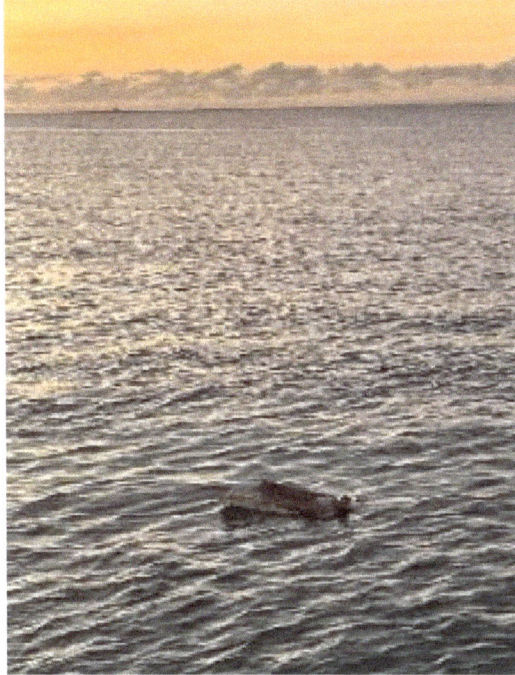

A fuel tank frame, photographed and released on site, floats away.

Hydraulic tubing consistent with the other B-26's found in Delaporte and Acklins.

Stainless steel case from the B-26 in Clifton Bay, likely to store ammunition.

Fuselage and door locking mechanism from the B-26 found in Clifton Bay.

Diver heading from the RAF ASR Base in Lyford Cay to *Kimber-L.*, November 2022.

Supplies for *Kimber-L*; adventure requires logistical support.

Chapter Ten:

Great Exuma, Historic 1930 Wright Bros. Engine

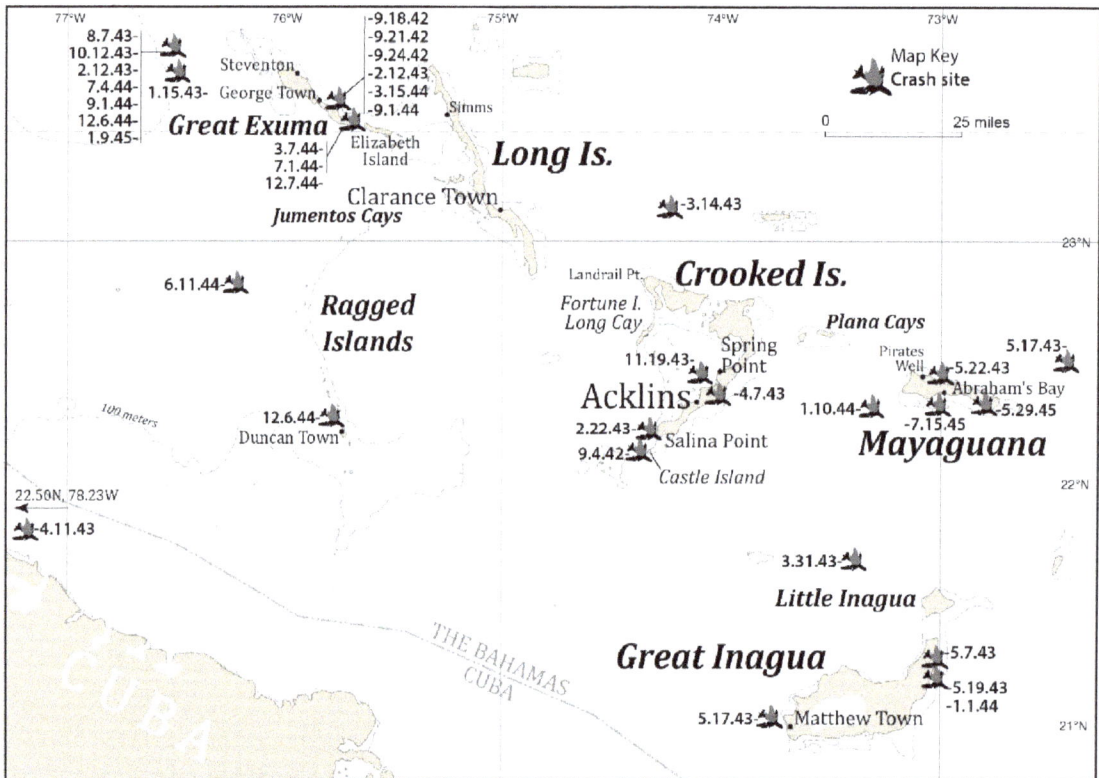

In 1930, two significant historical aircraft, one with a life-long-crippled man as radio operator, the other with a solo Australian aviatrix, crashed in The Bahamas, in Andros and Exuma. Because the woman quickly retrieved her aircraft, and the Exuma wreck was burned after it flipped and caught fire in a swamp and was abandoned, little attention was paid to either plane. That changed in 2020, when a radio historian in California wrote to the pre-eminent aviation historian in The Bahamas, my mentor Captain Paul A. Aranha, and more attention was brought to the crashes. Paul offered me a chance to find the historic aircraft in Exuma. Five days in the field, have taught us there are three strands to this story: what the aviators did before The Bahamas, what happened in their brief stay there, and what happened to their aircraft and those seeking it since.

The story began to make headlines on the early morning of April 2, 1930: an airplane which had set out to fly to Bermuda from the continental United States had recently gone missing. This was a rare Stinson aircraft and its engine was made by the Wright Brothers. The same year three men left New York in an attempt to be the first to fly to Bermuda and survive. According to the endurance limits, the plane could not still be flying after a certain number of hours. Yet the three men (Pilot William Alexander, Navigator Lewis Yancey, and Radioman Zeh Bouck, who could not walk without crutches due to a bout of childhood polio), had in fact landed on the bosom of the ocean in their seaplane named *Pilot Radio* for their sponsors in Lawrence, Massachusetts.

Having sailed to or from Bermuda 32 times, I am in awe of the fact that these men slept afloat, then in the morning were able to take off from the high seas and make it inside the large barrier reef to the north of Bermuda. There they ran out of fuel and anchored, radioing for support. The savvy Bermudians brought fuel to them and they took off once more and landed in the harbor. At first, they were threatened with fines and arrest. However, the tourism upside to the marketing and publicity accompanying the new visitors soon dawned on the local officials and the aviators were given a warm(er) welcome and even a large prize purse. Importantly, from an artifact perspective, since their aircraft was damaged during the flights, they gifted both a propeller and a gyrocompass to their Bermudian patrons. Then they shipped the plane back to New York.

At that time, it was incredibly competitive in the aviation world—hundreds of people were pushing boundaries every day it seemed, and fame could be immediate and lasting: Charles Lindberg, Amelia Earhart, Beryl Markham, Antoine de Saint-Exupéry, the Wright Brothers, Jean Batten, Kingsford Smith from Australia, Francis Chichester, and many others were vying for fame. Some of these aviators also wrecked in The Bahamas, including young Jessie Maude "Chubbie" Miller, the Australian woman aviator. Her flight over in late November 1930 from Cuba to Florida involved such bad weather that she ditched on a beach in Mangrove Cay, Andros, hiked alone many miles, took a ferry to another island, then a fishing boat to Nassau, and a flight to Miami before going back to retrieve her plane.

In such an intensely competitive milieu, the captain, navigator and radioman of *Pilot Radio* undertook a massively ambitious airborne good will tour covering much of South America. That same year, they flew from Mexico counter-clockwise down the Andes, up the east coast, to the Dominican Republic, then over Cuba and towards Miami via Bahamas. There the plane still remains. California radio historian Robert (Bob) Rydzewski has skillfully tabulated all the details. On September 14, 1930, in a piece titled "Yancey Describes His Plane Crash" the *New York Times* recounts how *Pilot Radio* (NR 487H) was a Stinson SM-1FS monoplane, 47' wide, 32' long, with room for one pilot, and capacity for six passengers. The engine was a Wright J6 9-cylinder, 300-hp Wright Whirlwind. The frame was made out of fabric was stretched over steel or aluminum tubing, rather than wood, so in a fire not everything ought to go up in smoke. However, the engine, struts, and much of the cabin superstructure was made of high-quality steel, particularly the oleo legs and anything associated with the landing gear, the fuel tanks, and support for the heavy engine, as well as piping and communications equipment.

The *New York Times* and Yancey, Burgin and Bouck (his *nom-de-guerre*) all detail what happened next. On May 14, 1930, the three men began their circumnavigation of South America; they were only an hour from completing it in Miami when their plane wrecked. At dawn on Thursday, September 11, 1930, they left San Juan for Miami. At 8 a.m. *Pilot Radio* flew over hurricane-ravaged Santo Domingo, Dominican Republic with the three men. At 1 p.m., after passing Port au Prince and the Windward Passage, they turned north from Cuba to the southern Bahamas. At 1:30 p.m. they were passing Raccoon Cay, in the Ragged Island or Jumento Cays, when their engine mounting broke a bracket, threatening to wobble out of its cradle at even the lowest rpm.

They made for Great Exuma, and passed Georgetown at about 3 p.m. As the vibrations reached emergency levels, the men desperately sought a place to land. Before 4 p.m. pilot Yancey espied what he believed was a smooth dry patch of packed sand at the base of gentle hills, and committed to landing on it. Unfortunately, the sand was swept by tidal currents and two feet of translucent water greeted the wheels of *Pilot Radio* on impact. Rather than coast a long distance, the wheels were caught in the mire. The plane carried forward and flipped onto its back. From that point they became the responsibility of the District Commissioner Pyfrom, local Justice of the Peace J. M. Bowe Jr. and residents of The Forest, Great Exuma, The commissioner cabled to Nassau that the aviators had:

"ENGINE TROUBLE TRIED LAND BUT COULD NOT LOCATE A SAFE PLACE STOP PLANE MADE A FORCED LANDING NEAR TELFAIR STRUCK MARL IN

MANGROVES AND OVERTURNED CREW HAD TO ESCAPE." Amazingly, all the men were alive despite the gear and equipment cascading down upon them and being hung upside down. In the words of the pilot: "An immediate landing was necessary and the only available spot not covered with rocks was a swamp. We glided in and made a still landing, but the ship went over on its back, piling crew, baggage and radio equipment in a heap. No one was injured in this, though all were bruised and shaken badly. The crew got out and managed to save some of the baggage when the ship suddenly burst into flames and was completely destroyed."

The men, Bouck unable to walk without crutches, were roughly 14 miles from Georgetown, in an area only visited by shepherds and artisanal farmers. They clambered out of the wreck, gathered what they could, and were sitting disconsolately watching the shell of their hopes and glory when a farmer ran towards them. He had seen that a spark was setting fire to the craft, and warned them to retreat further from the plane. Instead, Yancey raced towards *Pilot Radio* to salvage more materials, only for the plane's gasoline to explode as he approached, sending him hurtling 10 feet backwards and burning his right arm quite badly.

From that point onwards, they were at the mercy of their hosts. Justice of the Peace J. M. Bowe Jr. did an exemplary job of accommodating them. The commissioner was sent for, and he enlisted a doctor to assist. They did not arrive in The Forest (where artist Amos Ferguson grew up) until midnight, and saw to Yancey's injuries. Bouck, in crutches, could not move quickly or far, and they all slept in a crude fisherman's shack. Bouck says, "We spent the night in a native fishing hut, and on Friday started by a small fishing schooner to Nassau, arriving at 3 p.m. Saturday," September 13. Given the shallowness and lack of ports on the west side, it is likely they were taken by horse and buggy or possibly car east for roughly four miles to deeper waters to join the schooner.

The schooner *Louise* hurried them to Nassau, where they were photographed looking dejected, probably at the Royal Victoria Hotel. Then the men raced to Miami and New York to tell the story of their months-long flight around South and Central America and the Caribbean, and their near-miss survival. They never went back to The Bahamas, and no one went back to salvage *Pilot Radio*. The assumption was that the aircraft was destroyed, and no one is known to have gone looking for it, until 2022.

After Bob Rydzewski, who has had a life-long fascination with radios and aviation and never lets go of a story until all the details are known, wrote to Paul Aranha and Chris Curry in 2020 that "as far as I know its remains are still there somewhere today... I know that the best information sources are local. So, I was trying to reach someone in The Bahamas who might be able to check."

Then in the fall of 2022, over 72 years after the crash, the assignment fell onto my desk. Then, with characteristic hubris and overconfidence, and relying too much on technology, I made several mistakes. Determined to find the plane in a month or less, I obtained the commissioner's reports, which convinced me that everyone else was wrong and my hunch on the location of the crash was the right one. I corroborated this with grainy satellite images, and called Captain Steven Cole to arrange a guide, an off-road vehicle, and a hotel. In October 2022, I spent two days flying from Boston to Exuma. Thrashing around in the mangroves, I achieved almost nothing except nearly blinding my right eye, badly infecting my left thigh with a fungal bacterium for months, and spending more money than I could part with to simply canvas a broad area and return without spotting a shard of metal.

I helped organize an expedition with old sailing buddies and we anchored in Steventon near Rolleville, Great Exuma in January 2023, and immediately set out for the hamlet of Curtiss where Edison Rolle told us he had seen the plane near Richmond Hill. The reason why this account will leave readers in suspense is because the airplane has not been found. Only small bits of metal, possibly from a battery or radio, including copper, brass, melted aluminum, and steel, have been sighted and are being tested. Since *Pilot Radio* is arguably the most historically significant aircraft in Bahamian territory, we will have to wait until a sixth and seventh visit to the site.

The fueling idea was that the wheel struts and engine ought to be visible above the 'marl' or 'mash'—local words for marsh and mangrove. Bob informed me that "... towards the end of the journey, the landing gear had buckled a couple of times and was repaired at least twice, once by a convicted murderer at Devil's Island." Yet, one hundred hours in five days of very hard hiking, tramping, searching, much of it alone, has not yielded the 92-year-old mother lode... yet.

Many, however, including David Smith and Margaret McKenzie of Stuart Manor, and Ken Simmons, the conch vendor at Pompey House, teacher Everette Hart, and others, remember visiting the site of the plane. Ms. McKenzie was 10 at the time and says it was in the mud, and clearly was a plane. Ken Simmons says it lies in the grass among the tide, and that over time, sea algae and grass have overgrown and covered the site. Fisherman David Smith of The Forest questions what the big deal is—there is a bigger drug plane sunk further out to sea that is more intact and photogenic.

The war in Georgetown has left behind an impressive array of air and maritime infrastructure and wrecks. Inside, or west of Stocking Island was the site of almost all the mishaps and the nucleus of most of the rescue attempts. Rumors of enemy activity in nearby cays are unsubstantiated, since it would be difficult to think of a more hostile and useless area for Germans or Italians to patrol, and indeed none of them ever did. With a naval air station and naval operating base there, as well as a mailboat and rescue hub, Georgetown was the largest US base between Florida and Guantanamo, so it was a mouse that roared, with several sub-stations in Mayaguana and San Salvador. German U-boat commander Herbert A. Werner confirmed as much to me.

The US Navy historian of Squadron VP-92 described Great Exuma early in the war as: "Little more than a sand dune with a few barracks and a radio station, the harbor facilities were ideal. The beaching gear was adequate to efficiently handle a half-dozen aircraft. It was a marine base with wooden barracks, a small canteen, and an open-air theatre. The plane crews did most of the work; in addition to flying, they beached, gassed, and maintained the aircraft. VP-32 had a detachment there, and the men of both squadrons [VP-92] worked well together."

"The naval air station [NAS] on Great Exuma Island was constructed, under the Guantanamo contract, to support a squadron of seaplanes used for patrol operations along... the numerous passages through The Bahamas... 324 leased acres on the southeast tip of the island, which occupied a strategic central position. Construction was begun during December 1941, and the station was commissioned on May 15, 1942. The principal operating facilities, comprising a 50-foot timber seaplane ramp, a concrete parking area, 400 by 300 feet, and a 180-foot barge pier, were located on a partly natural and partly dredged-in beach adjacent to the seaplane landing and takeoff area. This area of water, 3 miles long, is protected from the open sea by Stocking Island, which forms a natural barrier one mile offshore, directly opposite the station."

"Seventy-nine buildings included... 28 Quonset huts... quarters for 80 officers and 180 enlisted men, a 10-bed dispensary, an administration building, storehouses, a chapel, a bakery, a power house, and several industrial buildings. Located on high ground adjacent to the beach, they occupied an area of 59 acres. The remainder of the tract was devoted to magazines... During the early construction period, pieces of rock and stone were picked up from around the island by local labor at a set price per yard, and broken into usable size by women laborers using small hammers."

"Dredging operations created a seaplane operating area with a minimum depth of 6 feet, improved the small-vessel anchorage in Stocking Harbor, and deepened the approach channel to the anchorage. A considerable portion of the 750,000 cubic yards of dredged material was used to reclaim the beach area needed for seaplane operating facilities. Fresh water for the station, obtained from seven drilled wells, was filtered, chlorinated, and stored in a 100,000-gallon underground reservoir built of concrete. No Seabee personnel participated. [The base was active for over three years, from May 1942 until] its disestablishment in June 1945."

On September 21, 1942, US Navy Pilot R. J. Finnie on a Consolidated PBY-5A Catalina in VP-92 began a sea landing off Stocking Island. Unfortunately, the landing resulted in a high-speed water crash, and the aircraft sank and was lost. Captain Finnie was killed and the PBY was damaged beyond repair. Generally, the USN salvaged sunken and damaged aircraft. PBYs are maritime patrol bombers for search and rescue built by the Consolidated Aircraft Corp. of Rhode Island, and is the most utilized seaplane of World War II, serving in all US service branches as well as under many nations' flags since. It accommodated ten-crew, was 63' 10" long, 104' wide, 21' 1" high, two radial engines each with three propellers, a max speed of 196 mph, range of 2,520 nm, bombs, two torpedoes, four depth charges, and five machine guns.

On Columbus Day, October 12, 1943, Georgetown received an urgent message from RAF Nassau relaying that there was "a plane with one engine afire and losing altitude" near Darby Cay, Exumas, roughly 40 miles north, and that "the plane was not theirs." Authorities determined that two other planes were in the vicinity, however, they were safe and undamaged by fire.

As usual with the No. 111 Operational Training Unit, over a dozen aircraft, day and night, were taking off in the vicinity of North Exuma and south of New Providence in training exercises from Oakes Field and delivery flights from Windsor Field. Per the daily base diaries for that day, all "aircraft completed the patrol without incident and landed." Nevertheless at 2;53 p.m., the US Navy dispatched a Martin P-5M Mariner aircraft "to make search surrounding Darby Island for aircraft reported." At 6 p.m., the plane returned after over three hours during which its crew lowered their heads and stared out the portals for their friends and barrack-mates, only to report that "results from search were negative." By dawn the following day, the bases logged that "the report shall be considered erroneous. (File Closed)." It was another Darby Island false-sighting; however, the appetite of realtors and others for salacious stories about

Darby persists today, notwithstanding that there are no facilities there to accomplish any manner of resupply for ocean-going submarines, who had their own supply subs.

A wide variety of tasks are undertaken by the personnel at these remote bases. A telegram from the Commissioner of Arthur's Town and Cat Island to the south arrived, detailing a wreck drifting between his island and theirs. The partially submerged derelict's mast stuck 50 feet out of the water, only 20 miles south of Little Exuma, and was considered a hazard to navigation, so the NAS agreed to use it as target practice and destroy it. At noon on July 1, 1944, an amphibious Martin PBM Mariner aircraft was attempting to take off from the underwater runway of NAS Georgetown. To avoid striking another aircraft in formation the pilot made a drastic turn, and the seaplane hit a navigation buoy. Given the high speed, it sank quickly, killing all six crew members.

As tragic as they were, such accidents were not uncommon. Less than three months later, on September 24, 1944, an airplane in VP-92 was trying to land on Exuma's sea runway while it was not lit, and crashed. Although the plane was destroyed, no one was killed, though several of the crew were injured. The following week, on October 1, a US Navy aircraft carrier was passing through The Bahamas *en route* from the US to Panama via Windward Passage when an aircraft landed on Exuma. At 3:49 p.m., the group simulated an attack by carrier planes, and 21 minutes later, stood by to recover the aircraft. Just before 5 p.m., 54 planes had made it back to the carrier. However, the carrier USS *Ticonderoga* reported an airplane missing. Within half an hour, the task force was searching for the missing aircraft with two planes launched from this ship along with smoke made to enable the pilot to return to the ship. By 6:22 p.m. the search planes were back on board and it was learned that the missing aircraft "had landed safely at NAS, Great Exuma," and the ships headed towards Guantanamo. Presumably, the plane later joined them from Exuma to Cuba.

On June 26, 1945, a USAAF Curtiss C-47 went missing off Ship Channel Cay, southeast of New Providence and in the northern Exumas. At 3:49 p.m., a B-25 was sent on a search and rescue mission from Nassau and returned at 7:07 p.m. Then a Grumman Goose was sent at 3:54 p.m., returning at 6 p.m. The search was joined by RAF crash boat HMS *P-191*. The plane was not found. Such are the tragedies and mysteries of war, in which the Exuma Islands and its resilient people participated, whether in building the bases; manning the many vessels supplying it; or operating, witnessing, and reporting wartime equipment.

The *Pilot Radio* crew (L-R: Yancey, Bouck, and Alexander) feted by a welcoming entourage in Bermuda, 1930—after initially being threatened with fines and arrest!

L-R: The Bahamas crew; Burgin, Bouck, and Yancey at *Pilot Radio*; 1930 publicity.

— PLAN of the ISLAND —
— of —
GREAT EXUMA

PLAN OF THE ISLAND
— of —
LITTLE EXUMA

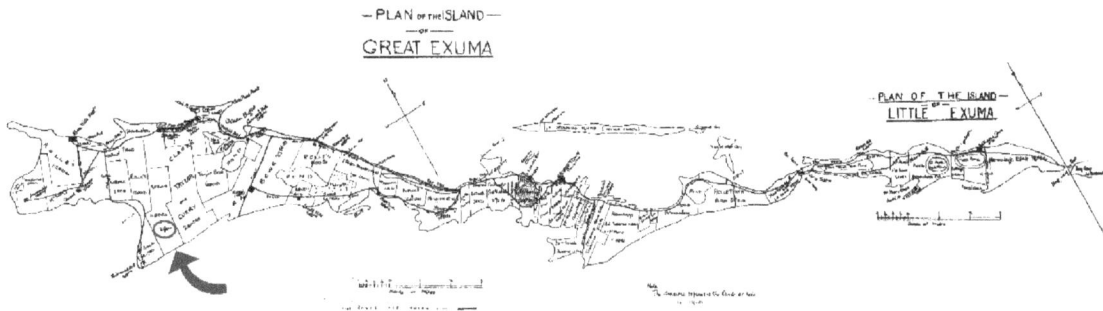

But where did the aircraft overturn? Map of *Pilot Radio*'s 1930 demise, Great Exuma.

Pilot Radio's ignoble end: flipped, aflame, and abandoned. Burnt metal was found on a fifth day of searching—but is it from this aircraft? Metallurgists will tell.

Pilot Radio in 1930 being refueled in Bermuda as the first to land there.

The despondent crew of *Pilot Radio* in Nassau after arriving by schooner *Louise* from Georgetown, Exuma in September 1930, before being flown to New York. Probably this is at the Royal Victoria Hotel, whose proprietress Clara Mallory-Munson welcome survivors Tapscott & Widdicombe of the *Anglo-Saxon* in 1940.

Intrepid guide Renardo D'Arville at sunset after seeking *Pilot Radio* all day in 2022.

Seeking *Pilot Radio* in often deep tidal brackish water, fall 2022.

Pieces of *Pilot Radio*? Found from *Parole* in January 2023.

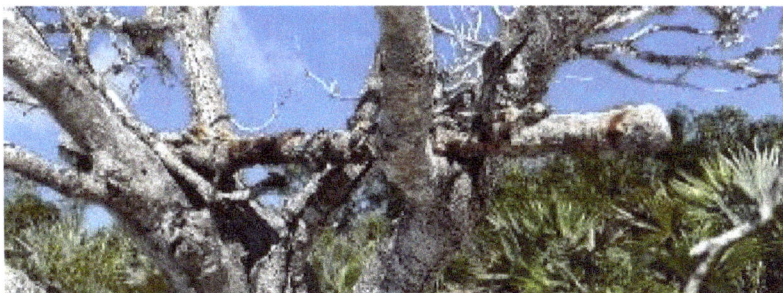

This heavy-metal strut could well be a brace from *Pilot Radio*; January 2023 expedition, fifth and final day, solo. *Pilot Radio* parts were immersed in tidal terrain.

These men paused making a tomb to tell Charlie and I about seeing *Pilot Radio*.

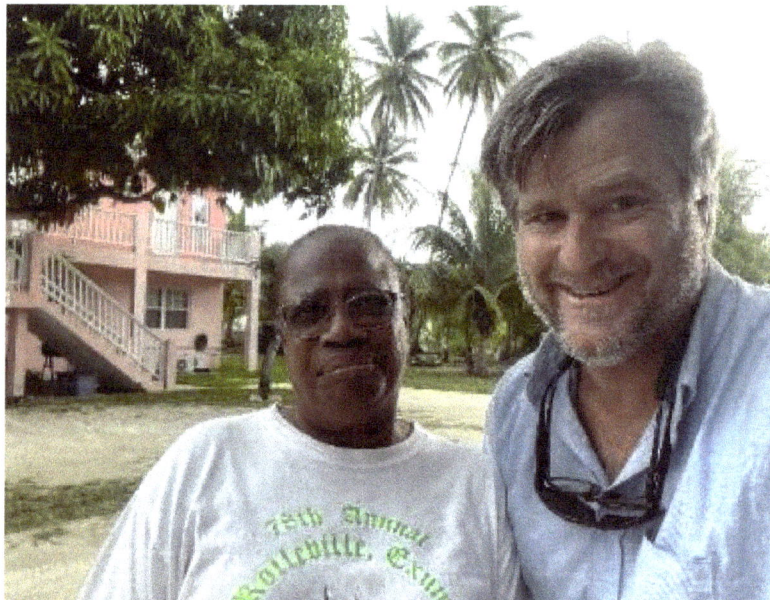

Ms. McKenzie was very helpful: she saw *Pilot Radio* as a 10-year-old child.

Are these metal fragments from the 1930 crash and wreck of *Pilot Radio*?

Pieces of various metals, some melted, found in January 2023.

Naval Air Station Great Exuma. The week it opened, the commander was dragged off the islands in handcuffs by men in a plane from Guantanamo for the sake or morale.

Left: Naval Air Station and Naval Operating Base, Great Exuma. Right: US Naval Air Station and Naval Operating Base at Great Exuma during World War II. The US investment into the infrastructure was considerable, but oddly enough, turnover at the highest levels seems to have been a recurrent issue, and the men posted there struggled with morale.

Could these shadows on the sea floor just west of Stocking Island possibly indicate one of the several aircraft which wrecked off George Town?

Chapter Eleven:

Tarpum Bay, Eleuthera, B-25

How does a majestic large bomber transition from ruling the skies to washing ashore in shallow waters in a populous island just east of Nassau, to slowly become a fishing spot for hopeful hand-liners? This is the Tarpum Bay target. Just before noon on Tuesday, June 6, 1944 (D-Day), the RAF in Nassau recorded that a "B-25 FW-154 FR was airborne at 11:16 a.m. upon A/S [anti-submarine] patrol No. 2. No W/T [radio] contact was made with this aircraft after 11:50 a.m., when a long dash [Mayday] was received. At 1:50 p.m. a signal was received from the pilot, via government channels, that the aircraft had ditched in the sea two miles north of Tarpum Bay, Eleuthera, at 11:48 a.m."

"The aircraft still had the RG's aboard [bombs] but these were at first [switched to] 'safe.' The crew were uninjured except the [wireless] operator who had facial injuries. The A.S.R. [rescue] launch HMS *P-712* was dispatched from Harbour Island and arrived at Rock Sound [then] Tarpum Bay at 6:39 p.m. Goose GB [Grumman amphibian aircraft] was airborne at 2:43 p.m. with the Chief Ground Instructor, medical officer and Staff present at the scene of the ditching. The aircraft returned to base and landed at 8:40 p.m., with the pilot of the ditched aircraft. The remainder of the crew were brought to Nassau in HMS *P-712*, which berthed at the Prince George Dock [Nassau] at 12:05 a.m. on the 7th."

The B-25 was a workhorse of the RAF's Bahamas training operations from 1942 to 1946. At 68 feet wide and 53 feet long, the aircraft was sent on thousands of missions, often for several days. Powered by two radial engines of 1,700 horsepower each, and armed with machine guns, torpedoes, rockets and bombs, it could achieve 272 miles per hour. The B-25 Mitchell was named after a pioneer in US aviation and was one of fewer than 500 type B-25 D-30's built in Kansas City in 1942. This specific aircraft began service in The Bahamas on December 2, 1943, and reported sighting a German U-boat on January 31, 1944. On May 26, she completed calibration exercises. Typically manned by a pilot, copilot, bombardier, navigator/radio operator, and gunner, in June of 1944 she was on her final certification flight before the four crew members would be approved for combat in Europe or the Pacific. Less than eight months before, another B-25 out of Nassau had crash-dived at Bannerman Town, southern Eleuthera.

Prior to the crash FW-154 FR was only airborne for 32 minutes, from 11:16 a.m. to 11:48 a.m. When the pilot of the aircraft realized that they would have to land in the ocean, he jettisoned the depth charges, which were set to 'live.' The crew appear to have extricated themselves (including the radioman who nearly blinded) from the craft and made their way ashore using the auto-inflate emergency rafts, perhaps with some assistance from nearby fishermen. That day US forces noted that "no serious injuries to the crew were reported, and rescue operations are being conducted at the Nassau station of the RAF." Later they added, "Salvage operations being conducted." The latitude and longitude given for "Tarpum Bay" was to the northeast, and on land.

In any event, the plane slipped 24 feet beneath the surface of the clear waters and out of public consciousness except for the fishermen who liked to hand-line or spearfish for fish and crawfish finding shelter around the engines under the fuselage. There were many witnesses then and since: four survivors, rescuing boat crews, senior leaders from Nassau, so this appeared to be a very findable wreck. The waters in the area are murky, particularly after storms, and the waters can be so choppy that many fishermen simply pull their boats out rather than moor them. The fact that all of the crew survived further suggests that the plane did not break up on impact. One strategy was to go to Tarpum Bay, inquire after fishermen, and engage one of them to take me to the site. There I could put on a mask and fins and find myself atop another historic bomber.

And I did make my way to Tarpum Bay in early 2023, but the boat we were on was too deep, the weather too bad. Rather than visit the site, we were able to interview well-respected fishermen and community leaders including Captain John McCarthy, known by his boat name *Big Mac*, Captain Andrew Hunt, and Captain Sanjay Sawyer. Tarpum Bay is a lovely community of roughly 750 persons nestled on the leeward, or western, side of Eleuthera between Rock Sound and Windemere Island. A member of the town committee, Lawrence Carey, was instrumental in introducing our three-man crew to the right people, and others including Cleveland Knowles, bus fleet owner Ken Devaux, former policeman Mr. Pinder in Hatchet Bay who rented us a car. Another fisherman named Tobias Carey facilitated helpful introductions.

Given the inclement weather, the fishermen were not afloat, so we were able to confirm from several of them that they had been eyewitnesses to the aircraft on the sea floor, had fished and dived near it over the years, and that remnants of it were still there. Big Mac—an immensely tall and friendly man—promised he would take his daughter fishing there again and tell us where it was. We, in turn, promised to hire him to take us there when we returned in better weather.

We needed to know that there was indeed a plane there. Fortunately, short of actually touching it, through the proxy of well-reputed mariners, we now know that it is. I asked folks who run a dive shop nearby, but trying to run their business without electricity was proving a more immediate focus of their energies. I hinted that that the site might have the potential to lure visiting divers as well as fish and crawfish, if left intact. And what an unusual and rewarding sight to see: a World War II bomber in translucent shallow waters near a picturesque town and 75 miles from Harbour Island.

Public fishing pier, Tarpum Bay, south Eleuthera, on the western, leeward side.

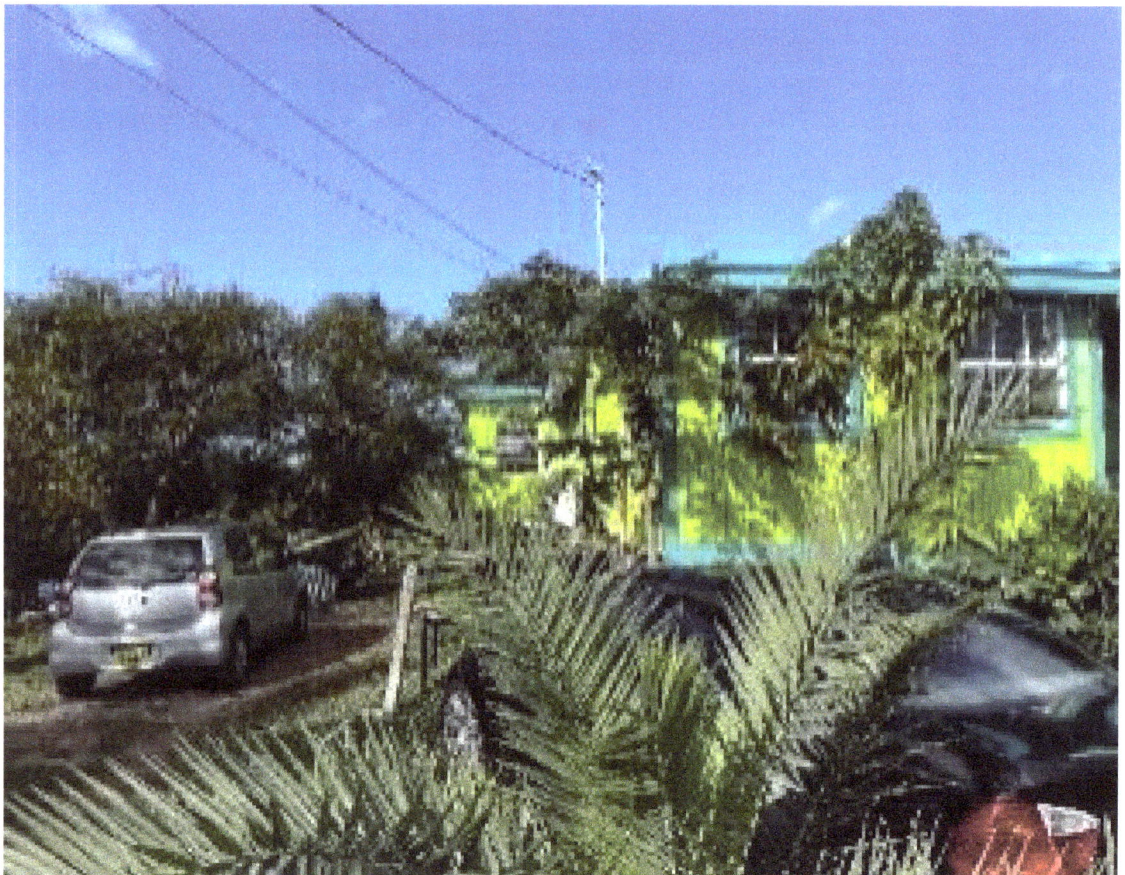

Home of fisherman who knows the B-25 wreck in Tarpum Bay, Eleuthera.

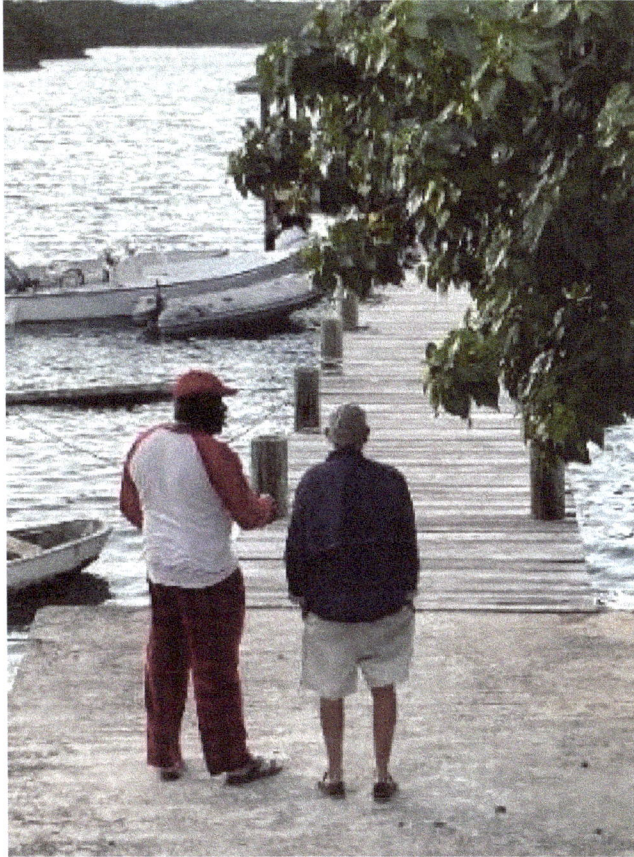

Captain Howard and a former police officer conferring in Hatchet Bay after a gale.

Damage and debris strewn about Gregory Town, Eleuthera after a blow.

Chapter Twelve:

Bannerman Town, Eleuthera, B-25

On the night of Tuesday, October 5, 1943, RAF Pilot R. Hastie calmly pointed his sizeable B-25 bomber towards the dark outline of South Eleuthera, just above Lighthouse Point. With one engine lost and the other one overheating, he managed to belly-land his nearly 70-foot, 35,000-pound airplane a mere 100 feet from the beach, gleaming white in the moonlight, without any of his men being killed. However, one of them was trapped unconscious in the back of the plane, which quickly filled with water, and all the hatches were blocked. Though they were already free from the plane and in inflatable rafts, two of the crewmen swam into the stricken plane which was settling in 10 to 15 feet of water through the bomb doors, and pulled their unconscious shipmate through a narrow tunnel into the air and safety.

This is the extraordinary story of a team of RAF pilots who, on the verge of being sent to Europe, found themselves being carried by stretchers organized by Constable Enoch McPhee of Bannerman Town, Eleuthera. They were taken by an American Jeep commandeered by Justice of the Peace H. H. Finley, and tended to by Dr. Norman Kerr in Rock Sound Hospital. The crew were led by the pilot, Warrant Officer R. N. Hastie, Flight Sergeant V. A. McLennan, Sergeant T. W. Allen, and Wireless Operator S. J. Trusson, all of them in the Royal Air Force.

Overall, they were airborne for less than 4 hours, crashed 70 miles from Oakes Field Nassau where they trained with O.T.U. No. 111, were driven 18 miles to the hospital, and then taken by boat another 64 miles to the Air Sea Rescue base at Montague Foreshore, Nassau. Their entire ordeal, from liftoff in Nassau on Tuesday to being hospitalized at the RAF base in Nassau, took nearly 20 hours. Members of the hamlet of Bannerman Town have confirmed to me that as children they played on the remnants of the aircraft, which today is being developed by Disney cruises.

Bannerman Town is the southernmost inhabited enclave of Eleuthera, with a population shared with John Millar of just 65 persons. The most accurate account of events is provided by a search for missing aircraft, from the base record books. It reads: "B-25 FR384 CM was airborne at 5:36 p.m. upon anti-submarine patrol No. 2f. At 5:40 p.m. [four minutes after take-off] the last W/T [Radio] contact was made with the aircraft. At 7:30 p.m. a signal was sent to [aircraft] CX requesting news of CM. The aircraft had no news to pass. Three aircraft were then detailed for air search... as far as Rum Cay. The aircraft were airborne between 9:38 p.m. and 9:42 p.m. A signal was sent to the RAF detachment at San Salvador, instructing the Widgeon aircraft to search... The Marine craft [ASR fleet], at Harbour Island and at Montague were ordered to stand by for air sea rescue, at 9:47 p.m."

"When Pilot Officer Thompson, captain of [rescuing] CX, returned from flight, he reported seeing CM jettison its depth charges and head for land. At 10:28 p.m. a signal was received from W/O Hastie, captain of CM, via Harbour Island that the aircraft had been ditched on Eleuthera's east shore. All were safe; however, one man was badly injured. It was requested that the Walrus [one-engine amphibious biplane] be dispatched. A signal was sent... to the effect that the missing aircraft had been found. The [searching] aircraft then returned to base [and] landed between 12:12 a.m. and 12:20 a.m."

The report then focused on what caused the crash: "The port engine of CM had failed to rectify the drag, and the captain had full boost to the starboard engine. This engine then began to show signs of seizing up. It was then decided to make a forced landing. The depth charges were jettisoned and the aircraft was ditched on a rock, about 100 yards from the shore. The crew were able to leave the aircraft. The rear gunner was unconscious with head injuries, and was extracted from the aircraft by the other members of the crew. The dinghy was launched, and the crew paddled ashore. The crew were taken to Rock Sound Hospital, where their injuries were attended to."

"The marine craft launch HMS *P-89* at Harbour Island was instructed to proceed to the scene of the crash and pick up the airmen. HMS *P-191* had proceeded [from Nassau] with a medical officer at Ship Channel Cay to render any assistance necessary. HMS *P-89* failed to locate the wrecked aircraft. A signal was received at 12:15 p.m. that all the crew were comfortable and in hospital at Rock Sound. HMS *P-89* was signal ed to proceed to Rock Sound to pick up the crew at 12:25 p.m. At 12:37 p.m., it was decided to send HMS *P-191* to Rock Sound and if insufficient petrol for the return was to await reloading. The medical officer arrived with HMS *P-191* and arrangements for the crew to be brought to Nassau were made. At 4:50 p.m. HMS *P-191* left Rock Sound Hospital, one member injured, and docked [in Nassau] at 10 p.m. The crew were taken to the [RAF] Station Hospital, and one member was detained."

Residents amplify how the plane looked, saying it sat on a rock in just 10 feet of water, 100 feet from shore. The policeman and justice of the peace arranged use of the truck from a US Navy base in the Governor's Harbour area to drive to remote Bannerman Town, load the stretcher case into it, and drive to the hospital in Rock Sound, which is a round-trip of some 100 miles. Two months later, the officer commanding O.T.U. No. 111 was effusive in his praise of the four men in the aircraft, submitting a report to his seniors which read, in part:

"On October 5, 1943, R. N. Hastie was captain of the Mitchell aircraft FR384 CM. Owing to loss of oil and the feathering mechanism of the propeller on one engine failed, and the consequent behavior of the engine made it impossible to maintain height on the remaining engine. Hastie carried out his emergency procedure accurately and thoroughly, in spite of the difficulty in controlling the aircraft, and his crew were at their correct crash stations before the ditching was made. He showed good airmanship and a thorough understanding of the capabilities of his aircraft throughout and made a good touchdown on the water. The gunner, Sgt. Allen, was in the rear compartment of the aircraft. F/Sgt. McLennan and Sgt. Trusson had already escaped, but on discovering that Sgt. Allen was still in the aircraft, they crawled back through the bomb tunnel, or bay, and with great difficulty dragged him out."

"The task of pulling an unconscious man through this small tunnel required strength and determination. The rear end of the aircraft was below water, so the hatches could not be used. McLennan and Trusson stood in grave danger of being trapped and drowned had the aircraft sunk before they could pull Sgt. Allen through the tunnel. Their prompt and gallant action prevented a very successful ditching from becoming a tragedy. The conduct and devotion to duty of Hastie, McLennan and Trusson was highly commendable throughout." Earlier, the crew on this aircraft had gone to render search and rescue aid for other aircraft in distress in Castle Island, Acklins Island, and Andros Island.

My colleagues and I journeyed to find the plane that swam on the shores and interviewed nearly a dozen persons in the communities of Bannerman Town, Wemyss Bight, John Millar's, Deep Creek, Cape Eleuthera, and Green Castle. These included Captain George Bullard, Clem Thompson, teacher Mrs. Randa Davis in Rock Sound, Herbert Richards (former staff to member of the Cotton Bay Club and owner of a restaurant, hotel, and bar at Green Castle), and Mrs. Justine Brown, roughly 90 years old, who welcomed us into her home. In Deep Creek, Germain Pinder (owner of the restaurant and bar as well as a car rental), and Chad and Chris (at Cape Eleuthera and Island School) were also very helpful, as were the rest of the Pinders. Altogether, this was very much a team effort, with the actual remains of the aircraft yet to reveal themselves—the site is situated on the ocean side and in winters it was very rough and the water was cloudy.

Interviewed in early 2023, Mr. and Mrs. Charles and Eleanor Rolle, and their neighbor, Phillip McPhee fondly remember playing on parts of the airplane, specifically the wings and fuselage. They said it was just off the beach about 100 yards, in 15 feet of water on the Atlantic side, less than 2 miles south of the end of public access to Lighthouse Beach. Phillip McPhee, whose uncle was the assisting constable, and Mrs. Rolle said that the men were stretcher cases, and the vehicle found to move them that night was borrowed from Americans in Governor's Harbour and was more like a Jeep than a truck. They added that lighter aluminum parts of the plane, such as fuselage and wing parts, were strewn along the beach and in the dunes on the way to Eleuthera Point.

Tangentially, London-born Dr. Kerr's daughter, Marilyn, rose to social prominence by marrying an Aide-de-Camp (ADC) to Sir Charles Dundas, governor of the colony up until the Duke of Windsor supplanted him in 1940. Marilyn became Lady Peek (later Quennell), wife of Sir Francis Henry Grenville Peek, fourth Baronet. Her and her children's portraits hang in the National Portrait Gallery in London; Sir Francis was the first governor of the Lyford Cay Club in New Providence.

As the sun set following a blow, when the seas had just started to settle down, I hid my phone behind some sea grass and ventured—alone and with no shore spotter—out to the reef, trying to find traces of the plane. Visibility was murky, and the sea was stirred up and cloudy, like lemonade. The sun was too weak for me to see much. The water went from so shallow that you might step on burning fire coral, to deep enough that you question whether sharks and moray eels might lurk therein. It was open water, and deep to the east: no land until Africa or Europe.

I was only there, in just shorts and a snorkel, for less than an hour on a winter evening. Those men in the B-25 crashed in the dark into the reef and ocean, and had only seconds to clamber out. They probably barely knew which way was up, and the instinct for self-preservation must have been paramount, ringing in their ears. But despite all that disorientation, going from air to sea to rock, they voluntarily went back, endangered themselves, and saved their shipmate. My hats off to them.

Parole entering the sheltered lagoon at Hatchet Bay, north Eleuthera before a storm.

Taking down the quarantine flag meant we have been welcomed into The Bahamas.

Hole-in-the-Wall Light, southern Great Abaco on the Northeast Providence Channel.

Charlie with Mr. Phillip MacPhee at Bannerman Town.

Near this idyllic spot off Bannerman Town a B-25 Mitchell ditched at night.

On or near this spot on the beach, north of the southernmost point in Eleuthera....

Chapter Thirteen:

Ragged Island; Amphibian, Yards from Shore

Ragged Island, a small but critical outpost in the southern Bahamas, has been attacked by Germans and Cubans flying Soviet MiG's. With less than nine square miles of land, they are a kind of Hawaii or Hong Kong to the archipelagic nation, situated at the elbow between the Old Bahama Channel and the Crooked Island Channel. Ragged is also located at the entry to the Windward Passage between Haiti, Turks and Caicos, and Cuba. To call the modest outcrop, whose population was recently close to zero due to government mandate, a strategic foothold is to understate it.

During World War II, Ragged Island witnessed a convoy battle in which three ships were hit by a U-boat nearby, and a seaplane powered right into the most populated island. These two distinct war events were both witnessed by Captain Edward Lockhart and others in the small community of Duncan Town, known for its salt pans, commercial fishing, mailboat captains, boatbuilding and bonefishing.

On August 7, 1942, the German submarine U-598 under *Korvetten-kapitän* Gottfried Holtorf cornered a fleet of escorted Allied merchant ships against southern Ragged Islands and struck three ships: *Standella, Empire Corporal,* and *Michael Jebsen*. This was the most ships struck consecutively by a single submarine in The Bahamas out of 130 hits in World War II. U-598 entered the area from Kiel on August 7, 1942, two days after losing Willi Bredereck, who drowned while refueling from U-463, and reached the Mayaguana Passage on August 10, then passed west of Inagua and motored up the Old Bahama Channel. In the crescent of deep water which forms the back end of Ragged Island, working alone against the British and Allied convoy known as TAW-12J for the 12th Trinidad, Aruba, Key West group of ships to head northbound, Holtorf deftly pinned the wounded and disorganized ships into a *cul de sac.*

The night before, the hapless Allied had been partially scattered in the Windward Passage in an action against convoy WAT 13 by U-658 under Senkel, U-508 under Staats, and U-600 under Zurmühlen, who vectored Holtorf to the vulnerable convoy. In an audacious dawn attack, Holtorf managed to hit *Michael Jebsen* and *Empire Corporal* both sunk, the latter with the convoy commodore on board. Though also badly damaged, another ship, the *Standella,* managed to limp into

Havana, where her crew had the dangerous and difficult task of locating and extracting the bodies of their six dead shipmates from the forepeak area before the bodies putrefied in the tropical heat. The *Standella* was owned and operated by the Anglo-Saxon Petroleum Company Limited, of London—the same owners which controlled the ship *Anglo Saxon*, whose two sole survivors washed ashore at James Cistern, Eleuthera in 1940.

Holtorf fired three spreads of torpedoes starting at 5:54 a.m. between Cay Santo Domingo and Magallenes Bank. After passing 20 yards ahead of the *Empire Corporal*, the torpedo struck the bow of the *Standella*, causing a 50-foot column of water to erupt there. Visibility at the time was good with a smooth sea and light breeze just before sunrise. Six Chinese crewmembers, who were in the accommodation in the forecastle at the front of the ship, were killed (Ping Chan, Yet Lo, Fat Chan, Mui Lum, Fook Wong, and Jok Wong) and ten others were badly injured.

The engine officers immediately stopped the engine, and Captain Loyn ordered the Chief Officer to bring a damage report. Finding his report unsatisfactory, the master went to see for himself. He found the bow to be completely demolished: the forecastle deck had fallen several feet, the pump room and store room were flooded, and there was a hold on the port side below the waterline. The captain decided, nevertheless, to proceed at half speed in the direction of the convoy, which by now had steamed out of sight. Within an hour, the officers were confident enough to increase RPM to full speed, and by 7:30 a.m., in a great show of seamanship, the vessel took up a position in the rear column of the convoy. Acknowledging the *Standella*, HMS *Churchill* signaled "I will be with you later—am sub-hunting."

At 11 a.m. HMS *Churchill* came alongside the slow-moving tanker and sent over Surgeon Lieutenant O'Brian to tend to the injured men. The doctor stayed onboard until 5 p.m., during which a frenetic search for any living members of the crew was conducted in terrible conditions and tropical heat. The *Standella* was instructed by HMS *Churchill* to peel out of the convoy and proceed to Havana independently for repairs. Arriving off that port at midnight, *Standella* cruised off the port waiting for a pilot, probably very nervous about either sinking or taking another torpedo near such an important port. The next morning at daylight, the pilot boarded her and the ship was berthed at 10:30 at the oil berth, and five of the men were admitted to a hospital in Havana.

At 11:54, U-598 fired two spreads of two torpedoes at convoy TAW-12J, south of Ragged Island. The first spread must have hit the *Michael Jebsen*, which sank immediately. One torpedo of the second spread missed the convoy commodore's ship, the *Empire Corporal*, which was then sunk by the stern torpedo. When the torpedo struck the *Michael Jebsen,* the damage was immediate and catastrophic. The projectile penetrated the boiler room and exploded the boilers located there, killing anyone in the engine space. Steam escaped everywhere, effectively cutting off the men in the bow from those aft. The funnel collapsed to starboard, crushing the lifeboats on that side and bringing down the aerials. At first, the *Jebsen* lifted to the side of the starboard, then it swung over to port and "within a minute turned completely over and sank." The *Jebsen* crew joined the 49 survivors of the *Empire Corporal* which was sunk the same morning in the same convoy.

The U-598 then moved down the column of ships on the port side of the convoy at periscope depth and, after firing its salvoes, hid under the ships themselves. Other reports by survivors have her on the surface at least part of the time. Though half a dozen or so depth charges were dropped by the USS *SC-498*, the sub was never pinpointed or pinned down. Another eyewitness account has the sub on the surface throughout the entire engagement. Hans Senkel in U-658 recorded on August 15, 1942, reported in his U-boat diary that "Southeast of Duncan Town, Ragged Island, an oil slick and wreckage." That was from Holtolf's attacks on the three ships from U-598 the day before.

Edward Lockhart heard this Battle of Ragged Island. He explained that he and others in Duncan Town could distinctly hear machine gun fire from Holtorf's U-boat U-598 and from military and merchant ships in the convoy about 35 miles away, in more than 2,000 meters of water. Edward survived Hurricane Irma as a hermit on this remote depopulated string of islands; he knows the islands well from a lifetime of observing it through both war and peace. He informed me of his World War II recollections as an aside—distraction almost—for research into the book *Mailboats of the Bahamas.* Captain Lockhart said, in 2020, that the airplane engine is still on the reef near their community. Today the mailboat *Captain C.* is ably run by Captain Jed Munroe. The difficulty is the long distance and uncertainty of location, though the engines are said to still be on reef. Also, a major hurricane all but wiped out the small traces of human life which hung onto the island, with the government at first considering closing it altogether.

Taxied to beach, hit trees, and sank: these seven words encapsulate a bad day for a dozen men. To this day, Edward Lockhart Sr., a captain from an island which has produced legendary shipmasters—Ragged Island—remembers what he saw and heard eight decades ago, from the World War II Battle of Ragged Island to that plane washed ashore with friendly men inside it.

As a child on the island, he went on to become a mailboat captain, and to work and live in Nassau. It is thanks to him that I learned of this crash while researching mailboats. Lockhart knows this case so well that he can even name some of the crew. Two US Navy crewmates named Kurt and Droddy captivated Lockhart, who actually met the survivors and rescuers alike. As a young man, Lockhart says a WWII bomber crashed in the sea off Ragged Island and of the several men, he befriended the two US aviators and others around 1944 or 1945 when their plane crashed. He said there were 22 airmen that landed at Duncan Town who were repatriated by Americans, probably to Guantanamo or Georgetown, Exuma via amphibious aircraft. Incredulously, years ago, he claimed to Brita Caldoret and I that the engine could still be found, right there on the reef.

On Sunday June 11, 1944, a US Navy Consolidated PBY-5 was damaged beyond repair during the taxiing phase of operation at Great Ragged Island. The problem began when, during an advanced base and overnight navigational training flight from the US, with NAS and NOB Great Exuma acting as a safety net in Georgetown, the plane lost the use of one of its two radial engines that boasted 1,200 bhp each, with three propellers. The pilot landed on the water to the east-southeast of Great Ragged. Being the only inhabited island nearby, the pilot made way towards it using the engines on the sea surface, and heading west-northwest probably somewhat clumsily and uncomfortably.

Mike Stowe, aviation accident report investigator, shared a critical file showing that a week after D-Day, the 13 trainees managed to wrestle a badly-disabled amphibian airplane out of the sky and onto the smooth surface of the sea. With that accomplished, the pilot decided to head to the welcoming embrace of a wide arc of beach north of Duncan Town, the primary settlement. Unfortunately, the overconfident amphibian aviators, mere hours from their Florida base, underestimated Bahamian reefs. What was hoped to be a smooth beaching instead left the aircraft impaled on stag coral as a reef made quick work of it, destroying the underbelly of the aircraft. The calm seas hid how dangerous they actually were. Cutting a corner with just 50 or so feet to spare turned out to be a catastrophic, but not fatal, mistake.

Despite drastic predictions by other military researchers, a team and I were led to the site by expert fishing guide and hotelier Captain Phicol Wallace and indeed, in just a few feet of water and visible from the shore, lay the Catalina PBY-4. Usually, the navy salvors completed their reclamation assignments, however, in this case, several aircraft experts from NOB and NAS Great Exuma, and even salvors with barges, failed to ever put this Humpty Dumpty back together again.

On that June morning, US Navy ensign Paul Charles Bernardy was at the controls, being monitored overall by Captain Leon Elton Robbins, and supported by Lieutenant Constantine James Economou. The aircraft was stationed in squadron VPB-2 OTU, at NAS Jacksonville, in northeast Florida, some 600 nautical miles from Ragged Island. The plane was a maritime patrol bomber built for search and rescue in Rhode Island. It became the most utilized seaplane of World War II. The United States gave 93 PBY-5s to the RAF under Lend-lease. Weighing 28,000 pounds, two radial engines of 1,200 bhp spun three propellers, meaning there should be a lot of heavy metal on a site where one sank, even decades later.

The 10 other crew members were ensigns Henry William McNair and Reginald Everett Jenkins; mechanics Peter John Pappas, Lee Imey Outlaw, Jr. Eugene Gerald Cratty, and Norman Alphonse Tremblay; and gunners James Joseph Jowdy, Willis Daniel Birch, William Andrew Doelle, and Thomas Edward Stokel—all of them in the US Naval Reserve, or USNR. They took off from Florida on a routine, over-water navigational training flight, also known as advance base training. Bernardy, the pilot, had 195 hours of flying experience with this type of PBY aircraft, and 409.3 hours of overall flying experience.

When the crew were practicing navigation on the western edge of the critical artery north of Windward Passage known as Crooked Island Passage, west of Mira Por Vos Islands, the weather was calm and settled. A light wind of 10 knots blew from the southeast along with just a slight swell from the same direction, undulating like the belly-breathing of a supine person. Then after noon, trouble came in the form of an engine malfunction, and by 1:15 p.m. doom had struck.

The official report, marked confidential by the US Navy, relates that "While the plane was circling an island in the Bahama Group at an altitude of approximately 800 feet, the starboard engine caught fire. Subsequent investigation determined that number 3 cylinder had blown out. The propeller was feathered, and the fire ceased; the pilot attempted to maintain flight on one engine. When it was determined that the plane could not maintain its altitude, a landing was made at sea. No damage occurred to the plane structurally incident to the sea landing. The Pilot [Bernardy] attempted to taxi to a sandy beach of Great Ragged Island, British West Indies at about one mile from the scene of the [water] landing. At approximately 20 yards from a point of land, the plane grounded on a reef. All attempts to remove the plane from the reef failed. Numerous holes in the hull caused the plane to fill with water rapidly. When the salvage crew and equipment arrived [from Exuma], the hull was damaged beyond repair."

All military units from Florida to Nassau, the Naval Air Station in Great Exuma, and the Naval Operating Base in Guantanamo and beyond were alerted that day of the "Jacksonville PBY forced down off Great Ragged Island." The report read that "At 11:25 a.m. a PBY from NAS Jacksonville reported to its base that her starboard engine had caught fire and was forced to land off Great Ragged Island. The PBY further advised that she had caught on a reef, and was taking on water fast. Her hull was gradually being broken up, and the aircraft requested instructions from NAS Jacksonville. At 12:39 p.m. (just over an hour after the mishap) the Gulf Sea Frontier commander advised the bases in Exuma and Cuba that the PBY was forced down, and that the plane was in a sinking condition, further stating that assistance was requested."

"At 1 p.m. NAS Great Exuma [approximately 85 miles north of Ragged Island], advised NAS Jacksonville that they were sending a boat immediately, and would advise, if possible, to tow the plane after contact was made. RAF Nassau advised at 2:50 p.m. that the following message was received from the commissioner of Ragged Island at 2 p.m.: 'PBY Navy with 13 men fell on northeast side of mainland [Great Inagua] at 11:30 a.m., now grounded among dangerous rocks. Every assistance for safety of plane and accommodation of men is being rendered." The original District Commissioner of Ragged Island's reports from 1944 at the National Archives of The Bahamas are not readily available. Overall, several similar messages with the urgent nature and need for assistance were transmitted that day from various stations.

Investigating engineers remarked at how the "hull bottom was crushed and broken. Stringers of remainder of hull loosened. No. 3 cyl. of stbd. engine was blown off. Engine case broken around base of No. 3 cyl. Corrosion of both engines, equipment & accessories of plane." Attribution of blame was "80% Pilot Error; 70% judgment; 10% technique, 10% pp, or engine structure, 10% misc.; airport, terrain, etc."—i.e.: reef. The worst remark from the third-in-command's perspective was the Commanding Officer's endorsement: "In the Board's opinion, Lt. Economou, the second pilot, disclaimed the proper responsibility. This officer has had varied experience aboard Navy ships. It is the further opinion of the Board that this officer should have advised Ensign Bernardy against taxiing toward shore, and that he, Economou, should not have continued taxiing toward the shore."

Mrs. Ilka Lockhart and dear Mrs. Yvette Lockhart assisted in bringing this search to the present day. She was introduced to me by French artist and traveler, Brita Cadoret. Konstantinos Economou in Greece helped to connect me to his namesake, Constantine Economou, on the American side of his family. Captain and entrepreneur Phicol Wallace, who was introduced to me by Brita and our brother John, led us to the partly exposed amphibian in mere moments.

Recalling that Edward Lockhart knew the names of two of the PBY crew; Kurt and Droddy, we dug into the documentation. In fact, the crewmen had similar names to those young Edward remembered: mechanic Eugene Gerald Cratty and gunner Willis Daniel Birch. They were repatriated by Americans to Georgetown, Exuma via boat or amphibious aircraft. Less than half a year later, two other large amphibious planes (capable of carrier takeoffs and known as OS2U Kingfishers) ran out of gas in the vicinity of Ragged Island on December 6, 1944.

A large VIP carrier, known as an Army JRF, as well as a pair of US Army rescue boats were sent from NAS Georgetown, Exuma to refuel them. First, they had to be located, as one was drifting off Ragged Island, and the other was further out to sea. Over two weeks later, on June 28, 1944, at 5:41 p.m., "N-ARB, C-9463 returned from completion of salvage of seaplane at Great Ragged," to NAS Great Exuma. Case closed for the PBY. Then, a year later, on July 1, 1945, a Grumman Goose GB amphibious plane landed at Great Ragged Island. It avoided grounding.

Crossing a salt flat between road and beach to find the aircraft.

Working in the cozy main salon on *Parole*. Ship-wide internet was a saving grace.

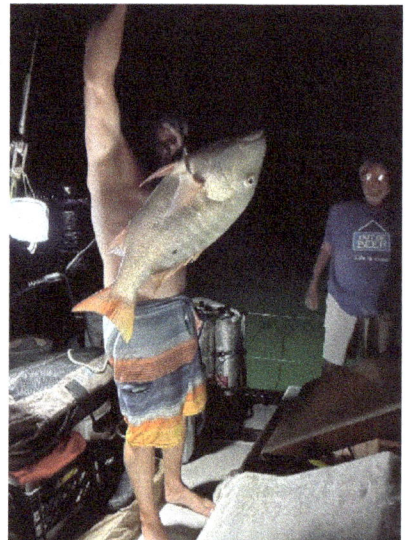

Life on board *Parole*; landing and fishing. L-R: James and Captain Howard.

Consolidated PBY Catalina, showing its amphibian nature and size.

Capt. Phicol helping the *Parole* crew find the beached PBY on Ragged.

Sideview of one of the engines from the turbulent surf zone.

The green parts clearly appear to be brass or copper.

Underwater image of piping.

Battle of Ragged Island, August 7, 1942, in which three Allied ships were hit by the German U-boat U-598 under Gottfried Holtorf despite allied protection. The tanker *Empire Corporal* under its former name *British Corporal* from John Crossland.

Reporting findings to Charlie and Phicol.

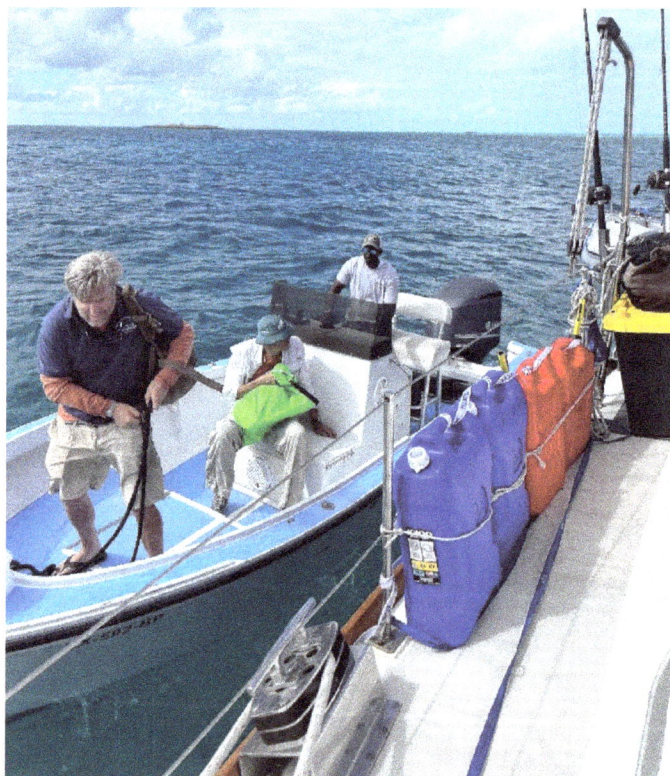
Transferring after a very surgical and precise insertion and return.

Chapter Fourteen:

Inagua

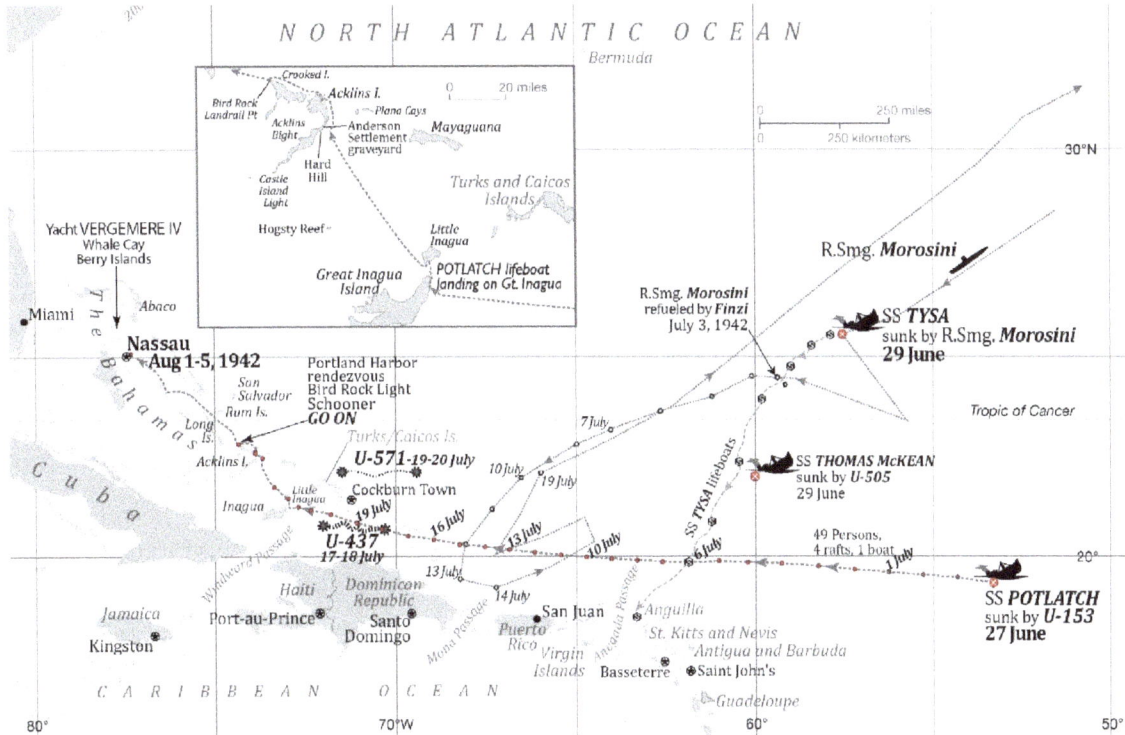

Great and Little Inagua present several World War II aviation mysteries to parse, though probably the aircraft to be found were lost post-war. The east coast of this 650-square-mile-island has no roads or airstrip, and is very rarely visited. U-boats and Allied military ships often transited the many channels around Great Inagua and reported sighting land. The confirmed rescues were of three US aviators (including John Bunch), who were without food for 17 days and rescued by fishermen in Little Inagua and taken to Great Inagua.

Then there was a tragic engine fire and crash of an aircraft under Pilot Inman where a US Mail pouch washed up on the east coast of Great Inagua, with no plane or body. And there appears to be an unclaimed cigar-shaped plane (possibly a 1970s cargo plane) in the dunes, a DC-3 which has been identified and visited, and another mystery plane with a parachute and body. As per the Nixon family, who have been park wardens there for generations, in 2022 there was one body and parachute found and buried in the coast Inagua area, and possibly the engines. Henry Nixon said his father found possibly a Curtiss C-46 and a dead man attached to a parachute, and that he buried him near the plane. Remains of the plane are still there, and were found over a decade ago by a Bahamian sleuth in a seaplane.

On August 10, 1942, U-598 under Holtorf logged "Passed through Crooked Passage. Lighthouses as in peacetime. In the twilight stayed close under Fortune Island, in accordance with... *American Sailing Instructions.*" Twelve days later, the U-boat logged that "SW of Inagua 2nd time small yacht in sight bearing 300°T. Same vessel as in KTB August 20, 7:50 p.m. Suspect stationed as a patrol." His colleague Hans Senkel in U-658 recorded the same day seeing "Glimmers of light from the lighthouse on Inagua Island and Castle Islands were distinguished at great range. The beacons are not dimmed." On August 29, 1942, U-600 under Zurmühlen, wrote "Great Inagua in sight bearing 305°T," then "West Caicos in sight bearing 95°T." U-108 under Scholtz logged on May 9, 1942 that "Inagua lighthouse in sight bearing 348°T. Sailing vessel in sight bearing 260°T."

On May 13, 1942, U-594 under Hoffmann wrote that "Glow of the Matthew Town Lighthouse in sight." And the next day: "Caicos Passage just E of NE corner of Great Inagua: A shadow in sight bearing 40°T. I see a small vessel with target angle 0 to 10°, estimated range at 800 to 1,000 meters. I take the vessel for the reported destroyer and have the impression that he approaches me quickly." On May 11, 1942, Werner Winter in U-103 wrote, "Continued west of 'Inagua' to the Windward Passage. Beacons on Inagua burn as in peacetime. [Then] avoided a dimmed vessel. Not distinguished, if fisherman or patrol vessel." Witt in U-129 wrote on June 14, 1942, logged "Little Inagua Island in sight." On August 22, 1942, Klaus-Peter Carlsen in U-732 recorded that "I head for Little Inagua Island, to download there under the protection of land." [The U-boat then made the unusual step of pausing a war patrol, between Little and Great Inagua]. Clausen continued, "Boat is one nautical mile west of Little Inagua in the wind-shadow [lee] of the island. Downloaded one from bow and one torpedo from stern, by 6:30 a.m. deck was clear..." With just one mile from shore, would men have been tempted to step ashore? If so, they did not record it.

Then on March 5, 1944, the commander of U-154, Garth Gemeiner, logged that "No traffic, no patrols, no beacons. Inguna [Inagua] Island abeam. Nothing seen. Surfaced to charge and ventilate...." Clearly, Inagua and its lights were often seen by

German and Italian submarine invaders, and Little Inagua was used for shelter as it was by men in lifeboats from SS *Potlatch* in July 1942, and by the survivors of an air crash as well. Between July 27 and 30, 1942, the 48 survivors of the torpedoed SS *Potlatch*, under Captain Jack Lapoint and Lieutenant Dorsey Lybrand, landed on the northeast corner of Great Inagua. They stayed for two nights after following jackasses to water, then sailed the metal lifeboat to Little Inagua where they found almost no sustenance and left for Acklins Island, from where they were rescued and taken to Nassau by Joe Carstairs in her yacht, *Vergemere IV*.

On March 21, 1943, USS *Hambleton* attempted to rescue Allied survivors in the vicinity of Inagua, however, this was carried out instead by USS *Moffett*, which "reported picking up two survivors, but a thorough search of all floating objects in this vicinity revealed no further signs of life." That was "northeastward toward Inagua" from Guantanamo. Later, Inagua had the misfortune to be the place a member of Miami's 36th Street Army Air Field lost one of its own, Private D. E. Goldbeck, who on February 25, 1945 "was overboard from Army Vessel [USS] *H-121* on February 16." All stations with any air-sea-rescue capabilities in the wider area were instructed to keep an extra-vigilant look out for him but to no avail.

On May 17, 1943, a US airship was mistakenly reported as sunk off Great Inagua when "the commissioner at Great Inagua reported a blimp down in the sea 6-to-8 miles offshore in the direction of Matthewtown. This blimp later landed at Guantanamo with the crew safe and no damage to the airship," making it seem like Mark Twain's famous quote that "rumors of my death are greatly exaggerated." On July 27, 1943, at 10:55 a.m., aircraft BAH-VP, which was part of an amphibious squadron, departed Naval Air Station Great Exuma for Inagua Island. At 4:30 p.m. the following day, the same plane landed back in Georgetown, Exuma from Inagua.

The Axis powers were not the only parties describing Inagua during the war—the RAF in Nassau sent out airplanes to reconnoiter as well, including this demonstrative example: "Reconnaissance Exercise. Liberator BZ883LW was airborne from Windsor Field at 12:43 p.m. upon a recco of Inagua. The cloud base was low and visibility poor and in consequence the photos taken were not satisfactory. The aircraft landed at 7:48 p.m."

Henry Nixon, head warden of parks of Great Inagua, and his family and colleagues know a great deal about the island. On the east coast of Great Inagua are three known wrecks: DC-3 from the 1980s with no bodies, and an unidentified, scattered aircraft on the northeast coast. Mr. Nixon's father found this wreck, with the cadaver and parachute. Also, there is a Piper on the north coast quite recently. On May 8, 1943, a Curtiss C-46 cargo plane piloted by William B. Inman experienced a fire on its left engine. Other aircraft heard the Maydays in quick succession and some saw smoke trails. The last known position was just to the west of Providenciales, Turks and Caicos. That places it in the sea off the east coast of Great Inagua. "When last contacted, plane had bad engine on fire and plane was going down." To most hardened aviators and rescue personnel, the most likely outcome was the death of all four men in this crash at about 12:59 p.m. They were Capt. Inman, Joseph W. Mitchell, Jr. (a civilian aviator), F. L. Deitz, and Harold D. Carter (2nd Lieutenant, a pilot student). The cause is described as "fire in flight."

In a letter to the family of Joseph Mitchell dated March 11, 1946, from the Commanding General US Army Air Forces, it was stated that the aircraft "operated in contract cargo service by Eastern Air Lines for the Air Transport Command, departed Miami at 8:54 a.m. on May 8, 1943, with a full load of cargo, destination, Natal [South Africa]. A t 12:03 p.m. the plane sent their final position report, giving no indication of trouble. Then the pilots sent to Miami a distress message reading "We got bad engine. Wait, it's getting… SOS, WQ 99 [callsign], bad engine. We going down now… is burning, on fire." At the same time, a plane going in the opposite direction, from Borinquen to Miami, supplied the following phrase: "Left wing on fire." No further word was received since the transmission was cut short." Three aircraft were immediately vectored to canvas the area in search of the downed airplane, so that "all available aircraft were dispatched to the area for search. The next day, some 30 airplanes completely scoured the area… No wreckage of any kind was sighted. On May 9, 1943, the search was continued over a wide area, but nothing was sighted." Air Force Colonel Robert W. Witty continues observing that on May 7, a small convoy near the crash was sighted, with the personnel later questioned about what they saw, yet none of them had seen a crash or debris. Later, however, "On May 21, 1943, two (2) [locals] on the island of Great Inagua picked up a pouch of US mail which was later identified to have been on the missing 5180. An investigation was conducted on the island to determine if any other articles or pieces of wreckage had been found. It was determined that nothing except the mail pouch had been seen."

The owners of the aircraft, Eastern Airlines, "concluded that the aircraft was on fire to such an extent, [it] had broken up in the air and had never reached the surface of the water intact or under control." Further, they believed the crew never had time to use the parachutes, life raft, and other safety equipment due to smoke inhalation. They conclude the letter by observing about The Bahamas in World War II that "most of the islands in this area capable of supporting life are inhabited and that this area was covered in war time by extensive air and naval operations. Had any personnel survived for an appreciable time, it is inconceivable that aid could not have been summoned."

On May 2, 1943, a USAAF A-20B Havoc was lost 100 miles north of Haiti. In 2022, an article from 1996 was given to the author from Mrs. Carolyn Lowe of Green Turtle Cay, Abaco, to solve. It is a letter to the editor in *The Nassau Tribune*, dated Saturday, July 20, 1996. It was signed 'Jo Watts,' daughter of John Bunch, in New York. The letter reads in relevant part: "I would very much like to contact Mr. Emmanuel Matthews or any of his descendants. Regretfully, verbal thanks is all I can offer from my family to theirs, but I feel that it is important that I do so if possible." Her father, John H. Bunch enlisted in Oklahoma City, Oklahoma on July 23, 1940, in the US Army Cavalry. He was from Coal County, Oklahoma and enlisted for the Philippine Department. He was a farmhand with three years of high school education, aged 18, single, and without dependents. His mother, Merle Propps Bunch, said that as a child, he pretended to be a soldier, carrying a tree branch on his shoulder and marching around the property.

Years later, Bunch's daughter, Jo Watters, recreated the scene where the military informed her grandmother that her son John was presumed dead when the plane went down: "I pictured the man knocking on the door with a telegram in his hand. I imagined I could hear my grandmother sitting down in her chair and insisting that it was a mistake. She never believed it. It read: 'Regret to inform you that your son Staff Sgt. John H. Bunch, is missing on a flight to a secret destination. Search was immediately instituted and we will advise any develop. Signed, Colonel Wm. L. Plummer, Commanding.'"

"Bunch was an aerial gunner and had been stationed at Homestead, for several months. He entered the army three years ago (at age 16) and would have been 20 years old in July. The last letter his parents received from him was dated Sunday, May 6, 1943. Col. Plummer's letter on May 31 was equally cold and without hope. How does a mother react to the words 'It is my disagreeable duty to inform you that I hold out very little hope in this case? We will probably carry this plane as missing for some little time; You will continue to receive your allotment until all hope is abandoned.' Col. Plummer covered himself by implying that the pilot took off without waiting for the flight leader and that his (the pilot's) decision was the cause of the ship and crew being lost at sea. In fact, there was no flight leader! Against their better judgments, the fliers took off after informing the colonel that the plane had engine trouble."

"After just a few hours, the plane did go down with only minor injuries to the crew of three. They floated on a life raft for two and a half days before coming into sight of a small island. It wasn't much more than a sand bar surrounded by reefs of razor-sharp coral. As they got near the beach, the surf and a strong undertow capsized their raft and they lost everything: boots they had removed because of swollen feet, food, tools, weapons, and precious water. Even though they were wearing their "Mae West" life vests, which helped them to float, their bare feet were cut to ribbons on the coral as they waded ashore."

"During the night, the men were attacked by flies and other insects that were attracted to their bloody feet, which soon became infested with maggots. They knew there had to be water on the island because they had spotted some wild burros. Walking on their infected feet caused unimaginable pain, but they desperately needed water so they searched as best as they could. It was torture for them in that Caribbean climate in early summer. There were no birds, turtles, or fish—only flies. Sgt. Bunch, the pilot and navigator ate the fruit from prickly pear cactus. They used the sharp coral to scrape the spines off the leaves so they could suck the moisture from them. It was their only sustenance for 15 days."

"Hanfred Cartwright, a Bahamian fisherman, owned 50 percent of his boat and used that influence to convince his two partners to go to the island known as "Little Inagua" before returning to their homes after several days of fishing. The other two didn't want to go. All three knew there were no fish there; they were tired and wanted to take their catch home to Great Inagua and their families. They argued, but Mr. Cartwright remained steadfast; after all, he owned half the interest in the boat. They agreed to go to Little Inagua. His partners asked him why he would do such an unreasonable thing, and he told them that there were some American flyers there. He had had a dream the night before: Three American servicemen were on Little Inagua and needed help. Skeptical, but deferring to the man who owned half the boat, the partners agreed to go there and have a look. As in the dream, they found the three on the beach, waving their hands and shouting."

"On the boat, the grateful men were so hungry that they made themselves sick eating turtle eggs, and a barracuda and corn meal stew that the fishermen prepared for them. The people on Great Inagua loved Americans and welcomed them with much fanfare and celebration. The Bahamian in authority even flew an American flag!

124

Dad says they feasted for three days until the US Coast Guard could come for them. They told the men that it was the most important thing ever to have happened on that island. John Bunch and his friends were treated for minor injuries and exposure. They had been without shelter for more than two weeks, 17 days to be exact. Dehydration and sunburn were serious. He survived to return to Homestead AFB, then to duty in North Africa weeks later. He became a P.O.W. in Italy, escaped, and was recaptured at least twice."

On May 20, the RAF base logged: "Crew of Missing A-20 Found; the British Security Officer has received a report from Matthew Town, Inagua, that three survivors from American plane 413466, which crashed between Haiti and Puerto Rico, have been found at Little Inagua. This is the Army A-20 plane which departed Homestead, Florida at 7:30 a.m. on May 19 *en route* to Borinquen Field, and was reported overdue with a crew of three. The survivors, Lt. R. L. Clark and gunners Bunch and Murray, are in the hospital at Matthew Town, Great Inagua, suffering from shock and exposure. They were without food for 17 days. RAF Nassau requested NOB Guantanamo to send a plane to remove the survivors to a military hospital for proper treatment." After three years in the army, Bunch was honorably discharged in February 1944 with a medical diagnosis of chronic dislocation of the jaw. After the war and his liberation from the P.O.W. camp, Bunch was given a medical discharge and returned to Oklahoma, where he met and married Bonnie Lee (Sue) Robertson. When the USAF was formed in 1947, Bunch rejoined the military, remaining in the armed forces to complete 22 years before retiring from the USAF. He served in Korea, and on several bases in the States.

Bunch's daughter, Jo Watts of Newfane, New York wrote "we will be forever grateful to Hanfred Cartwright and we pray that God has blessed him and his children as we have been blessed. Using an ad in the local paper, she located Cartwright in Matthew Town when he was nearly 80 years old and in good health, in 1995. He and his wife have raised 10 children, the youngest graduated from college. Mr. Cartwright and John Bunch became correspondents, exchanging letters and small gifts. She informed her Bahamian audience that her father died in 1998.

Sgt. John Bunch, USAAF, courtesy of his daughter Jo.

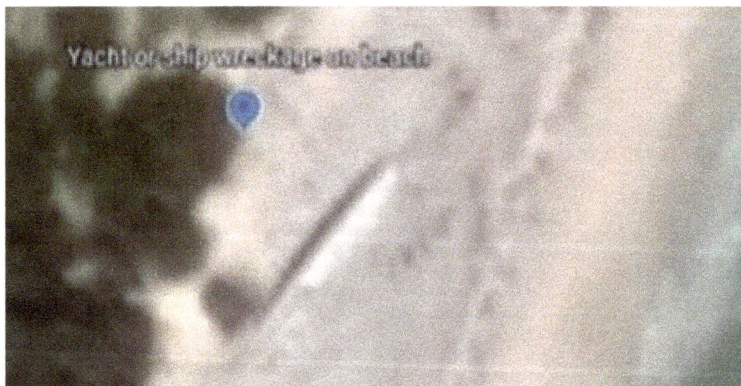

Yacht or shipwreckage on beach

Plane fuselage plainly visible on east coast of Great Inagua from space. This piece of fuselage (if that is what it is) only shows 55' out of sand.

Sam Nixon, first park warden of Great Inagua, holding adolescent flamingos. He buried a pilot with parachute. His son Henry Nixon is head of parks for Great Inagua.

Chapter Fifteen:

Royal Island, Eleuthera, PBM Mariner

On the night of Wednesday, July 19, 1944, at Royal Island, North Eleuthera, Lt.(j.g.) H. L. Hayes crashed while landing in a turbulent sea. No injuries to the personnel occurred, but both wing floats were torn off the plane and the starboard wing tip bounced on the bottom and finally sank in 20 feet of water. The plane was damaged beyond repair and was later surveyed." Squadron VP-208 reported that the plane landed at Royal Island, and in doing do "water-looped to such an extent that the plane was struck off charge. Major damage." An expert explained to me as I set off to swim and find part of the plane that "usually a water loop will pitch a wing underwater after it loses its outer wing buoyancy, and crinkle the wing and adjoining fuselage, making it unflyable. If no resources to repair anywhere near they could have purposely sunk it after stripping it. But they probably would have taxied to somewhere deeper to do so."

In January 2023 I swam a tiny acre of the hundreds where parts might have become hidden in crevices, yet found no clues. The fishermen at Spanish Wells adjacent know every inch of their waters, and I rationalized that if they don't know about it, it is probably not there. I called Elon Pinder, mailboat captain and owner in Spanish Wells, and he told me he has never heard a fisherman reference a plane wreck near Royal Island. My conviction that there is no wreckage of that crash there was borne out with the following message while we sat at anchor off Royal Island, which now aspires to be an elite resort.

Aviation historian Doug Campbell kindly shared that "Plane was P-19; pumps have hull leaks under control. Need flotation gear for both wing tips." So that tells me they didn't sink right away, but they did sink. Next day: "P-19 sank in 20 feet of water. Salvage operations taken over by Headquarters Squadron 12." So that's probably your answer." Plane salvaged, nothing more than a few nuts and bolts to find, if that after 80 years. We pulled the anchor of our expedition boat *Parole* and headed south to seek shelter in Hatchet Bay from an impending cold front. The exercise proved how important it is to have experts advising, an internet connection, and persons with you who are experienced divers and mariners. And when to give up.

On September 20, 1943 a Martin PBM-3S Mariner suffered a water loop while landing, spinning out of contol in proximity to USS *Christiana* in Pelican Bay. The large amphibian plane was struck from active service in squadron VP-208. On March 11, 1945 largest air sea rescue effort in Bahamas of World War II began with the simple statement in the Gulf Sea Frontier commander's daily diary that "at 8 a.m. Miami advised ComGulf that Air Transport Command in Jacksonville reported a PB4Y was lost at sea." When a land plane hits the water, usually the search is called off in hours or days. But given that amphibs can float for months, the search can drag on inexorably. Many dozens of aircraft, hundreds of servicemen on land, in the air and afloat deployed to find the missing 14 men, who were never found.

Liferafts were retreived not belonging to the same plane, a plane was reported ablaze and sinking a mile west of Governour's Harbour, Eleuthera (it was a boat), a large piece of rectangularly shaped metal was reported on Nunjack Cay, Abacos, and lights were seen flashing well east of the islands, all for naught. The main focus was on Paw Paw Rocks, northwest of Little Abaco and southeast of Walker's Cay, with nothing conclusive ever found. Airman Charles John Nickerman, from Salt Lake City, Utah, never made his 20th birthday. His parents were informed he was simply "missing in action," and he was awarded the Navy Gold Star for death in the line of duty.

On August 24, 1944 on the open ocean east of James Cistern, central Eleuthera, a PBM Mariner aircraft was given assistance by RAF rescue boats who ultimately were not up to the task. After a distress call was sent from the plane, a B-25 bomber based at Oakes Field diverted to its reported position. Then a signal sent to launch at Harbour Island instructing it to put to sea to locate the drifting Mariner, which the training crew in the B-25 located and returned to base. USS *Christiana* at Royal Island took over from the RAF air-sea rescue crash boat HMS *P-339*, which reached the Mariner, but could not tow it to shore, as its tow-rope was unable to stand the strain. HMS *P-339* then returned to Eleuthera.

What aircraft could be better in an archipelagic group of islands than an amphibian one which could land almost anywhere? After all the vast majority of space in The Bahamas has the sea for a surface, and most of that is shallow enough for a plane to anchor in. This is underscored by the fact that Sir Harold Christie and the founder of Pan Am, Juan Tripp, as well as many others were fond of using amphibious aircraft to island hop in The Bahamas.

Sir Harold was as firm believer in selling beaches and owned and operated a fleet of aircraft, many of them amphibians, to show prospective clients around. On one occasion rueful guests were forced to jettison their many pineapples and coconuts given them at Hatchet Bay or Three Bays farms so that the aircraft could take off. These were no doubt subsequently salvaged along the beach.

USS *Christiana*, IX-80, YAG-32, seaplane tender in Royal Island Eleuthera and Pelican Bay, Abaco, Bahamas, during World War II.

Sunrise off Royal Island, storm brewing.

Chapter Sixteen:

Grand Bahama

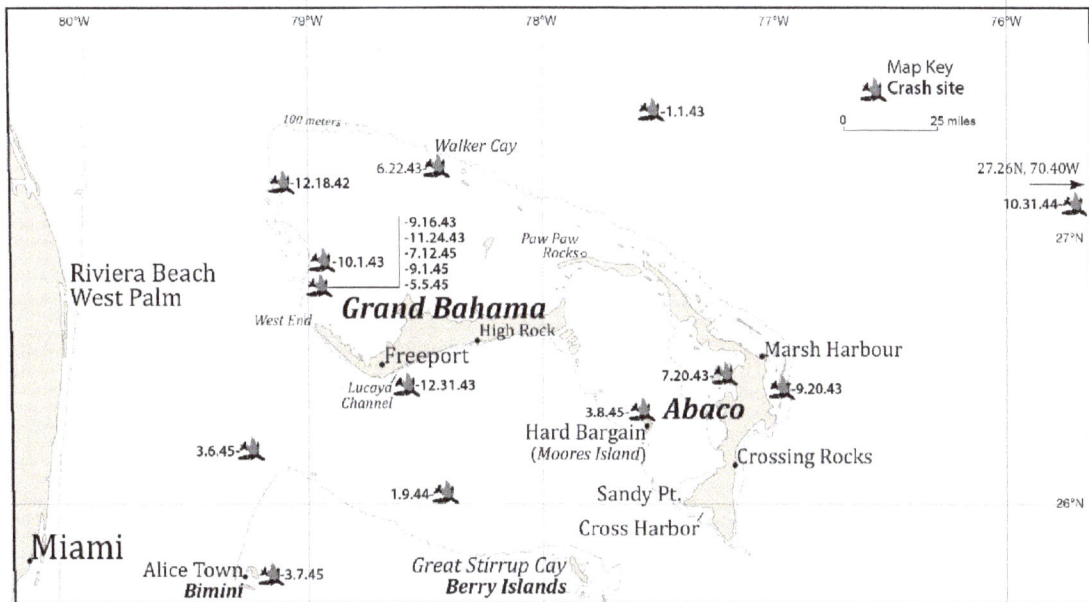

The story of Grand Bahama in World War II can be summed up in two words: proximity and volume. The proximity of Settlement Town, which is now known as West End, to Florida, and its connection to the northbound Gulf Stream, meant that it had a front row seat to the war. For six years tens of thousands of vessels, possibly millions of persons passed West End going North-South between nodes like Halifax and Panama, and East-West, Houston to Liverpool. Also, over 100 enemy submarines and innumerable training flights, patrols, training missions, planes were being delivered to the Caribbean. Though crashes and shipwrecks were few there, the biggest mysteries were never solved.

West End sat at the lip of much World War II activity, both friend and foe. Aside from intense smuggling and rum-running, it had yet to experience the mass industrialization of the post-war years which saw Freeport's rise to global-grade ship ports, airports, shipyards, oil terminals, and tourism. Back then the westernmost community in the country was a shallow fishing port with an airstrip. In days of yore, West End has been seen as a place to get away from the industrial areas and find quality seafood, conviviality, and a degree of privacy and seclusion, as shared in the popular song *West End Move*, by Phil Stubbs.

Though Grand Bahama, including the shallow banks to the north, is massive, what little military events happened were mostly at West End, Walker's Cay to the far north, and little-known Paw Paw Cay near Little Abaco. Aside from a few smaller planes and bombs, no significant lost planes were found on Grand Bahama, making it a high-volume low-yield artifact hunting ground.

On May 25, 1942, the German submarine U-558 under Gunther Krech logged, "Surfaced in Straits of Florida: 'Gun Cay' lighthouse (Grand Bahama Island) in sight." A few weeks later, on July 17, his colleague Rudolf Schendel in U-134 passed south of Grand Bahama heading west, and noted that "Nothing seen up to the entrance to the Florida Straits, no surveillance." On September 1, 1942, he "suspect[ed] that traffic now passing on the east side in the northern part of the Florida Straits is in fact close to the Great and Little Bahama Banks."

New Year's Day of 1943 heralded a dramatic rescue of half the crew of a B-26 Marauder that ditched east of the base at Walker's Cay, north of Crown Haven, Little Abaco. Since it was out on the open, heaving sea, it is little-known in Bahamas. Earlier that day, four Marauders left together from Myrtle Beach, South Carolina, bound for Nassau. While just beginning to overlap the northwestern Bahamas, one of the airplanes "caught fire and crashed at 11:30 a.m." Out of the six crew, three managed to escape the doomed aircraft by exiting the fuselage with their parachutes, avoiding being hit by the tail or getting tangled up, and landed on the sea. Fortunately, for them, their colleagues in the other three planes were witnesses and radioed in a Mayday on their behalf. The other three men either crashed with the plane into the sea, or did get out but did not survive the fall and the subsequent floating time. The air traffic controllers ordered a navy yard patrol vessel to the scene, and PBY and PBM amphibians were dispatched from Banana River, Florida. One of the PBM Mariners was able to both locate and rescue three of the aviators, and returned to Banana River with them.

On May 22, 1943, members of the USN VS-39 Squadron went to the assistance of Bahamian mariners without food in a sailing smack; in other instances, this required jettisoning their depth charges for a safer waterborne landing, but not in this case. Seaplanes were performing search and patrol anti-submarine missions from

Walker's Cay south when at 6:15 p.m. "a small Bahama sailing boat was sighted in distress. One of the planes landed, and three men were found aboard who had been without food for five days. A quart and a half of water and a package of emergency rations were furnished to them, and they were advised to stay where they were and [that] assistance would be provided." Following a report being made, the air traffic controller assured the pilot that "a Coast Guard vessel would be dispatched to the position indicated."

At 3:50 p.m. on June 22, 1943, a Vought-Sikorsky OS2U-3 Kingfisher observation seaplane crashed into the water off Walker's Cay, killing the radioman and leaving the pilot injured, but alive. This is one of the most carefully documented crashes in the theater, and the plane and all occupants, dead and alive, were recovered. Lt. (j.g.) Lester F. McDonough, USNVR, took off from the sea at 3:38 p.m., supported by radioman Franklin J. Sobolak. There was a sister plane flown by Lt. H. Basore, the senior pilot. As the first to lift off, McDonough turned left at 500 feet to observe the other craft takeoff, but in the midst of his climb he changed his mind in favor of observing a larger J2F seaplane approaching land. On making a steep turn to the left, the plane looped left, "causing a rapid loss of altitude which was climaxed by the crash." McDonough "failed to fully recover from the turn, and crashed into the sea in a nose-down attitude." This was a quarter-mile northwest of Walker's Cay, in about 12 feet of water.

Immediately, civilian managers from the base nearby set out by boat and arrived in 15 minutes. By then the plane was capsized, with the pilot clinging to the float that extended 10 feet from the sea surface. They quickly pulled him into the boat. The men dove repeatedly to the cockpit area of the upside-down aircraft to extricate the radioman Sobolak, but he was trapped "in the rear cockpit enclosure of the plane," and the current was very strong. After the rescue boat returned, several vessels (including a rearming barge) were sent to the scene where recovery and rescue operations went on for two days, day and night. Just after midnight the following day, the plane was towed to the beach near the seaplane ramp at Walker's Cay and Mr. Sobolak's remains were removed. Both men were considered well-qualified.

At 9:30 a.m. on August 29, 1943, a F6F fighter plane left Vero Beach on a short flight of 40 minutes, and was last seen just west of West End, Grand Bahama. Once the plane was declared overdue at 11:15 a.m., the blimp USS *K-120* set off from Palm Beach to Little Abaco, via West End. Just over an hour later, the airfield at Fort Lauderdale sent six of its TBF fighters, a first wave at 1:44 p.m., and another six being sent at 1:47 p.m. to scour the area around Banana River. By midnight, there was no further information on the missing aircraft.

At 11:55 a.m. on September 13, 1943, a USAAF B-25 operated by seven men took off from Greenville, South Carolina bound for The Bahamas. It was *en route* to West End loaded with enough fuel to last till 1 a.m. the following day, when at 1:30 p.m. it transmitted its last message reporting speed of 153 mph and course 156 degrees. All the men had life jackets, and there were two life rafts aboard as well. At the time of its last message, the B-25 was roughly 65 miles east of Florida, and north and west of The Bahamas, heading southeast to Grand Bahama. It is believed "that the plane may have overrun Settlement Point." Searches were conducted by the RAF in Nassau, and US vessels and planes were sent from Dinner Key, Miami, Walker's Cay, Banana River, and Richmond, including five search and rescue planes from Morrison Field, later West Palm Beach. Sadly, it was all to no avail, as the seven were never seen or heard from again. The patrols lasted at least four days, till September 17.

Two weeks later, on October 1, 1943, at 11:35, a small airplane crashed at West End. The district commissioner informed RAF in Nassau that "search was made, but no bodies found. Piece of a clockwork time device and one large bomb-shaped object [were] found in three feet of water. While the US forces were not aware of a missing airplane fitting the time and place, it was agreed that a mine-disposal officer would be dispatched to the location and if necessary, action taken to defuse explosives."

On November 24, 1943, the US liaison in Nassau informed them that a US aircraft of USN Squadron VS-41 "had crashed off Settlement Point... at 11:40 a.m. in 30 feet of water. The hull is upside down and it is, at present, impossible to recover the bodies, because of bad weather and lack of equipment." The plane was a SB2A-4, marked VS-41, which departed Vero Beach, Florida at 10:59 a.m. on what was known as a short "navigational hop," a training exercise. However, 41 minutes later they were dead. The navy sent a sister SNB plane from Vero Beach "to view the scene," with instructions to advise "if assistance is needed." In these circumstances, the navy typically went to the site with heavy-lift equipment and retrieved the bodies, and where possible, the plane or security-sensitive equipment as well.

On January 31, 1944, a USN notice was circulated regarding unexploded depth charges at Grand Bahama. It reported that "the mine disposal officer was alerted of the unexploded depth charges and requested that the district intelligence officer at Nassau ascertain whether the charge was on land or in the water. The District

Intelligence Officer replied that the charge was believed to be on land or in shallow water, since the original report stated that the charge was staked." On February 19, 1944, amphibious Scouting Squadron 39 (VS-39) flying out of Walker's Cay, dedicated the midday to searching for a navy aircraft "forced down two miles west of base. Pilot and crew safe. Plane towed to base by crash boat."

Though there are always extraordinary exceptions, once it is known that a plane is overdue or missing, usually the searching for them ends in hours if over water and in days if over land. These cold calculations err on the side of optimism for amphibious craft. Because they could land safely at sea anywhere and have the water and food to last for weeks, hope can be held out, though usually the crew would be able to send some kind of radio, light, or smoke signal to enable rescue.

A US Navy Vought OS2U-2 Kingfisher seaplane crashed with one fatality on June 22, 1943, at Walker's Cay, Grand Bahama, the northernmost air base in Bahamas. A significant portion of the island has port and runway infrastructure.

Chapter Seventeen:

Mayaguana

Mayaguana Island was the site of at least two significant World War II air crashes, a small rescue boat base, and other important activities. Being north of the trunk route from Palm Beach to Borinquen, its main role was strategic, in that it was the first and last land at the entry to several key shipping passages dissecting the southern Bahamas. These passages connect the Panama Canal with Halifax and the UK. That is why the New Zealand refrigerated ship *Makatana* wrecked on Plana Cays near Mayaguana early in the war; it was *en route* from Panama to New York with agricultural produce and frozen meat. Thousands of ships passed Mayaguana to enter or leave the Caribbean. Though millions saw the island in passing, almost none of them stopped, since the only facilities was a small boat dock.

Mayaguana gets its name from Lucayan for "lesser middle land." This is appropriate as to many, the island's small population of 275 on 110 square miles, and the tiny settlements at Abrahams Bay, Betsy Bay, and Pirates Well, may seem just a footnote. The island is roughly the size of New Providence at 25 by 6 miles, yet with vastly fewer people. An anthropologist writing his thesis on the social habits of the islanders before the war observed that, in the absence of roads and an ability or opportunity to operate boats, many of the womenfolk were reliant on the monthly visits of mailboats to socialize with persons from other communities, at time going over a decade without visiting villages only a mile or two away.

An Anglo-American treaty signed on September 2, 1940, granted US access to air bases in Mayaguana, as well New Providence, Exuma, San Salvador, and Eleuthera. Thereafter, the US Coast Guard and US Navy constructed a station, Abrahams Bay, consisting of "rescue station, barracks, canteen, support facilities, generators, water-makers, radios, radio towers, and a good timber dock, where they tied up PT-type boats." Mayaguana maintained a 104-foot rescue boat operated with air-sea-rescue for the USAAF, to aid downed aviators and mariners in distress. This was a form of highway patrol or insurance policy, with eyes and ears on the marine chokepoint which is the Crooked Island Passage.

The small Allied steamer *Mariana* was torpedoed and sunk off Mayaguana by U-126 under Ernst Bauer on March 5, 1942. Despite calm conditions and the Germans watching survivors getting clear of the ship, all 36 men under Captain Ivan Elroy Hurlestone of the Cayman Islands were lost. Yet, they were only 25 miles upwind from the island. Did they land at the uninhabited end and perish there? Later that year, one of many German submarines and some Italian invaders made log entries about sighting Mayaguana. On August 21, 1942, U-558 under Günther Krech logged "Land in sight bearing 300° true; Mayaguana." One wonders what the residents and American soldiers and sailors were doing at that moment, being watched and reported by a German sub.

Then on May 17, 1942, the Dutch steamship *Fauna* was sunk by the U-558 some 25 miles east of Mayaguana. Two were killed and 27 survivors ended up in Providenciales the same day. On January 21, 1943, the aircraft FR-372 landed in Nassau from Dorval and received a report from the USN that the civilian motor boat *Paddy Halfready* was overdue at Nassau from Abaco. The B-25 FL-184 ascertained that the motorboat was located 30 miles west of Mayaguana, having drifted some 350 miles from Cornwall, Abaco.

Mayaguana was the site of an exhaustive search starting May 22, 1943, when a B-25 was reported missing and overdue. That day at 6 a.m., the district commissioner of Mayaguana reported that "a plane crashed on the north side of the island some distance out to sea in a northerly direction from Curtiss Creek about 6 am. No large boats here at present to investigate." The search authorities added their input to this report that, "The B-25 [missing] was last reported the previous day and its limit of endurance would not carry it through 6.00 a.m. the following morning, so this report cannot refer to it. No other planes have been reported missing... in this area."

The day after, on May 24, an RAF B-25 with tail FR-375 CJ went in search for the eight missing aviators at sea near Mayaguana. They searched for a reported crashed aircraft, and did succeed in finding white planks and smaller pieces of painted wood. When these were observed floating, the pilot then circled in the B-25 but failed to locate the missing plane. More searches were made in the vicinity of Mayaguana where a crashed aircraft was reported. However, although the area was thoroughly searched, nothing was found. The plane continued landed back at Nassau, and the search was called off without finding the men.

During the same week, on May 19, 1943, three men led by USAAF Capt. Clark had to ditch their stalled A-20 somewhere east of the Turks and Caicos and north of Haiti, and escaped in a dinghy. As several days later they washed ashore in Little

Inagua, and because they were lost between Florida and the Caribbean, it might be possible that their lost aircraft was the one spotted crashing north of Mayaguana, and that they drifted south. This is, however, unlikely, and it does seem to contradict the HQ's idea that there were no other planes missing at the time of the search for the B-25 on May 23.

On January 9, 1944 regional war diaries by the US and UK reported a B-24 still overdue and unreported, noting that six aircraft from Nassau and five from Guantanamo as well as one from Georgetown were searching for it. There were 14 persons aboard the missing plane that was *en route* to Trinidad from Morrison Field. A USAAF plane reported smoke rising from the north coast of Mayaguana at 10:30 a.m. that morning. So, a plane from Great Exuma searched the area, but without any fruitful result. It was agreed that the Gulf Sea Frontier would discontinue its search the following day.

NOB and NAS Great Exuma were the closest military installations, so naturally, there was traffic to and from the islands. On April 7, 1944, a Grumman Goose was airborne from Florida *en route* for Mayaguana when adverse weather forced it to land at NAS Great Exuma and remain there for the night. The following day, it flew to the small boat base located there and two days after that, returned from Mayaguana.

On May 27, 1945, Sam H. Marcroft was piloting a Douglas C-47B from George Field, west of Louisville, Kentucky, to the Caribbean. The plane was reported missing, however, it managed to make it to less than a mile from the island. Following engine failure, he ditched it into the sea .8 miles off Mayaguana. The aircraft was damaged beyond repair, though it is believed the crew made it to shore. The air-sea-rescue base on Mayaguana's mission was to support wayward, lost, or ditched aircrews of the USAAF, RAF, RAFTC, RAFFC and those from Guantanamo, Puerto Rico, Trinidad, Cuba, Bahamas, US, and Canada.

On July 19, 1945, the USN destroyer escort USS *Carter* (DE 112) under command of Lt. Commander Francis John Torrence Baker, USNR of Sewickley, Pennsylvania left a convoy protecting USS *Guadalcanal* during a search for a lost plane. At 6:48 p.m., USS *Carter* "left formation to investigate life rafts on Mayaguana Island." The convoy was passing through the Crooked Island Passage bound from Mayport Florida to Guantanamo Bay at the time. After the war, a large US air base was built for missile and space asset tracking and retrieval purposes. Mayaguana is home not only to one of the largest airstrips in the nation, but also the largest mailboat fleet in the land. Of the 23 boats to serve Mayaguana since the early 1900s, 15 have been or are owned by the Taylor family from Pirates Well.

A 1945 Douglas C-47 (aka Skytrain, Dakota, DC-3) ditched north of Nassau in 2020.

Mayaguana Island with Abrahams Bay (lower left) and Pirates Well (upper left), shows where Curtis Bay is, and if a plane wrecked there, where that might be.

Chapter Eighteen:

Andros

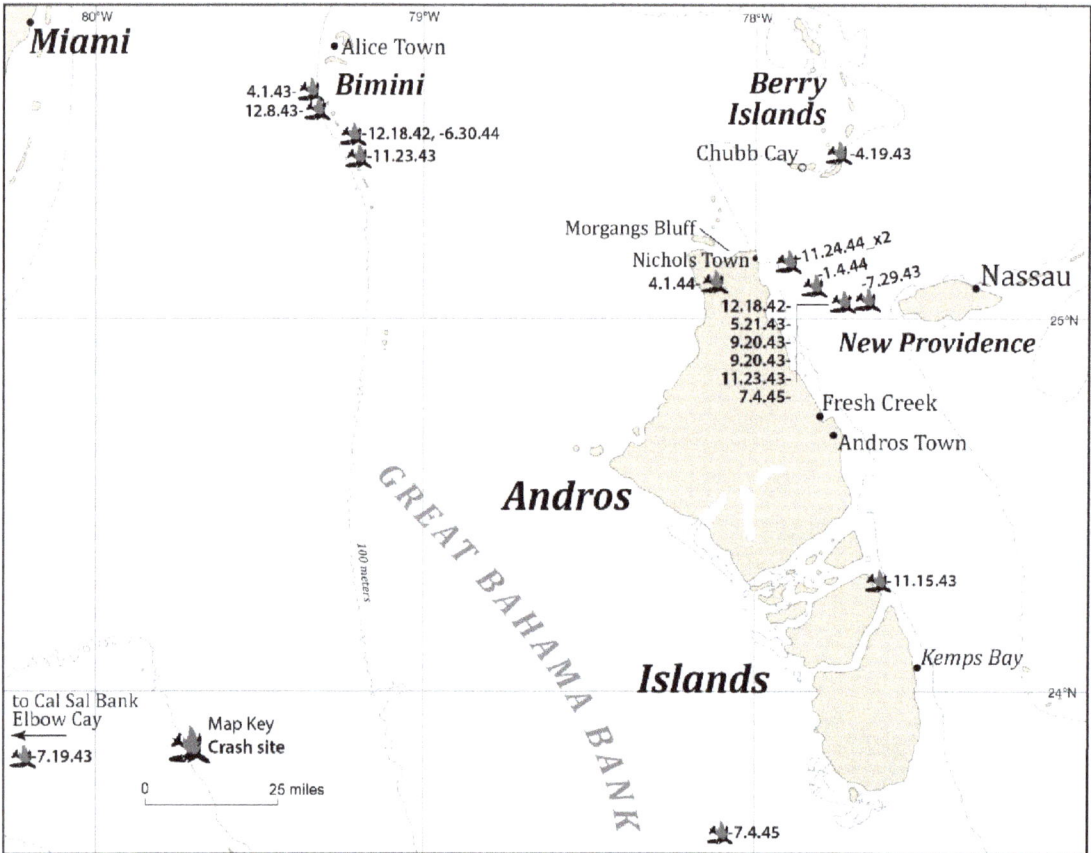

Andros is underappreciated in the national conscience in terms of the water it provides, the mailboats it has acquired, and the incidents of aircraft wrecks on its shores in the air races of 1930 and during World War II. Only New Providence has seen so many plane wrecks in The Bahamas. This is due to the sheer size of Andros' three islands, their position straddling both the training grounds, and the routes from the US to the Caribbean and Cuba. Once you are west of New Providence, Andros is the only body of land left in the country. Because of the nascent infrastructure, as there were no large bases there, most of the rescues and recoveries at Andros were undertaken by boats, seaplanes, and even a blimp sent from New Providence, southern Florida and the Florida Keys.

Andros comprises some 2,300 square miles, with massive shallow banks to the west, north, south, and southeast comprising many times that amount. The islands are girdled by the third-largest barrier reef in the world. Andros is rich in timber and freshwater lenses; however, the terrain further west is severely and often indented with creeks, channels, and marshy wet surfaces ideal for swallowing airplanes. Thus, the islands represent harsh, sparsely-populated terrain, with only 7,500 people today. The overwhelming majority live in eastern settlements near the deep Tongue of the Ocean. The northeast corner of Andros, from Nichols Town, Mastic Point, Morgan's Bluff ship terminal, Joulter Cays, and east to Chub Cay at the bottom of the Berry Islands, were the locations of the most wrecks, with a few hundred feet determining if a plane was forever out of reach or visible from 30,000 feet.

The shallow banks girdle Andros like a whale-bone dress of yore. On May 1, 1942, the German commander Harro Schacht ordered the U-507 to surface and recorded that a "tug bears 65°T, with course for the Bahama Bank." He was skirting the deeper waters south and west of Andros, known as the Old Bahama Channel. On February 10, 1943, a USAAC A-20 Havoc crashed into the shallow waters off Andros. The crash was just over 20 miles west of Windsor Field and the ASR base at Clifton Bay. They were fortunate that a larger B-25 under Wing Commander McBratney saw them. He dropped a rescue and survival kit in a Thornaby bag to the crew to hold them over until an RAF ASR launch went to their aid. When the site proved too shallow even for the boat to reach them, a Catalina flying boat managed to rescue all of the Havoc's crew.

Wing Commander McBratney was involved in several searches out of RAF bases on New Providence: one on the afternoon of December 19, 1942, and another for a US B-24 lost from Nassau. On February 3, a civilian aircraft flying between Miami and Nassau reported seeing a boat drifting with three occupants, and McBratney went out in the B-25 FR383. However, nothing was observed and the plane returned. With so many training, transport, civilian, and military flights over the area, it is not surprising there was confusion at times. On February 27, an aircraft at 8,000 feet altitude saw searchlights from Andros' northern tip, leaving the pilots unsure whether it was sent from land or sea.

Since they felt it was an effort by stranded aviators to secure attention, they reported the flashes of 30 to 40 seconds. Prior to that, they had seen a large fire on

Andros, in waters too shallow for ships. The personnel believed to have been signaling were thought to have been from a B-24 lost between Savannah, Georgia and Batista Field, Cuba. The following day at 10:45 a.m., a marine crash boat at the north end of Andros heard a Mayday on 4220 kilohertz reporting a position nearby before it faded, and the transmission was caught in Palm Beach Florida as well. Regretfully, these intriguing signals did not result in a rescue. Perhaps someday the evidence will be found showing who was sending these signals.

On June 28, 1943, B-25 went down five miles north of Morgan's Bluff, Andros. Though an oil slick, damaged dinghy, wheel, and spare parts were found and retrieved, none of the crew survived this training accident. An oil slick was seen by rescue launch HMS *P-190* and HMS *P-63*. Their men managed to find one of the aircraft's dinghies, with no crew but the plane markings. The launches also took a plane wheel and spares aboard their boats back to New Providence as evidence. There were significant search patrols sent out on May 23, with events and observations recorded in the base record book as follows:

"B-25 FR282DD airborne on a parallel track search for aircraft FR382DD missing since the previous night on an exercise patrol carried out as detailed aircraft turned to starboard from its course to investigate a glint seen in the sea, no results, disturbance was observed on the water and upon investigation this proved to be a shark, landed back to base having sighted nothing. B-25 FR384CM airborne on an air-sea-rescue search, object sighted on port bow was a small motor vessel, oil streaks seen gave no results upon investigation, patrol completed, and aircraft landed back to base with nothing further to report. B-25 FR381DC airborne on air-sea-rescue search, area detailed covered by parallel track search, nothing sighted, landed back to base. B-25 FR375CJ is airborne on a search, completed the detailed patrol and having sighted nothing landed back to base." One of the aircraft, with tail number CA dropped a smoke float on the site.

On November 19, 1943, the RAF Naval Liaison Officer in Nassau relayed that the District Commissioner at Mangrove Cay, southeastern Andros, reported finding aircraft wreckage. This was identified as being the B-24 missing since the day before from a flight plan between Morrison Field, Florida, and Battista Field, north coast of Cuba. The commissioner "revealed that the wreckage found was thrown up in shattered bits along the coast. These pieces were salvaged by [residents] from Pleasant Bay to Little Creek, Andros, a distance of 25-to-30 miles. No survivors were found."

At 1:20 p.m. on September 16, 1943, Captain Bullock reported having seen a "small freighter aground on a reef on the northeastern tip of Andros Island." He added that a medium-sized vessel was standing by to assist and appeared to be engaged in lightering, or taking cargo off the larger vessel. The pilot did not see any people and was described as "not very familiar with the area." A plane then flew over to corroborate Bullocks' account, but was unable to. A report was made about a 75-foot vessel in the water in the area, without activity being noted or confirmed.

On September 21, 1943, a USAAF Baltimore plane left Morrison Field on a delivery to Windsor Field. They landed instead in the swamps of central Andros, upside down. With some help from colleagues and without air brakes, they managed to survive. They "crash-landed on beach on NW point of Andros." RAFTC and Montague ASR boat HMS *P-339* was sent. Pilots used the dinghy to attract attention. The water was very shallow, and on high tide an airship from USN picked them up and dropped them at Windsor where they were hospitalized. The ASR launch returned back to New Providence.

Once it was clear the airplane was overdue on a relatively short hop, a large search and rescue operation was put in place, calling on aircraft from Florida to Exuma including a number of blimps, or airships. The topography hampered rescue: "... aircraft upon air exercise Number 1, instructed to look out for the missing aircraft, landed without having seen anything. [Douglas C-47 Dakotas] FL-534 and FL-535 airborne but returned to Satellite having sighted nothing, three airships airborne from Exuma, reports received via RAFTC that blimp had sighted a raft and flying boat was proceeding to reported position. Commanding Officer instructed ASR launch, [HMS] *P-339* was to be dispatched from Montague Bay to scene of the raft, flying boat instructed not to become waterborne as sea was choppy, RAFTC ascertained that Baltimore had been landed on beach on northwest point of Andros, dinghy had been put to sea to attract attention. Launch [HMS] *P-339* unable to approach near shore because of shallow water, launch instructed to stand-by and await high tide and then approach, signal received through USN that blimp had picked up two survivors and was landing on Main Field. Airship landed and survivors taken to US Hospital, signal sent to [HMS] *P-339* to return to base."

This is a well-documented, even animated case, with the Gulf Sea Frontier on September 23 relaying how "it was the pilot's first flight to Nassau, and he simply got lost, could not find his way, nor get help by radio. So, he attempted a power landing with 45 minutes of fuel on board. At the end of his landing, the wheels hit a soft spot and the plane flipped over on its back. The pilot became asphyxiated and drenched by the gasoline and vapors and passed out. The radio operator had to cut the plane to get him out. All confidential and secret material was destroyed. The men spent a miserable night in the rain, but managed to extract food and personal effects from the plane, then sat under a tree on the beach. In the morning of September 21, they were spotted by a PBY and by a PBM, neither of which could land, but one of which dropped an emergency kit." The aviators reported that only the plane's windows, fins, and one propeller were damaged and it was salvageable, and parachutes and the life raft remained on board.

Next is the account of the pilot of the USN airship USS *K-65*, that went before dawn on "a special mission to search for an A-30 Baltimore bomber… which was last heard from at 1:58 p.m." the day before. They set out from NAS Richmond, Florida, at 4:45 a.m. with [USS] *K-70* and [USS] *K-53* starting sweeping the area at daylight." After receiving intelligence as to the location of the Baltimore, the pilot noted that "immediately the search was discontinued and all airships proceeded to the scene of the landing to attempt to rescue the two members of the crew." The pace of the narrative then quickens considerably:

"I arrived at the crash at 12.45 pm. The plane was overturned… I located the crew on a nearby beach by following their footprints, and shouted to them that I would pick them up. After valving helium and making several runs to affect a landing on the beach, I shouted to the survivors to grab the short lines and slow down the [air] ship. This they did, and after the ship hit water, it slowed considerably, but [still] did not stop. I instructed the two men to come to rear door and within thirty seconds both were aboard. One was pulled in by a line which was thrown to him and which he tied around his chest. The other was pulled in by the airship rigger, who laid face down in the car, with his body hanging out the door from the waist. When both were safely aboard, I took off on one engine, heading out to sea. The landing wheel and tail wheel were both in the water and the ship cleared the water within 300 feet of the beach before the water had gotten four feet deep. The survivors were First Lt. Bruno A. Carr, USA, and George P. Kelly, USA, radio operator. Both men were in fairly good condition, although they sustained minor cuts and bruises."

The reports conclude with "Admiral Munroe today expressed his personal appreciation of the rescue and safe delivery at Nassau… of the two survivors." He cited it as "another example of the usefulness of airships to the Frontier and that this task was well done under unusual circumstances." The US diarists added that "the RAF at

Nassau, under Group Captain Waite, provided everything possible for the requirements of the airship and the comfort of the men," as well as for servicing the airship.

On January 9, 1944, a B-24 was missing over Andros *en route* Florida to the Caribbean, and it was believed to have gone down off Andros with a crew of eight. The airplane left Boca Raton for Windsor Field, and when the arrival was overdue, search efforts were initiated across Andros. No sign of the B-24 emerged until, three months later, RAF planes were asked by the US to "investigate wreck on beach, at the west end of Andros." Those new planes also failed to locate the B-24. On January 10 and 11, "a request was received by the RAF from the Officer Commanding ATC for an aircraft to search Andros for the B-24 missing since January 9. The B-24 BZ744 LL was airborne, carried out a local flight to search Andros for the missing aircraft, but landed having sighted nothing."

On February 24, 1944, the officer in charge of US Army Transport Command set out from Lyford Cay to inspect the flipped Baltimore from which the two aviators had been rescued. However, in poor weather Major Brown's launch itself became overdue. Then B-25 FS-393 BF took off at 3:38 p.m. and returned at 5:08 p.m., without having found them. The following day, the boat was located west of New Providence, inbound from Andros. On July 4, 1945, the RAF base diary recorded the sad demise of nine servicemen under Captain Flight Leader Thompson thus: "B-24 LO airborne to search for B-24 MD NE of Andros, located wreckage, all crew lost... with negative results, the search was abandoned."

Captain Flight Leader Thompson set off for northwest Andros with eight other crew members and with no instructor on board to perform Leigh Light Homing exercises 47 there. As with several previous base aircraft, this ended disastrously, with all nine men perishing and none of them recovered. First, the B-24 LO set out at 10:26 a.m. to find B-24 MD, and located the wreckage, then vectored the ASR launch HMS *P-191*, presumably from Lyford Cay, to the position, without finding any crew. By 1 p.m. B-24 LO returned to Oakes Field.

The crash site was in shallow water in the vicinity of Morgan's Bluff, and there the HMS *P-191* found a deflated dinghy with markings of MD on it as well as portions of fuselage from the plane and of its tail still in the water. The aircraft LO and ASR launch HMS *P-191* continued their search of the area for survivors or remains, however results were negative and they returned to their respective bases. The search was abandoned.

What a far cry from the US Navy search for a PBY off Paw Paw Rocks that year, which went on for weeks, and early in the war when so many resources were contributed for so long. In 1946, the government utilized the Grumman Goose to make rescues, though the war was over but before the RAF pulled out. On February 2, "at the Colonial Secretary's Request, the Goose aircraft proceeded to Mangrove Cay, Andros in order to bring back a serious ambulance case." Perhaps the islanders who collected the remains of the B-24 on 25 miles of beach were being thanked.

Chapter Nineteen:

Bimini & Berry Islands

The Bimini and Berry Islands comprise less than nine square miles some 50 miles east of south Florida, and 30 square miles between Nassau and the Northwest Providence Channel. It is not their substance so much as their straddling stance which makes them strategic: they are like hundreds of branching islands through which commerce, recreation, submarine, aircraft, and vessels pass around or through, or allide with. Aside from several water crashes east of Bimini, and amphibian landings coupled with many unverified sights and sounds, the islands mostly served as goal posts or sounding boards for friends and foe to gauge their progress as they passed to and from the mainland and the open Atlantic, or south into the Caribbean or Old Bahama Channel.

The first reference to the islands during wartime outside the frenetic ferry and freight system plowing past to connect Nassau with Miami was on February 25, 1942, when the German submarine U-558 under Gunther Krech surfaced in the Straits of Florida and observed wryly that "Gun Cay Light is in sight. Shadow in sight bearing 270°T. … 'Great Isaac' lighthouse in sight. Dived. Proceeded submerged in the center of the Strait." On July 17, Schendel noted; "Lighthouse Great Stirrup Cay in sight bearing 270°T. Lighthouse Bimini in sight. Lighthouse Cat Cays in sight. All burn as in peacetime." Reinhard "Teddy" Suhren motored past Bimini on May 6, 1942, in U-564, writing in the log that a "steamer makes for the 'Cat Cays'."

The RAF operational diaries rarely mention Bimini—it was largely the province of US forces probing east from Florida. The US Army asserted in a confidential circular on November 15, 1943, that "The Army has rescue boats stationed in various locations from West Palm Beach [Morrison Field], to Havana, and at Cat Cay [Bimini] and Nassau. These boats are subject to call for any plane crash where their services are desired and can be reached directly on 4200 kcs voice [radio] or by the Controller through the Army Transport Command, Morrison Field. Since planes crashed in the Frontier involving any rescue of personnel are generally delegated to Com 7 Operations [Miami, 7th Naval District], the Controller calls to the Attention of 7ND Operations the Army boat nearest the position of the crash in order that they may avail themselves of its services if needed."

Only USN, RAF crash boats, and US Army amphibian aircraft mostly were utilized to rescue survivors in The Bahamas. Curtiss SBC Helldiver scout bombers were two-seat biplanes—with two stacks of wings, one on top of the other. They "entered [US] Navy service in 1937 and [were] the last biplane combat aircraft to see Navy service." A year after Pearl Harbor, on December 18, 1942, two of them were training east from Opa Locka when they were forced to make emergency sea landings; the first near North Bimini and the second off Andros. Both crashes were caused by running out of fuel between 12:30 and 1 p.m.

Ensign Z. P. Russon and his passenger J. N. Wilson in SBC-48 ditched off the western end of North Bimini, and both men were uninjured. Their colleagues, Ensign B. M. Richards and his passenger W. A. Underwood on the radio, also escaped injury after landing on the northwest edge of Andros. An Army transport amphibian JRF was sent from their home base at Opa Locka and retrieved all four of them, then flew them to Florida on the same day. Both aircraft flipped on their backs—upside down—upon impact. And though they crashed over 60 miles apart, their damage was almost identical. Both sustained broken propellers (they had a total of three on the single engine), and a crumpled top wing. The US Navy prudently was able to salvage both aircraft, although it was noted that "both engines require major overhaul and repairs, [which] will be made at NAS San Diego, California." How far away the Pacific must have seemed to Androsians who witnessed the crash and rescue.

On November 23, 1943, B-25 FV952FX was reported to have crashed at Northwest Channel Light, southwest of Chub Cay near Joulter Cays, which are northeast of Andros, and the entire eight-man crew perished. This is in the Berry Islands, which would make it the costliest aviation accident for that string of cays in the war. It has been difficult to precisely pinpoint the location; the Florida-based plane lost its signal abruptly at night, and the US Coast Guard reported a plane crashing into the sea near "NW Light, Bimini." That is vague enough that the location could be Northwest Providence Channel, as in Great Isaac's Light, Bimini, or Northwest Light, Miami; it is not clear. If the accident took place near Chub Cay, it would be near Joulters and Morgan's Bluff, Andros. The problem is that the sea is very deep there, and sufficient wreckage was not found to ascertain without a doubt that the crash occurred there, even after a year or more of deep-sea submarine trips for visitors out of Chub Cay recently.

Then an intriguing message made its way through reporting channels: B-25 FV-952 FX was airborne for night navigation exercises, but failed to return. A signal was received by W/T which terminated abruptly and only the first letter was received which was "F." This was presumed to be the first letter of the aircraft's callsign, and a signal was received from Miami to the effect that the Coast Guard had reported a plane crashing into the sea near Northwest Light. Another signal was sent to the aircraft FK, on the night navigation exercise, diverting it to the Northwest Light, Bimini, with instructions to search the area. B-25 FK-381 DC was airborne to carry out a search of the area in which the aircraft FX was reported to have crashed. However, nothing was sighted and the aircraft landed, search was then postponed till November 24.

That day the RAF sent a B-25 FW104 FH to search for FV952 FX at 11:30 a.m. The main focus of three other aircraft was the Bimini area, with Andros secondary, but there was still no result. Later yet, the aircraft was reported to have "crashed into the sea off Bimini." The RAF cooperated with the US, and "B-25 FW104 FH was airborne to search for missing aircraft FX, thorough search made of Bimini, no evidence found to presume existence of crew of missing aircraft, aircraft landed. B-25 FW- 132 FK, FV-951 PC, FW-123 FJ… searched the Bimini area and landed after…" This search pattern by a dozen or so aircraft was repeated for days. Tragically for the families and loved ones of the eight men aboard the aircraft, they have never been found. In some cases, family members post their finds and reports with locations on genealogy databases and forums.

On April 19, 1943, a USN Catalina PBY landed on the water near the privately-owned Berry Island named Whale Cay. Whether they were in distress or had business there or were on the kind of lark in which curiosity killed the cat, the ambulance-driving, speedboat-racing Queen of Whale Cay known as Joe Carstairs presumed the latter. Joe claimed to have gone towards them with weapons bared, warning them that hers was a private island, and she and her private militia were prepared to repel boarders. The crew backed off and flew away. At least, that was one version. The operational diaries relate simply that at 2:50 p.m. the RAF learned that "an American PBY had force-landed on Whale Cay. Two marine crafts [sic] were sent to search the area, and to give any assistance that might be required. At 3:38 p.m. aircraft FR381 was airborne to search the area, and aircraft FK180 was diverted to local flying to cover the area [Berry Islands]. At 4 p.m. a message was received that the PBY was safe, and the searching aircraft and the marine craft were recalled." Whatever her actions, and she was known to have been brash, Carstairs was not reprimanded. In August of 1942 she took the initiative to skipper her Bahamas-built speedboat

Vergemere IV to successfully rescue of 48 American merchant seamen from SS *Potlatch* from Acklins.

On January 9, 1944, a USAAF B-24 was overdue and presumed missing over Bimini, *en route* from Florida to the Caribbean. By January 10, a full-blown air-sea-rescue search by joint US and UK forces was under way. Word reached Nassau at 11:30 p.m. on the 9th, and by 5:35 the next morning, British assets were being deployed southeast of New Providence in search of the B-24. Six aircraft were initially committed, spread out two miles apart, and were airborne from about 11 a.m. to 5 p.m. but without result. From Boca Raton another B-24 and six Ventura's took off, all passing over Bimini and the Berry Islands. These were followed by three Hudson aircraft and another Ventura, none of which had observed the aircraft or debris by 6 p.m. and so they returned to Florida.

Then the doughty—and new—Bahamian mailboat M/V *Noel Roberts* found a raft from Great Stirrup Cay, unknown aircraft, on January 11, 1944. Built in Harbour Island the year before by brothers Earl and Gerald Johnson, the wooden-hulled *Noel Roberts* was 115′ long and 180 gross tons. Owned by an entrepreneur from the same island and from Nassau, Sir George W. K. Roberts, she plied between Florida, Nassau, and other islands and also hauled mail inter-island. Passing Stirrup Cay north of the Berry Islands and Bimini was thus on the motor ship's usual route. For several days, both US and British management tried to attribute the raft to a known casualty, a process not always as clear as one might wish.

Prior to the *Noel Roberts* report an RAF aircraft was sent to search in Andros for the B-24. Up until midnight, another Liberator, BZ744 LL, attempted to locate the sister aircraft without result. Then the RAF operational noted that "The master of the M/V *Noel Roberts*, which arrived at Rawson Dock, Nassau, this morning, picked up an American-type rubber dinghy, off Stirrup Cay, at 10:55 p.m. on January 11, 1944. Upon inspection, it was ascertained that the dinghy had belonged to the missing [B-24] Liberator aircraft." Based on the evidence, it is thus likely that the debris found was from the loss of 14 aviators on January 9. That would mean that a B-24 "*en route* to Italy lost the life raft which was found and retrieved by the M/V *Noel Roberts*." Later, this was corroborated by the discovery of two other rafts by a B-26 Marauder aircraft. If so, this would lend credibility to the crash site of the USAAF 52349 being off Berry Islands, in the Northwest Providence Channel, due to the concentration of debris found and retrieved in the area. In any event the men were never found.

When Air Transport Command (ATC) at Morrison Field initially reached out to RAF in Nassau on January 15, 1944, for help locating one of their planes which was overdue *en route* to Borinquen, the RAF did not have enough aircraft or information to assist. So, US Ventura's and others (numbering 20 airplanes) led the search through The Bahamas, from Boca Raton to Nassau primarily, and over Bimini. However, on the following day, January 16, 1944, a Ventura airplane was searching over Bimini between Nassau and eastern Florida for a missing ATC aircraft, without result. The previous day, a B-24 Liberator out of Nassau also flew over Bimini in search of a US aircraft missing in the western Bahamas. Search was initiated from Morrison Field, Florida through RAF Nassau on January 17, 1944, using three B-25s from Nassau starting before noon, lasting till 5 p.m., but not having seen anything.

At 2:20 p.m. on March 19, 1944, a TBF Avenger with three US airmen made a crash landing in the Gulf Stream roughly 20 miles west of Bimini. Although Naval Air Station Miami immediately informed the Gulf Sea Frontier, and two US Coast Guard vessels, CG-*38052* and CG-*47016* were dispatched to investigate, as well as a Dumbo airship from Fort Lauderdale, nothing was found of the men or their aircraft for nearly four days. Then a break in the case: witnesses called into Gulf Sea Frontier that the airplane had splashed 30 miles east of Hollywood, so another Dumbo airship was dispatched, this time from Dinner Key, south of Miami, to the scene where the men were sighted. Fortunately, at 3:20 p.m. on March 23, all three men were retrieved by an Army aircraft based at Morrison Field and taken safely ashore.

On March 25, 1945, a life raft was discovered off Bimini. A B-24 flying out of Boca Raton reported sighting "an orange object, which appeared to be a life raft, South of South Bimini Island [in a position 3.5 south-southeast of Port Royal] at 5:50 p.m." The commander of the Gulf Sea Frontier's dispatchers sent the blimp USS *K-114* on a night patrol and then to the site by dawn. Thereafter, the dirigible pilot was to search the area south of Bimini until the limit of endurance had been reached (PLE), then to return to base in Florida.

A Palm Beach socialite's motor yacht was sold to the US Navy for $1 and quickly lost in Bimini, stripped, and abandoned. "After more than 13 years of service to the Parsons family and extensive cruising from the Florida Keys to New England, the *Pleiades* lasted just over 10 months in the navy before a trained crew wrecked her in the Bahamas. During her civilian life, the crew required to man the yacht consisted of a captain, an engineer, and a small crew to serve guests. In all likelihood, Parsons manned the wheel only occasionally. Within six months of Germany declaring war on the US, Parsons gave *Pleiades* to the US Navy. For his patriotism he was remunerated the princely sum of one dollar on June 8, 1942, while the yacht lay in Miami (she was "accepted as a gift"). Two days later, on June 10, the Chief of Naval Operations directed that she be delivered to a US Navy conversion yard and placed in service post-haste."

Barnett Harbour is little more than a cluster of rocks peaking barely above sea level, but constitutes a destination or waypoint for vessels coming across the Gulf Stream from Florida and accessing the shallower and comparatively sheltered waters. It is just 3 miles north of Gun Cay, only 44 nautical miles east of Miami. On Friday, April 8, *YP-453* was intentionally beached.

The navy and coast guard personnel continued to try to save her for a week or so, since there was a further entry regarding USS *YP-453* on April 15. That entry indicates that the former *Pleiades* was "aground on Bahama Bank and damaged beyond repair." Then the little ship's death knell was struck: "Authority was requested to strike it from the Navy list and destroy the hull after salvaging the engines and other removable material." A postscript relates that "all possible machinery and material [were] removed and stored; hull has broken up."

Indeed, on July 28, 1943, USS *YP-453* was formally stricken from the United States Navy Register and given up for good. "Most likely, with her fittings and machinery gone the YP-453's wooden hull and beams would have disintegrated quickly, and there would be almost nothing left of the vessel and its hull except stringers, fasteners, and odds and ends from her construction in the Bronx in 1929. Even these would be likely buried deep in the sand or covered with coral in the intervening 73 years."

On the morning of June 30, 1944, the intelligence desk at the Seventh Naval District in Miami noted that one of the US Navy's spy planes, a Grumman TBF Avenger which had been sent "on a photographic mission" over their allies' islands in The Bahamas, "crashed at sea" at 11:10 a.m. The airplane was 40' long and 54' wide, and would become the "most effective and widely-used torpedo bomber of World War II." Capable of 278 mph thanks to a three-bladed Wright R-2600-8 Twin Cyclone engine, nearly 10,000 of them were manufactured. Fortunately for this pilot, who was alone in the three-seater at the time, he orchestrated a smooth enough landing that he was able to escape in an inflatable life raft. The crash site was two miles east of North Bimini Island, and the capital settlement of Alice Town. Two search aircraft were dispatched from the Coast Guard station in Dinner Key, Miami, to assist. Ultimately, it was another aircraft, this one sent from NAS Miami, that managed to rescue the floating flyer only 45 minutes after ditching, at 11:55 a.m. the same day.

Just a few weeks earlier, another aircraft gathering intelligence was shot down by the Japanese over Wake Island. Although his crewmates died and others were captured, killed, and partially eaten, the pilot survived and was rescued by the submarine USS *Finback*. After being awarded the Distinguished Flying Cross and returning to the flight deck of USS *San Jacinto*, he went on to become Vice President and President of the United States. His name, of course, is Lt. (j.g.) George H. W. Bush.

The fortified fiefdom of Great Whale Cay, Berry Islands, the property and base of speedboat racer Marion Joe Carstairs in the 1940s. She both rescued and repelled mariners and aviators in distress.

Joe Carstairs on Whale Cay, which she owned.

Chapter Twenty:
Cay Sal Bank

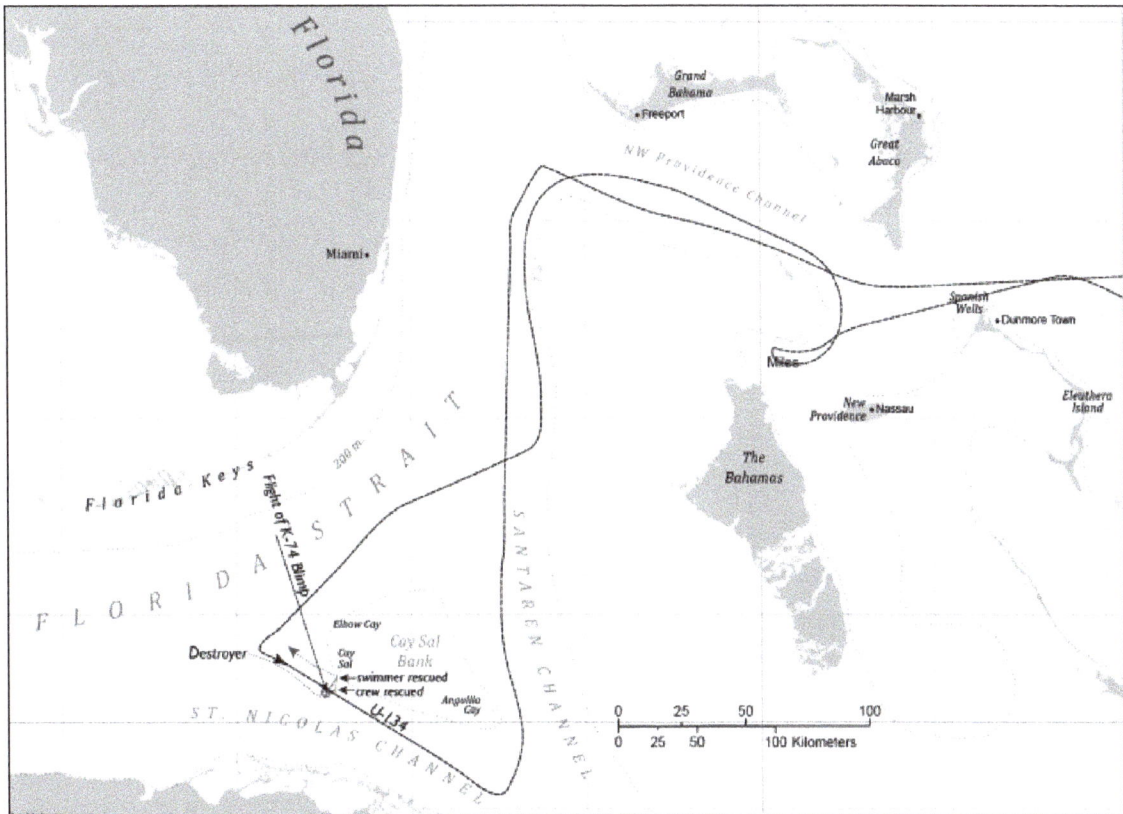

It is now proven by access to all of the logbooks that no German or Italian submarines were lost in Bahamian waters in World War II. The closest were off Cay Sal Bank and the St. Nicholas Channel bordering Cuba. There were two "vessels" sunk near the Cay Sal Bank; one of them was a blimp (USS *K-74*), the other was the *Gulfstate*, which was sunk closer to the Florida Keys. Cay Sal Bank in the southwest of The Bahamas has six crash sites near it. German commander Hans-Günther Brosin in U-134 was refueled by U-170 west of the Azores on his way to achieving the unique feat of bringing down a US Navy airship during his patrol. Entering Bahamian waters on July 10, 1943, Brosin motored west for Hole-in-the-Wall, Abaco, arriving on the 15th.

By the following day, U-134 was in the Gulf Stream heading south in the Straits of Florida. Two days later, near midnight on July 18, 1943, while off the northwest tip of the Cay Sal Bank, the U-boat was spotted and (inadvisably) attacked by the US naval airship USS *K-74*. Contrary to standing orders, the observation blimp dove in for the attack but the little-used release mechanism for the depth charges failed to work, and Brosin's deck crew were able to shoot down the dirigible.

Afraid that the charges would explode when they sank, the crew swam for their lives towards nearby Elbow Cay. Some claimed to see the U-boat approach the blimp to cut away samples of the material for analysis back in Germany, though this seems doubtful, given the danger this would have placed the submarine in, presuming that their position would have been radioed in to the Allies in nearby Key West. This was the only known case of an Axis submarine bringing down a navy blimp during the war, and when he drowned on the cusp of rescue, US Navy seaman Isadore Stessel became the only Allied personnel so lost during the conflict. U-134 was soon counter-attacked the following day by the US Ventura aircraft piloted by John C. Lawrence. Three depth charges found their mark, severely damaging the forward battery compartment. After this, Brosin performed a box maneuver southeast of the Florida Keys, and turned back towards the relative safety of the Northwest and Northeast Providence channels. On the 22nd of August, the submarine doubled the distance from Great Isaacs's Light, heading east past Nassau and emerging over the north coast of Eleuthera.

Years later, on February 27, 1945, Americans would revisit Cay Sal Bank, this time without casualties. Early that morning, a US Navy submarine named USS *R-15* "went aground at Cay Sal Bank. She was unescorted due to failure of the USCG *Cuyahoga* to make rendezvous at Key West." The sub worked itself free and simply added eight hours to its transit time. She fared better than USS *Dorado*, a submarine which is believed to have been sunk by friendly fire from the skies in the region.

One of the Cay Sal Banks' many cays, seen from space.

Eastern cays of Cay Sal Bank.

Elbow Cay, where the blimp USS *K-74* was shot down and Isadore Stessel died.

Final night, leaving Cay Sal for Key West, with a storm approaching.

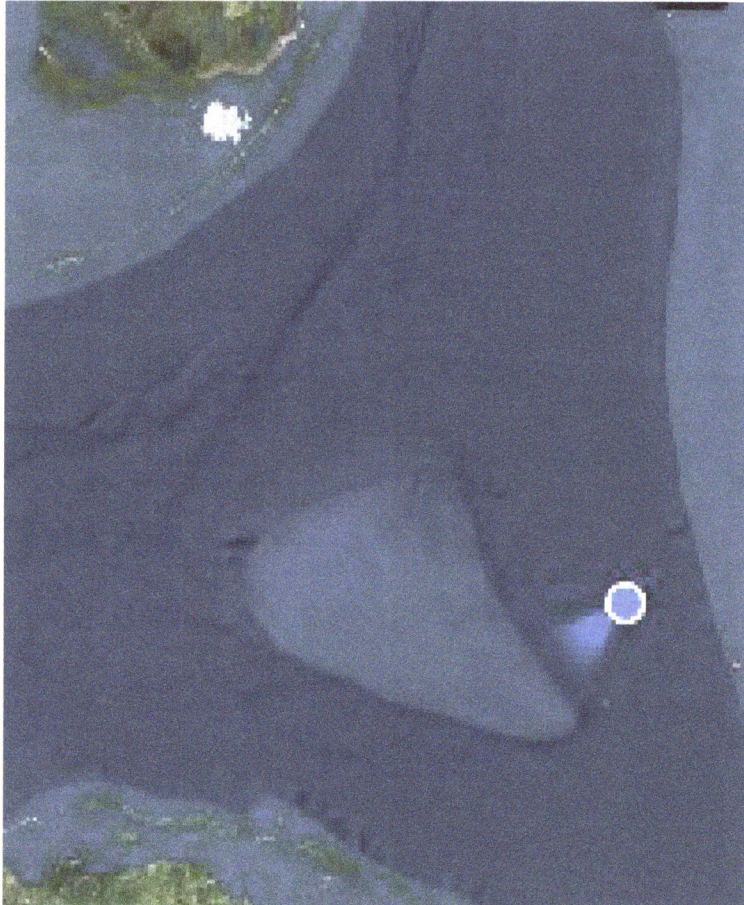

Our boat *Parole* is the blue dot, before we crossed the northern tip of Cay Sal Bank.

USS *K-74* being sunk by U-134 off Elbow Cay, Cay Sal Bank.

Chapter Twenty-One:
Personal Motivations & Impressions

Because this case took me from age 15 to 50 to solve, and I found two other planes before finding it and was dismissed for confusing types of craft, the B-26 Marauder off Marley Resort at Delaporte Bay was an integral search which galvanized the others. Plus, our mother's illness provided the opportunity and motive to never give up and perhaps show my tenacity to her and distract our anxious father with good news. Also, it took place at the doorstep of our family business.

Castle Island: This was the only case in which searching from space led to an actual aircraft in just minutes on the ground. It was the turning point from trench work (35 years) to *blitzkrieg* (5 minutes) to find a plane, using all available technologies. It proved that a precision and highly focused approach could work, though a later one-night flight to Exuma proved this approach could as likely fail.

The Hannah, or Portland Plantation, in the bush of Acklins between Salina Point and Pompey Bay, was unique as a land-crash. It featured parachuting, huge salinas so dense you can walk over them, and the ruins of plantations and livestock walls everywhere. Over 35 miles of hiking, the terrible labor exacted from the slaves haunted my guide and me. It was eerie, quiet, and disorienting, and viewing such a huge machine embedded in the earth was surreal.

The ghost-like vision of pilots emerging from bush with parachutes, the wedding dress aspect, the seaplanes landing to take them away, and bombers terrifying young children all made this an evocative, other-worldly experience, particularly as three of those who helped the most were reverend ministers: Forbes, Rolle, and Williamson.

Acklins shallow landing: This was the only case of intentionally destroying an aircraft from a US destroyer, which of course made it a lot more difficult to track down the deck logs of the vessels and crews who blew the plane up, but also the much smaller pieces which have yet to be found...

Royal Island water landing by seaplane: This was a case of wariness going into it, and following one's gut. The reason neither I, nor anyone else, ever found parts of this large aircraft turned out to be simple to understand: because it had been salvaged.

Ragged Island: Everyone told us that it could not be true; a large Catalina seaplane could not possibly still be sitting there just 20 yards from shore, sticking out of the water waving and waiting for us to find it in our shoes if we wanted. We were told that islanders would have stripped it long ago. They were wrong, the guides on the ground were right, the documents were accurate, and we found and left it as it was.

Tarpum Bay, Eleuthera: We knew fisherman would know about this wreck, and they do. We also knew conditions were tenuous, and they were poor the day we visited. So, it was a case whereby when you have an eyewitness pointing to the spot and telling you where it is, within a line of sight, you say: "Ok, solved!" and move on to the next site until conditions permit you to return, which they will.

Bannerman Town: This was a tricky one since "100 yards off Bannerman Town" was suspiciously too easy. Well, in a way it was since we didn't even know which of three coasts around Bannerman Town the plane lay in! A kindly woman welcomed us into her home where her elderly parents were pleasantly sitting. In a few minutes, they told me they had played on the plane, where we might find it, and who else could help us! Magnificent. This case also reminded me that if a Bahamian went door to door in other counties looking for crashed relatives, they might not have so warm and welcome a reception, and that I, in other locales, might be met with hostility. So, thank goodness, indeed, for the genuine trusting and helpful hospitality of the many hosts on many islands in many communities I was shown.

On Moore's Island, we knew the plane had to be nearby, yet we were anxious to approach the shallow island off the main shipping lanes. This is because we had just learned the hard way that "we are on a deep boat in shallow waters," by running aground. Now we tested a new approach. We sent our most senior officer, owner Captain Howard, to the community center to declare simply that "we are looking for the eldest person in this community." It worked! Mr. and Mrs. Jonathan Dean saved the day and showed us to the plane, which is precisely what we were looking for. Thank you.

Clifton and Lyford Cay: There were many reasons to want to solve this riddle; a greatly respected family friend and dive expert had already found what he described as a similar aircraft nearby. I grew up going to the school in Lyford Cay and had many happy—and also sad—memories of the bay. In fact, just a year before we scattered the ashes of my godson Henrik there, and my close friend Nicola and her sisters lost their Papa in the same bay. With so many casualties on the aircraft itself, we approached this wreck with great deference. And it turns out that Stuart was correct: he found the same plane but before censorship was lifted, so we both found the same plane at different times under different names! A tribute, indeed, to Henrik and Mr. Hepburn.

Exuma and *Pilot Radio*: This story is as much about trust, as it is hubris and tenacity. For years, folks who knew about this case watched me perform and find the World War II planes before they entrusted me to the *Pilot Radio* 1930 case. I was thrilled but also over-confident. During a flight from Bermuda to Boston (which was turned around due to a fuel leak) I felt I had found the wreck of the plane online, after I had uncovered the District Commissioner's reports in this case for a novel approach.

Well, the pride and hubris were burst after an expensive two-day jaunt to Exuma from Boston where I was jabbed in the eye by a pricker, got lost in the mud up to my waist, and found no metal at all. And I had severe rashes deep in the skin which lasted months and covered many square inches. But with team work, I was able to return and keep on looking. The team, and those who know more than anyone about this case, never gave up on me and while we are not going to solve it in 30 days as envisioned, it should be cracked by 2024, again with a large dollop of patience, cooperation, and doggedness.

Andros blimp rescue from mud: I like this story because of the derring-do and unscripted rescue. The American blimp pilot did "the necessary" to extricate his colleagues using a rope! As a longtime offshore captain with crews I often don't know, I am a firm believer in improvisation.

New Zealand man in Andros: I found the image of young Alistair Cleary haunting, not only because he looked young, brooding, rebellious, and a lot like me at his age, but since I sailed a boat, I met in Nassau to New Zealand and traveled there many months. Here are the details:

On Friday, May 21, 1943, RAF Coastal Command logged that during navigation exercise—"Mitchell II FR365/CD took off at 5:45 p.m., captained by Flight Officer J. E. Thomas, RAF, being the only one of five aircraft engaged on the five-hour exercise which failed to return. Last heard from at 7:51 p.m. about 120 miles northeast of Nassau. Searching aircraft and ships could find no trace of FR365 or its six crew."

Their B-25 plummeted into shallow waters, with the dinghy automatically deploying. It was found north of Morgan's Bluff. Then an oil slick was spotted, however, rescue boats and planes found no persons. HMS *P-190* and HMS *P-63* confirmed that the dingy bore the markings of FR365, and they were able to pull an

aircraft wheel and spar, or mast, onto their ASR boats for the return voyage to Nassau, about 30 miles east.

Young Alistair Grant Cleary of New Zealand, was a member of the RNZAF. His parents were Peter Morris Cameron and Frances Louisa Cleary of Christchurch, Canterbury. At age 21 he was killed five miles north of Morgan's Bluff, northeast Andros when his B-25 crashed on May 21, 1943. An oil slick was subsequently seen by the air-sea-rescue boats HMS *P-190* and HMS *P-63*. Sadly, seven of the crew were killed. Their remains were not recovered. Alistair was remembered fondly by his uncle as being mischievous, having a sly sense of humor, and being a good bloke to be around. Except for Cleary, the six others: Thomas William Vincent Atkins-Tallentire, Ernest William Durrant, M. E. G. Gedelian, Howard Watson Guinter, and Eric Douglas Todd were Canadian.

The day after the crew went missing, several training aircraft were still airborne on a parallel track search for aircraft FR-365 DC missing since the previous night on an exercise patrol carried out as detailed aircraft turned to starboard from its course to investigate a glint seen in the sea, with no results. A disturbance was observed on the water and upon investigation this proved to be a shark, landed back to base, having sighted nothing. B-25 FR384 CM airborne on an air-sea-rescue search, object sighted on port bow was a small motor vessel. Oil streaks seen gave no results upon investigation, patrol was completed, and aircraft landed back to base with nothing further to report. As for the others, the results returned included "area detailed covered by parallel track search, nothing sighted, landed back to base," and "having sighted nothing landed back to base."

Conclusion

Bomber on a budget.

That's what I chose to name my pyrrhic missions to find the metal and scraps of World War II aircraft in our country. While it may seem glamorous, the main ways I find things are still quite basic: research the hell out of the topic in every database and archive you can, get to the site and ask as many people as you can about what they know—often what they don't know is more informative and indicative that you are in the wrong place—and finally: get dirty, get wet, and get cut up. If you don't, you probably won't find the plane.

An important person in this process, as I began it middle-aged and recently divorced, having been away from home from ages 12 to 52, was our mother, Jane McDermid Wiberg, who passed after a long illness at Christmas in 2021. I went home to Cable Beach to see her for a week, which turned into a month. Unable to mope around at home, I fixated on the first World War II plane I found, and went out alone swimming after it in Delaporte Bay, sometimes at dawn, midday, and even dusk, up to five hours a day.

My tools? A $50 inflatable pool raft which I named *Clementine* due to its orange color, and as it was also Churchill's wife's name. I bought a dumbbell and tied a floating ski rope around it and used that basic equipment and a $60 children's mask, snorkel, and fins set I bought to find the B-26 Marauder. I never used a motor, but a kindly captain did tow me to shore once when I was sinking, trying to drag the cowling of a large engine half a mile to shore.

What is my point? It's simply that most of the 170 air wrecks from the war in The Bahamas took place either on land or in shallow enough water that the planes could be found by basic methods. Most errors and collisions took place taking off and landing at airfields, and pilots in distress were smart enough to head for land to improve their chances of survival. This means that most of the wrecks, even the ones going back to the 1930s, are accessible to people in The Bahamas, and that, for the most part, a sturdy pair of shoes, mask, snorkel, and grit and determination are enough to find them.

I was extremely fortunate in that nine persons loaned me vessels, whether 20' or 59', for between 20 minutes and over a month. The generosity and empathy of those kind souls, as well as the hundreds of volunteers in archives, in genealogical sites, on the ground, and in cities, ports and villages we visited, and just the friendly, helpful people online who helped me with so many details, all deserve my thanks.

If I were to inspire others to attempt feats like going from 'found no aircraft' to 'found 10 of them' in 14 months, I would say that it is up to each of us to become well-informed about our chosen interest, and then be able to communicate, to package and highlight what you've learned so as to effect, infect, inspire, and motivate others to assist—often not with direct investment, but rather with giving and lending their time and expertise. That is why I am so grateful to the editors of the *Nassau Tribune*, for ZNS presenter Spence Finlayson, to the RBDF who came out to help me, publishers, readers, and Howard, Amanda, John, Rich, Phicol and the many others who shared their resources.

I would encourage others to find something they are genuinely interested in and passionate about, try to focus on areas which have not already been combed over, be ready to pivot, as I did, away from U-boats and maritime to the RAF and aviation, since the latter offered many more accessible WWII wreckages.

Lastly, our mother inspired us to give something back; as a child I watched as she spoon-fed an elderly woman who had worked for us in her home behind Nassau. She has donated scholarships, for girls in particular, to buy tennis equipment and get a start in the sport she so loved. *Do it*, she would encourage us as we practiced tennis before school: *do it*. It goes back to Goethe, and really inside each of us:

"Whatever you dream you can do, BEGIN IT."

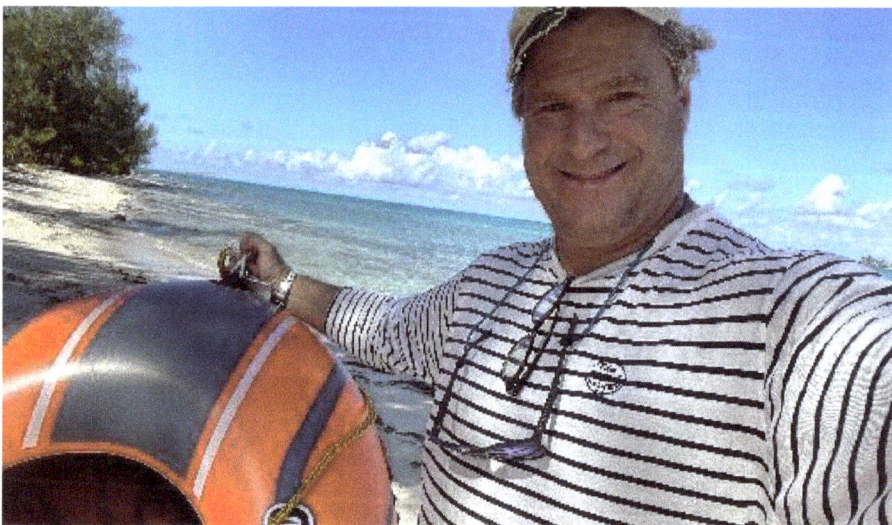

Before three power boats were loaned, it was just me and faithful *Clementine* combing Clifton Bay together, to no result.

Postscript

If, after around 80 or 100 years, details of what happened in The Bahamas are still being uncovered almost entirely *en masse*, then there is obviously a massive trove, and troves upon troves of military documentation, data, and physical remnants that have survived. Further, if a hundred or so (mostly novice) civilian volunteers can succeed—without pay—to find nearly a dozen of these aircraft in a short period of time (every six weeks or so) then it seems that an extraordinary opportunity exists for more discoveries, for more men and women missing in action to be found, and for more families in The Bahamas, Canada, New Zealand, the UK, Greece, Australia, South Africa and beyond to learn of their family members' fates.

Finding old aircraft in such a peaceful setting is one way to give back, by framing the history of The Bahamas and its impact on world events. Three percent of the entire global population perished as a result of World War II. The Bahamas were the headquarters of the Allies' trans-South Atlantic aircraft delivery system during that war. Now that it is known, and before the metals are reclaimed and reabsorbed into the planet by rust and hurricanes, let us find, document, and share this compelling history. The islands were not a forgotten drawer in the war; they were a crucial cog in the aviation supply chain. And in their web, 170 machines were caught, with many of them still findable today. In the words of Admiral Samuel Eliot Morison, PhD., who sailed The Bahamas extensively retracing Columbus' route:

"Dream dreams, then write them. Aye, but live them first!"

I did, and I encourage readers to as well.

New Aircraft Cases

New case one: USAAF B-24 Liberator *en route* to Italy crashes, 10 MIA/KIA.

Part I: Before we solved this mystery, I wrote:

On January 9, 1944, a USAAF B-24 Liberator was overdue and presumed missing over Bimini, *en route* from Florida to the Caribbean on the standard route. By January 10, a full-blown air-sea-rescue search by joint US and UK forces was under way. Word reached Nassau at 11:30 p.m. that night, and by 5:35 the next morning, British assets were being deployed southeast of New Providence in search of the B-24. Up until midnight on day one of the search, Liberator, BZ744 LL attempted to locate the sister aircraft without result. Then six aircraft were committed, and spread out two miles apart, and were airborne from about 11 a.m. to 5 p.m. without result. From Boca Raton, another B-24 and six Ventura's took off, all passing over the Berry Islands, followed by three Hudson-type aircraft and another Ventura. By 6 p.m. none of the fliers observed the aircraft or debris, and so they returned to Florida. Based on the evidence, it is thus likely that *Noel Roberts* found parts of USAAF 52349 off Berry Islands, in the Northwest Providence Channel. In this case, meticulous warplane cataloguer Doug Campbell turned up more details from a 'cold case file' of a bomber missing somewhere between Florida and Trinidad. Then an accident report specialist Mike Stowe, who has been solving aviation mysteries since he was a teenager, provided a detailed accident report. They were able to dig deep enough to positively match what the captain of the *Noel Roberts* found with dinghy with markings of the plane from 459th bomber command to 15 AF AAF #42-52349, C/N 1066. Key to patching all this information through was the US air transport command, or ATC 459BG 756BS.

This granular information was sent to Bob Livingstone in Queensland. His father flew B-24 Liberators in Nassau for the RAF in World War II. Bob also became a pilot and expert on B-24's; he has published books and articles, and was a consultant to the film and book *Unbroken*. He was able to deduce much from the very short length of flight time and distance covered. He explained that since the plane had some 2,500 gallons of fuel, it was not likely to have run out of fuel, but would also have been volatile if that large fuel capacity was ignited. Bob wrote that "likely causes were fire then engine failure, or without fire. Relatively green crew moving aircraft into combat ops in Italy. Early in flight, so not likely to have been fuel, and no weather events reported nearby, and plane was on course so not navigation error." The official reports include "Overdue ex-Morrison to Waller Field Trinidad no sign. USAAF plane saw smoke on N Coast of Mayaguana… Likely cause is fire and/or sudden catastrophic loss of one or both engines resulting in water crash."

Bob embellished with, "I ran January 9, 1944, against my listing and had one strike only and it fits the bill and I see the partial serial is in your report so there is no doubt that this is the correct aircraft. …It is rare (and lucky) to have both an accident report and a MACR; accidents usually do not create missing crew… The crew list is appended in two parts. To put this in perspective, this was when the 15th Air Force was just being populated in Italy and the 459th was a new bomb group raised in the US and transferring to Italy in January to February, 1944, so this is a green crew of the 459th ferrying the aircraft to 15AF to begin combat operations."

He continues: "ATC is Air Transport Command, which was responsible for these ferry operations; the aircraft and crew were assigned to ATC for this flight. They would have been re-assigned to the 459th after arrival in Italy. …. since wreckage identifiably from 42-52349 was found quite quickly, it must have been on track, so the loss was due to some sort of major mechanical failure. Multiple engine failure could be one reason, either mechanical or faulty, mismanagement of fuel transfer could be the other one. Fire is always suspect."

We remember those missing in action from this air crash:

1. Brooke, Edward B., Asst. Radio Operator, S/Sgt.
2. Goff, Roy E., Engineer, S/Sgt.
3. Hamilton, Robert B., Gunner, S/Sgt.
4. Lankford, Cyril I., Navigator, 2nd Lt.
5. Medos, Floyd J., Radio Operator, Cpl.
6. Martin, Paul D., Gunner, S/Sgt.
7. Mulroy, Maurice R., Bombardier, 2nd Lt.
8. Reed, Charles T., Gunner, S/Sgt.
9. Savage, Andrew M., Copilot, 2nd Lt.
10. Webb, Charles F., Pilot, 2nd Lt.

New case two: A large US Navy PBY force-landed at Walker's Cay, Abaco.

North of Grand Bahama and Abaco, the US Navy fortified tiny Walker's Cay as a seaplane base for rescue, escort, and anti-submarine activities. Doug Campbell has researched the fates of hundreds of thousands of aircraft. He helped parse these facts: on February 19, 1944, a PBM Mariner amphibious aircraft attached to VS-39 Scouting Squadron was reported by Advance Base, Walker's Cay, Bahamas, BWI. The operation diary states that from 11.50 am to 12:20 p.m. Squadron aircraft "searched for Navy BuNo 09491 forced down two miles west of base. Pilot and crew remained safe. Plane towed to base by crash boat." An event with a non-fatal ending.

New case three: Two B-25 Mitchells collided at Oakes Field on running away.

On Sunday, May 9, 1946, a B-25 Mitchell with RAF tail number KJ583 "was warming up on Oakes Field when it ran away during startup and collided with KJ670," another B-25 on the apron nearby. There were "no reports of injuries, however both aircraft were declared DBR, damaged beyond repair, and scrapped." At the time Oakes Field was being wound down, as the war had ended in Europe a year before and in Japan less than a year. Both aircraft were built in 1944. Many free market businesses and businessmen went to Nassau from Peru and other nations, and Sir Harold Christie invested in the purchase of several amphibian aircraft to promote real estate sales.

New case four: Ventura belly-landed in Abaco, sighted next month.

On August 12, 1943 B-25 FR375CL reported seeing the turret, tail, and engines of a Lockheed PV-1 Ventura along and in a shallow lake. Since it the carrier of this news landed at Windsor Field, it was assumed that the wreckage they saw was on approach, and thus in either Lake Killarney or Lake Cunningham, near Windsor on New Providence. But with the help of Paul Squires, an expert on PV-1s, it was recognized that the sighting had taken place 30 minutes and 100 miles away at Abaco. Thus, it was actually the PV-1 wrecked in Great Abaco under USMC Major Boyd Whitney. And since all the men on that plane walked away from it, we had details, but with such a massive area as the Marls west of Great Abaco, it took this new report by the B-25 to narrow down the search area. That allowed us to focus better on what happened and interview rangers and bonefishing guides in the Abaco area.

New Photos

This section illustrates that even after 80 years, history is not static; photos, stories, and diaries are still being found in attics and shared by volunteers online.

Stephen Smollett of Nassau's mother Dorothy E. Parks Smollett kept a wonderful photo album of wartime Nassau including men and women from several services and countries. Her husband was serving in the RAF Stephen generously shared these.

Taken by Dorothy Parks Smollett of Eleuthera and Nassau who married a British serviceman, this shows military personnel of all ranks and roles being welcomed into the United Services Canteen. The club owed its existence in part to an insistence by the Duchess of Windsor, against those of the IODE who preferred abstemiousness, that the club offer alcohol, dancing and various social entertainment beyond board games and tea. For both persons in uniform and those who helped run the busy club, this became the center of social life on New Providence and many dances were held there. Given all the dangers and accidents, it not surprising that clubs, hotels, and bars were busy during the war and a quarter of the capital's population were in the military and in transit to the front. Courtesy of Stephen Smollett, from his mother Dorothy Parks Smollett.

The United Services Canteen occupied the Bahamian Club on West Bay Street, in what is now the Dockendale corporate complex, just east of Xavier's Lower School. As Capt. Aranha clarified, a similar looking ruin near Fish Fry and Arawak Cay was the home of H. N. Chipman. near what is now the Arawak Fish Fry. Courtesy of Stephen Smollett, from his mother Dorothy Parks Smollett.

Parade, the Nassau Cathedral at left, Government House top left, and what is now the Pirate's Museum to right, with British Colonial Hotel off to right out of sight.

BAHAMIANS SERVE IN AMERICAN FORCES: Sgt. Bertram Aspinall, left, in the American Army Air Corps Troop carrier group. Staff Sergeant Alexander Maillis is a qualified Paratrooper in the United States Army

CANTEENS
Provide
Refreshment and
Fun for
Service Men

—Photographs by Stanley Toogood

The Popular Bahamian Club of prewar days has been transformed into a United Services Canteen. The Duchess of Windsor takes a personal interest in running it and is often to be found there. At the right is the games room

Private Barbara Duncombe, A. T. S. of Nassau, marries Corporal Joseph Ings, "somewhere in England"

F/O Reginald Ponting, R. A. F., of London, was married in October to Miss Cynthia Johnson of Nassau

Busy afternoons are spent in the U.S. Canteen's kitchen and dining room. On duty are Mrs. D. S. Graham (left), in charge of the former, Miss Leonard and Mrs. E. D. Sears, waitresses being Mrs. Lewis Phillips, Miss Daphne Sears, Miss Iva Parks and Miss Dorothy Parks. On the buffet at right are cakes, sandwiches, bananas and oranges. Bacon, eggs and other favourites of service men are much in demand

Miss Wendy Moore, elder daughter of Mr. and Mrs. Bruce Moore, left Nassau for England recently and has been accepted in the A.T.S. Her fiancé is P/O John

Two members of the R.C.A.F. in Nassau P/O Cleland Lamb of Lethbridge, Alberta and P/O Joseph Webb of Victoria, B.

Mr. and Mrs. John Bothell, the former Miss Hilda Van Zeylan, are among the newlyweds

Possibly in the gardens of the Royal Victoria Hotel where many RAFTC pilots stayed.

Bahamian F/Lt. Lester Brown is in middle left of this image and other recognizable Bahamian names.

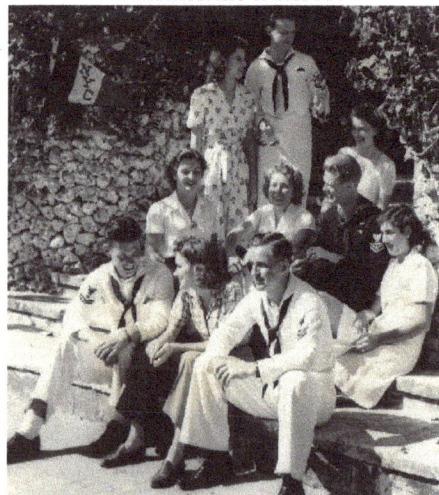

In 2021 Ted and Jen posted on Flickr these images of their relative John William James Spiller, RAF, in the Bahamas as well in other images, in many theaters, including Europe. They did an exceptional job of preserving his memory with images, medals, log books, and more. The beach in this scene is Old Fort Bay, just a mile or two west of Windsor Field, where we played as children and relatives kept a home and my brother worked, and a French film was made post-war. I felt that his relatives' candor about "Spiller (thin leg)" was endearing, and seeing he and his mates gamboling around and rowing in the rushes made him very human to me. When in June 2023 while in final edits I saw him name among those missing, presumed lost, it was genuinely saddening, though of course I did not know him or his family. John Spiller was lost on Tuesday, April 25, 1944, when his B-24 Liberator BZ759LP was reported overdue while training north of Eleuthera, "missing in ocean, no traces." There were nine men on board that aircraft. A volunteer reserve in the RAF, Spiller was aged 20 when he died, leaving his parents Francis Gilbert and Edith May Spiller of South Brent, Devon bereft. Here is the aircraft (LP) in which these many men perished; together with the aircraft they are in the Bahamas still.

Ted and Jen, for John Spiller, Flickr.com, 2021.

111 OPERATIONAL TRAINING UNIT NASSAU 1943/44.
Training of airmen for conversion to Consolidated Liberator aircraft.

Spiller (thin leg)

John Spiller and his friends weren't the only ones to enjoy Old Fort Bay – here the evacuee students from Belmont School in Nassau, trapped by a German U-boat blockade for the duration of the war, piled into the headmaster's automobile for a spot of archery in the sand there... Thanks to David Sanctuary Howard's memoir *The Unforgiving Minute.*

Here aircraftman George Pythian records a day-to-day aspect of RAF life rarely depicted; yet, if the maintenance is not properly carried out, the chance of mechanical mishap rises significantly.

This image of planes being worked on at Windsor Field by George Pythian is similar to other images taken by a different photographer months apart… It also reminds the reader, from the men's proximity to the propellers, that at least three fatal accidents occurred in Nassau due to propeller strikes on the ground.

Liberators with tail numbers NA and LB are clearly marked in this photo.

We have two B-25 Mitchells in one photo, possibly a third far left, a tractor for moving heavy items, a pool in which men were dunked, a US Navy blimp, and at least a dozen servicemen!

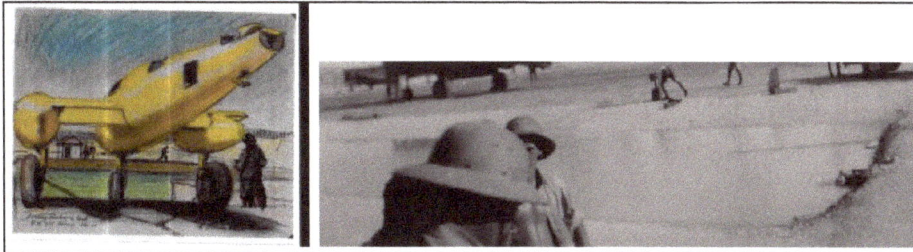

Each image is so rich with detail; here we see the pool that aviators were dunked into per the yellow fuselage painted by Australian artist R. Malcolm Warner visited the Bahamas to paint. Caption: "This painting is one of few records of Empire Air Training Scheme training in The Bahamas. It depicts 'ditching training,' practicing how to exit a plane after an emergency landing in water. A stripped American B-25 Mitchell fuselage sits before a pool of water into which the fuselage would be pushed. R. Malcolm Warner, *Ditching Practice in Tank, Nassau, December 1944, pastel and ink on paper, ART24149.*"

Australian Imperial War Memorial image showing B-24 Liberator either FL964 LD or possibly BZ946 LD at the hangar in Windsor Field. FL964 LD flew to and from Texas, Miami, Bermuda and on numerous anti-submarine, navigation, and training missions in Bahamas July 1943 to August 1945. Though it arrived in Bermuda short on fuel, it didn't crash during that time.

Thatching the roof of a Bahamian home with tight-stitched straw, as chronicled by George Pythian.

Nassau Court looking across Marlborough Street (now West Bay Street) at the base of East Hill Street, towards the British Colonial Hotel, recently purchased by gold magnate Sir Harry Oakes. The man appears to be having his shoes shined. Photo by George Phythian, broadcaster. This is the hotel's southern entrance which now boasts a large statue of Sir Woodes Rogers (1639-1732)

One of the larger hotels on New Providence, possibly the swimming area of the Emerald Beach Hotel at Cable Beach, West Bay Street, New Providence, by George Phythian, RAFVR. Note the goats or sheep in the driveway and the silk cotton tree right of center.

This image of allied servicemen on a labor detail was taken by George Phythian.

Another image of a work party by Phythian, this one with puppy and pith helmets.

A B-24 Liberator with tail number LT at the tarmac—the plane behind seems to have a number "N" visible.

Government House, base of the Windsors for much of the war, though they left before V-E Day.

School children receiving outdoor lessons in Nassau, by George Phythian, ZNS.

Parading and drill practice as seen through barbed wire on New Providence, George Phythian.

Marching in Nassau, by George Phythian.

An RAF burial of several airmen concurrently at the time when the cemetery was only recently completed. Note the freshly built wall, wooden crosses, and absence of any buildings nearby. Both the RAF Hospital and cemetery were purposefully located between Windsor and Oakes airfields to make access more equitable to both. From Aircrew Remembered.

The Duke of Windsor on parade inspecting troops; these photos from Roy Evans.

Soldiers with sponge smack sirens along what is now Woodes Rogers' Walk in Nassau. Fitting to capture the enjoyment of life when death was dealt so quickly in the air over The Bahamas at the time.

Jim Lawlor of the Bahamas Historical Society shared this image of RAF officers in The Bahamas in Living Memory, *The Bahamas Weekly*, November 14, 2010. Chris Hoyle's father Arnold Hoyle served with the RAF in the Bahamas and he very generously shared these images with us:

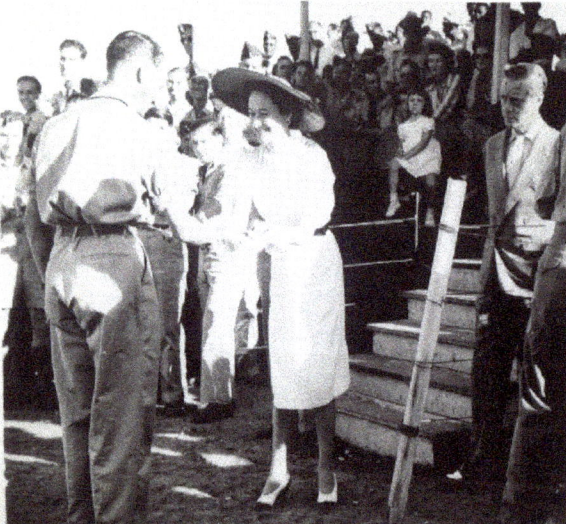

Arnold Hoyle. These images courtesy of Christopher and Arnold Hoyle.

As this book went to press, Lucinda (Lucy) Jay in Dartmouth, South Devon, England kindly reached out to me, and the Bahamas Historical Society, saying that her relative, who she knew as Uncle Roy, had some photos from World War II in the Bahamas, which she and his family were happy to share. Of course, Jim Lawlor, Paul Aranha and myself enthusiastically offered to help facilitate her finding and sending over a dozen high-quality images belonging to her uncle, Flight Lieutenant Roy Vincent Evans (1920-2003) who was based with the RAF in the Bahamas during the war.

Lucy, now living in the UK, forwarded these images and shared the back story. Essentially her grandmother's niece, born "in the early 1940's, was named Joyce Fitchett, a beautiful young woman who decided to move out to the Bahamas, and there Joyce married a man called Peter Tivy (sadly no longer with us). They lived in the Bahamas from late 1950's onwards and had three children (my second cousins): George, James and Sarah. Joyce Tivy is therefore the cousin of my mother, and also the cousin of F.L. Roy Vincent Evans."

Lucy continues, by relaying that "Joyce Tivy and her husband, Peter, were apparently friends with the Wibergs throughout the 1960s, whilst all living in the Bahamas, before Joyce and family moved to Florida, where Joyce still lives. Eric found Joyce, first via his parents, then via a 'Vintage Bahamas' website, but Joyce didn't have any pics of her cousin, Roy. However, her eldest son, George, had just flown over to England and he and I had spent the day together, having not seen each other since I was 7 and he was 11, nearly 50 years ago. Joyce emailed me, knowing that Roy Evans' widow, Elizabeth, was still alive (age 91) and living in South Devon, England, just ten miles away from where I live in Dartmouth. Joyce thought I might be able to find some photos if I went round to my aunt's for a cup of tea and scrummaged in her wardrobe, which is exactly what I did. So that's the story of how it all happened. What a wonderful world!"

"The best part about this for me, is that I knew Uncle Roy very well, since he was brought up with my grandma, and they were best friends, and shared a common love of gardening, greenhouses and geraniums. Roy was at all of the Devon family gatherings, as far back as I can remember, but since he'd never spoken to me about the war, I had no idea he'd trained in the Bahamas, or that the Bahamas had anything to do with WW2 ... in fact, I had no idea about any part of his five years in the RAF. When I got the email from my mum's cousin, Joyce, introducing a man called Eric, who believed Roy had served in the RAF in the Bahamas, I honestly thought they'd both gone mad, and that I was being sent on a fool's errand into the wardrobe in search of photographs that obviously did not exist. Imagine my total shock upon discovering pictures of Roy in shorts, in the sunshine, in a military line-up, being inspected by an exiled King Edward! I was utterly flabbergasted, and am left thinking, we should all look in the wardrobe more often. Who knows what else we'd find?"

Christ Church Cathedral is the backdrop for this RAF parade image. Roy Evans.

RAF Flight Lieutenant Roy Vincent Evans (1920-2003), from Lucinda (Lucy) Jay.

An RAF parade down Bay Street, downtown Nassau, with signs read "S. H. Thomas, Shoe Store," at left on black, and "The Albury Drug Store" upper left. Roy Evans.

These images of HRH the Duke of Windsor inspecting RAF troops in Nassau during World War II are shared by Flight Lieutenant Roy Vincent Evans and Lucy Jay.

These two group photos have Flight Lieutenant Roy Vincent Evans (left at bottom, second from left, middle row at top). It is not possible to confirm a location. Lucy Jay.

The poem which most encapsulates the polyglot airmen who died in Bahamas for me, and which inspired me to complete this book, and which I sang, often loudly, from the bow of Parole as we sailed towards yet more crash sites, is *An Irish Airman foresees his Death*. In it, poet William Butler Yeats (1865-1939), questions the conundrum faced by young men from far corners of the world brought to the Atlantic to fight for Britain.

I know that I shall meet my fate
Somewhere among the clouds above;
Those that I fight I do not hate,
Those that I guard I do not love;

My country is Kiltartan Cross,
My countrymen Kiltartan's poor,
No likely end could bring them loss
Or leave them happier than before.

Nor law, nor duty bade me fight,
Nor public men, nor cheering crowds,
A lonely impulse of delight
Drove to this tumult in the clouds;

I balanced all, brought all to mind,
The years to come seemed waste of breath,
A waste of breath the years behind
In balance with this life, this death.

from *The Wild Swans at Coole*, The Macmillan Company, NY, 1919, poetryfoundation.org

For those who died in The Bahamas during World War II.

Plane Types Lost in The Bahamas

Martin 187 Baltimore

Vought OS2U Kingfisher

Douglas A-20 Havoc

Boeing B-17 Flying Fortress

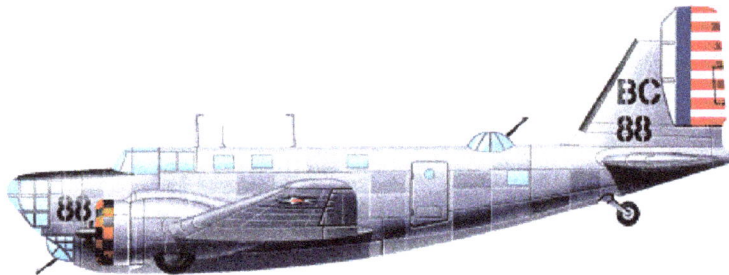
Douglas B-18 Bolo

Consolidated B-24 (Liberator in RAF)

North American B-25 (Mitchell in RAF)

Martin B-26 (Marauder in RAF)

Boeing B-29 Super Fortress

Curtiss C-46 Commando

Curtiss SB2C Helldiver

Douglas C-47 Skytrain (Dakota in RAF)

Douglas SBD Dauntless

Grumman F6F Hellcat

196

US Navy Blimp; airship USS *K-74*

Grumman F4F (or FM2) Wildcat

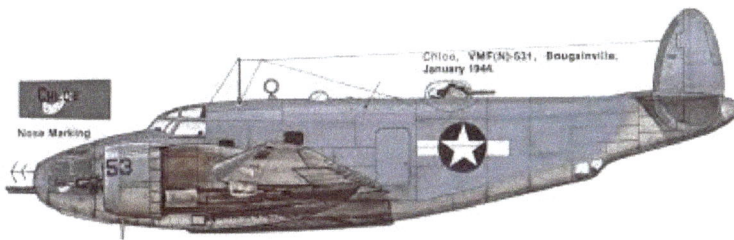
Lockheed PV-1 Ventura

Lockheed Hudson IIIA

Grumman G-21 Goose (JRF in RAF)

de Havilland DH.98 Mosquito

Martin PBM Mariner

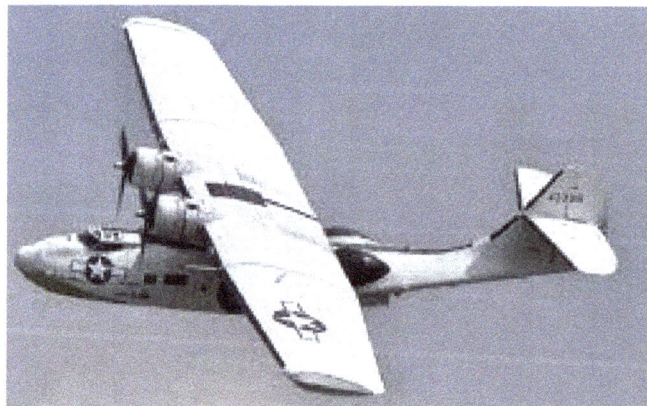
Consolidated PBY (Catalina in RAF)

Appendices

Appendix 1: Master List of War Crashes in The Bahamas

DATE	ISLAND	STATUS	FIND	PLANE TYPE	BRANCH	TAIL/SN	KIA	LIVED	KIA, NAMES	SURVIVORS NAMES	SHORT SUMMARY
12/6/1944	Ragged Island	Salvaged	N	OS2U	USN	Kingfisher	0	2			2 OS2U amphibious boats ran out of gas, Army JRF, 2 US Army rescue boats were sent from Exuma NOB to refuel them, 1 found Ragged I, other at sea
12/6/1944	Exuma Water	Salvaged	N	OS2U	USN	Kingfisher	0	2			2 OS2U amphibious boats ran out of gas, Army JRF, 2 US Army rescue boats were sent from Exuma NOB to refuel them, 1 found Ragged I, other at sea
1/19/1943	NP Oakes	Insuff. Info.	U	A-20	USAAF		5	0			Havoc A-20 Douglas crashed into sea off NP fm Oakes Field
5/19/1943	Inagua	Deep, can interview Inaguans	N	A-20	USAAF	MSN5796, 41-3466	0	3		Clark, R. L., Bunch, John H., Murray	Havoc left Homestead AFB, FL for Borinquen 7:30 AM 19th, not heard of till 17 days later June 9th. 3 men drifted in raft to Little Inagua, no food, rescued by fishermen, Great Inagua, US boat, Little Inagua 17 Days, no food, taken to Great Inagua, Cuba, US

Date	Location	Status	Y	Type	Operator	Serial			Names		Notes
2/22/1943	Acklins, Castle I.	Found	Y	A-20B	USAAF	BuNo 5261, 41-2931	0	3		Libby, D. A., White, Murray, Veronko, J. S.	Forced Landing Due to Engine Failure, allocated to USSR Air Force. Libby suggested White eject as navigators on water landings often went through the nose. He refused, when they landed on saline lake he ejected and oleo injured his right leg. Other planes vectored a rescue PC, went to Guantanamo. Discovered by ETW & Ken Williams 8.5.22 pickled in lake
3/18/1943	NP Windsor	Airfield, burnt out	Y	A-30	RAF	FA354, 27936	1	1	Hollowell, Donald Terence	Atwell, A. F.	Baltimore IIIa, took off from Oakes, RAFTC to Trinidad, stalled on overshoot and crashed, burned 1 m from Windsor, all 2 KIA
3/25/1943	NP Airfield	Airfield, burnt out	Y	A-30	RAF	FA340, 27922	1	0	Glen, Ian Simpson		Crashed making circuits solo. In attempting to land aircraft took a hard bounce. The abrupt impact caused pilot to be thrown out onto the ground, and killed, aircraft caught fire
3/27/1943	NP Oakes	Airfield, burnt out	Y	A-30	RAFTC, 4 Ferry	41-27796	0	4		Twiston-Davies, M. P.	Accident on "Farm" Field, Oakes Twiston Davies had his passport catch fire in a crash per diary
3/28/1943	NP Windsor	Airfield, burnt out	Y	A-30	RAF	FA427	2	1	Walmsley, Elwood Palmes, Morris, William Frederick	Taylor	Accident on "Farm" Field, Oakes Twiston Davies had his passport catch fire in a crash per diary

Date	Location	Disposition	Burnt	Type	Service	Serial	Deaths	Injured	Crew	Notes
4/13/1943	NP Windsor	Salvaged	N	A-30	RAF	FA317, 27899	0	3	Houldin, A. J., Downey, S. R., Anderson, M.	Test landing overshot runway, all 3 men survived, test observer Anderson injured right foot, airframe damaged beyond repair, engines were salvaged
4/17/1943	NP Windsor	Airfield, burnt out	Y	A-30	RAF	FA121	0	1	Pienazek	Not yet attained flying speed when the failure occurred, he could not maintain height necessary to loop back to the airfield aircraft completely burnt out, Pienazek escaped
4/29/1943	NP Windsor	Airfield, burnt out	Y	A-30	RAF	FH365	3	0	Harris, Albert, Anderson, Robert Venable, Thomson, George Somerville	Hudson crashed taking off, 1-5 m from Windsor, aircraft veered to port, slightly at first, port wing dropped down and struck earth, at which point aircraft crashed aflame
5/6/1943	NP Airfield	Salvaged	N	A-30	RAF	FA130	0	1	Russell, J. C.	On landing caught wing, tire blew, ground looped off edge of runway, extensive damage, pilot uninjured
5/8/1943	NP Windsor	Salvaged	N	A-30	RAF	FK400	0	3	Hutchison, Tutt, Bisson	Belly-landed uninjured; propellers bent back
5/24/1943	NP Windsor	Salvaged	N	A-30	RAF	FA124	0	0	Lee, E. W.	Lost port tire and aircraft veered into trees on its belly, solo occupant Lee uninjured.

Date	Location	Disposition		Type	Service	Serial			Crew	Crew	Notes
5/27/1943	NP Windsor	Airfield, burnt out	Y	A-30	RAF	FA448, 28030	0	1		Parson, Gedye, Hunt	Aircraft was damaged at the fuel tanks on its belly forward and a long cable ran along the port side the length of the craft. Fabric over the tank was ripped. To prevent the hanging and loose belly tanks from striking ground and exploding the wheels were lowered and Parsons "made a low approach and perfect touch-down, and ran down the runway with the starboard undercarriage wobbling." Then the undercarriage folded up and the plane's belly sank, struck the ground and caught fire
5/30/1943	NP Airfield	Airfield	Y	A-30	RAF	FA227, 27809	3	0	Chouteau, Henri, Lyons, Joseph Paul, Somerville, Cyril J.		Airfield crash, engine cut taking off, test flight
6/7/1943	NP Airfield	Salvaged	N	A-30	RAF	FA481	0	2		Coe, E. W., Thorburn, R. W.	Belly-landed successfully on runway since starboard undercarriage would not lock. Very little damage to aircraft.

Date	Location	Recovery	Y/N	Type	Service	Serial			Crew (fatalities)	Crew (survivors)	Notes
7/13/1943	NP Windsor	Findable by boat	Y	A-30	RAF	FR383DX	6	0	Daschuk, Billy, James, Wilcox Thomas, Johnson, Wilfred, Koepke, John Barth, Meehan, Robert Paul, McArthur, James		Windsor, 5 nm, ATC saw smoke, ASR Lyford found 1 nm oil slick, Wireless comms ceased at 15:45, aircraft failed to return, aircraft located an oil patch and wreckage in the sea 5 nm south west of Clifton Point, no survivors found, surface vessel recovered small pieces of wreckage
7/3/1943	NP Airfield	Salvaged	N	A-30	RAF	FA177	0	2		Alderton, R, Bake, C. E.	Tail wheel off runway, ripped off, damaged tail when tail wheel caught the lip of the tarmac on taxiing following a fuel consumption test flight
7/19/1943	NP Windsor	Salvaged	N	A-30	RAF	FA134, 41-27716	0	0			Damaged in takeoff
8/25/1943	NP Airfield	Salvaged	N	A-30	RAF	FW359	0	3		Learmont, G., Cunliffe, T. J. J., Atkin, J. W.	Port engine faltered, plane ran off runway, bomb bay damaged

Date	Location	Findability		Type	Service	Serial			Name	Description
9/20/1943	Andros North	Findable, difficult terrain, marsh far from roads	Y	A-30	USAAF	FW409, 43-8566, New Castle, DE	0	2	Carr, Bruno A.	Landed upside down, radioman rescued pilot from fumes. Sighted on beach NW of Andros by a USN blimp, didn't stop, rescued the 2 men, landed them at Oakes Field. Crash "landed on beach on NW point of Andros." RAFTC and Montague ASR boats HMS P-339 sent. Pilots used dinghy to attract attention, water very shallow, on high tide an Airship from USN picked the 2 survivors up landed them at Windsor, hospitalized, ASR back to NP. USN airship, K-65 went before dawn on "a special mission to search for an A-30 After valving helium and making several runs to affect a landing on the beach, I shouted to the survivors to grab the short lines and slow down the [air] ship. This they did, and after the ship hit water, it slowed considerably, but [still] did not stop. I instructed the two men to come to rear door and within thirty seconds both were aboard. One was pulled in by a line which was thrown to him and which he tied around his chest. The other was pulled in by the airship rigger, who laid face down in the car, with his body hanging out the door from the waist." Crashed before delivery to RAF, to 27th FRS, 2nd FRG and damaged in landing accident

											at Andros. Morrison Field, overdue to Nassau ran out of fuel *en route* Exuma
3/9/1944	NP Windsor	Salvaged	N	A-30	USAAF	FW739, 43-8896	0	1		Froude, James W.	From New Castle AAF, DE, crashed/ditched at NP, NTU, to 63rd FRS, 2nd FRG and w/o in landing accident at Windsor, SOC Jun 27, 1946
12/27/1943	NP Airfield	Salvaged	N	A-30 MKV	RAF	FW603	0	1		Jackson, J.	Undercarriage collapsed running up engines on apron, solo occupant escaped
3/2/1944	NP Water	Insuff. Info.	U	A-30A	USAAF	FW733, 43-8890	0	1		Allen, Robert E.	New Castle AAF, DE, to ditching off NP, crashed before delivery, 12 FRS, 2nd FRG ditched in Atlantic
1/15/1943	Bahamas Water TBD	Insuff. Info.	U	B-17	USAAF		0	0			Missing *en route* to Borinquen (Fold3)
2/3/1944	Bahamas Water TBD	Insuff. Info.	U	B-18	USAAF		0	0			Missing 150 nm E of Jax., *en route* Cuba-Miami

Date	Location	Findable	Y/N	Type	Service	Serial			Crew	Notes
9/4/1942	Acklins, Castle I.	Findable by boat, have PC & Borrie deck logs	Y	B-18A	USAAF	37-539	0	7	Ginther, Richard F., Hammer, Arthur J., Smith, John W., Perkins, Charles V., Oakes, George W., Boener, John F., Soar, John S.	Forced landing, 1 nm S of Acklins, halfway to Castle Isl. 7 men rowed met by constable and son. USS Borie DD-215 bombed wreck next day with a PC from USS Talbot, have deck logs both ships
8/15/1943	NP Airborne	Salvaged	N	B-24	RAF	BZ761	0	2	Meers, C. J., Staples, P. A.	While instructing firing, the aircraft hit turbulence, causing an uncontrolled firing, 2 X .5 cal. Bullets in starboard wing, fired by instructor
9/4/1943	NP Airfield	Salvaged	N	B-24	RAF	BZ806	0	3	Johansen, E. U.	Despite checks the undercarriage failed, nose wheel collapsed on landing, causing damage
10/29/1943	NP Water South	Findable by boat	Y	B-24	USN	BuNo 7628	0	0		B-24 went missing Morrison to Borinquen, on Nov. 2, thought a life raft signal seen, was not confirmed left 5:30 AM, wrecked, found a tobacco pouch, wreckage, shattered piece 72 miles bearing 164 degrees True from Windsor. 4 explosions were heard Nov. 2, NE of Green Cay

Date	Location	Condition	Status	Type	Service	Notes	#	#			Description
11/15/1943	Andros South, Mangrove Cay	Findable by boat or swim, difficult, broken up	Y	B-24	RAF		0	0			May be 29 Oct 43 wreck, explosions off Green Cay: 3 days later, Nov. 18, parts washed up in "scattered bits along the coast," "salvaged by natives from Pleasant Bay to Little Creek, Andros a distance of 25-30 miles. No survivors were found. Wreckage found in Andros Mangrove Cay southeast coast.
11/16/1943	Grand Bahama Water	Insuff. Info., deep	U	B-24	USAAF		8	0			B-24 going Charleston SC to North Point near Walker's Cay, Grand Bahamas was overdue, 8 men onboard.
1/9/1944	Andros TBD	Insuff. Info.	U	B-24	RAF	BZ TBN	0	0			B-24 BZ missing over Andros from Florida to Caribbean. Plane left Boca Raton FL for Windsor, overdue, searches sent from SE of NP to N of Andros. No sign. Flying searches turned up nothing, possible this is the aircraft went off course, landed Florida.

Date	Location	Disposition		Aircraft	Service	Identifier			Crew	Survivors	Notes
1/9/1944	Berry I. Stirrup Cay	too deep, disintegrated on impact	N	B-24	USAAF, 459th to 15AF	AAF 42-52349, C/N 1066, ATC 459BG 756BS	10	0	Brooke, Edward B., Goff, Roy E., Hamilton, Robert B., Lankford, Cyril I., Medos, Floyd J., Martin, Paul D., Mulroy, Maurice R., Reed, Charles T., Savage, Andrew M., Webb, Charles F.		Likely causes were fire then engine failure, or without fire. Relatively green crew moving aircraft into combat ops in Italy. Early in flight so not likely to have been fuel, and no weather events reported nearby, and plane was on course so not navigation error. Overdue ex-Morrison to Waller Field, Trinidad, no sign. USAAF plane saw smoke on N Coast of Mayagauna, C/N 1066, MACR#1484, ATC 459BG 756BS *en route* to Italy. B-24 life raft from NOEL ROBERTS mailboat then 2 rafts, by a B-26 confirm crash site of the USAAF 52349 sunk off Berry I in NW Providence Channel, debris in area. 459th ferrying the aircraft to 15AF. Likely cause is fire and/or sudden catastrophic loss of one or both engines resulting in water crash.
2/2/1944	NP Airfield	Salvaged	N	B-24	RAF	BZ718	0	3		Ross, McKercher, Fisher	Following B-24 down runway, lost brakes, veered off runway, lost nose wheel, pump not activated, damaged beyond repair

4/25/1944	4/6/1945	4/10/1945
Eleuthera Water North	NP Windsor	NP Airfield
Deep, insuff. Info.	Findable, Insuff. Info.	Salvaged
N	Y	N
B-24	B-24	B-24
RAF	RAF	RAF
BZ759	BZ722	LF968
9	0	0
0	0	1
Aitken, Philip Raymond, Cameron, Kenneth John, Fussell, Denis William, Pearce, Frederick Archibald, Powell, Kenneth, Seaforth, Stanley Henry, Smith, William Francis, Spiller, John William James, Thomas, Peter Henry		
		Creed
Liberator missing in ocean N of Eleuthera, no traces	Crashed on approach to Windsor Field	Nose wheel wouldn't extend/jammed on landing, damage to front of plane

Date	Location	Status	Findable	Aircraft	Service	Serial			Crew	Pilot	Notes
5/22/1945	NP Windsor	Salvaged	N	B-24	RAF	KK366 NM, 45 Group	0	0			During landing Windsor tire burst, undercarriage collapsed
6/2/1945	NP Water	Findable by boat	Y	B-24	RAF	BZ811MB	8	0	Allbut, George Robert, Brookes, John West, Burns, James Williamson, Franks, Robert Henry, MacDonald, John Blair, Neilson, John, Parker, Kenneth Gordon, Swinbanks, Joseph Hancock		Crashed into deep sea c. 8 nm E of NP c.3.5 nm N of Cabbage Beach, or Paradise I., located wreckage and guided ASR launches HMS P-89 and HMS P-181 to the scene; they found a dinghy matched to BZ811 MB, tried towing a portion of the fuselage 3m to shore yet were unable, so prior giving up, ASR officers requested US Navy vessel destroy remainder of the fuselage to avoid a hazard to navigation. No bodies recovered.
7/4/1945	Andros, N Morgans Bluff	Findable by boat	Y	B-24	RAF	BZ813 MD	9	0	Thompson		Water crash off Morgan's Bluff, N Andros, ASR HMS *P-191* found dinghy, tail, crash site was in shallow water, HMS P-191 found deflated dinghy, markings of MD, portions of fuselage, tail, in water.

Date	Location	Disposition		Aircraft	Service	Serial			Names	Crew	Narrative
10/13/1943	NP Airfield	Salvaged	N	B-24J	USAAF	42-73066	0	1		Hoff, Burton M.	From Memphis MAP, TN, to forced landing NP. Left US on 7.10.43. 4th Ferry Group 93 Ferry Squadron, diverted to NP urgent landing. Records say it crashed on takeoff from Windsor, no MACR. Appears aircraft was repaired and flew further east with no casualties.
2/26/1943	NP Delaporte	Findable on land	Y	B-25	RAF	FK176AX, 2331	3	4	Bullard, Louise, Bullard, Charles, Bullard, baby girl	Uncle	At about 3:45 AM, 3 RAF aviators on night training bailed out of their stricken B-25 bomber and parachuted to safety, yet the plane continued ashore and hit the home of young newlyweds, their 1 y/o daughter, all KIA, but uncle escaped.
3/19/1943	NP Airfield	Airfield, burnt out	Y	B-25	RAF	FL697, 12759	2	0	Daiken, Alex John, Zdan, Benjamin Henry		Airfield Crash, No.113 Transport Wing, an engine caught fire immediately on takeoff, and the plane slipped into the scrub, or low brush, and burned out in the area of Soldier Road, between Oakes Field and Windsor Field. Although an ambulance reached them and both men made it to hospital, they died there.

Date	Location	Findability	Status	Aircraft	Service	Tail #			Crew		Remarks
4/9/1943	NP Clifton	Findable by boat	Y	B-25	RAF	FR379DA	7	0	Schafer, Gordon Wellsley, Waton, Alvin Bernard, Goodman, Benny Baldwin, Farnsworth, Ronald, Fenton, George, Tompkins, George William, Burchell, Robert Lloyd		Ditched at sea, crashed SW of NP, Clifton Bay, Yellow Orange light found by Lyford ASR, 7 KIA, 15 nm SW of NP Windsor aircraft on exercise sighted empty dinghy—area searched with no further result. Dinghy retrieved by surface craft, empty, damaged. 12 days later ASR boat found an aircraft dinghy prob. belonging to B-25 FR379DA, possibly to a "FU" tail # but at nearly identical location, 25N,77.50W
5/9/1943	Bahamas Water TBD	Insuff. Info.	U	B-25	RAF	FR378CL	0	0			Boca Raton FL
5/21/1943	Andros North	Findable by boat	Y	B-25	RAF	FR365CD	7	0	Cleary, Alastair Grant, Atkins-Tallentire, Durrant, Ernest William, Gedelian, M. E. G., Guinter, Howard Watson Thomas, Thomas William Vincent, Todd, Eric Douglas		Crashed 5 nm N of Morgan's Bluff, Andros, oil slick seen by ASR HMS P-190 and *HMS P-63*, dinghy found 5 nm N of Morgan's Bluff, oil slick spotted, dinghy found no persons, markings of FR-365, took wheel and spares on ASR boats
6/21/1943	NP Water East	Findable by boat	Y	B-25	RAF	FL184	3	0	McLean, James Robert, Tickler, John Earle, Vallance, John		Crashed 10 m E of Nassau or 8 m SW of NP

Date	Location	Status	Y/N	Type	Service	Serial			Crew	Pilot	Notes
6/28/1943	NP Water West Old Fort Bay	Findable by boat	Y	B-25	RAF	FR382	7	0	Beaulieu, Arthur Joseph, Keayes, James Brian, Ogren, Carl Eric, Smart, Charles		Mitchell II 111 OTU took off 2:45 PM, radio comms lost at 3:15 PM, found empty dinghy and oleo leg just 3.5 nm NNW of Old Fort Bay, not east in pos. 25.09N, 77.53W, no trace of survivors found
7/13/1943	NP Clifton	Findable by boat	Y	B-25	RAF	FR393DX	0	0			Ditched at sea, SW of Clifton Point all KIA, later B-25 was located by RAF
8/7/1943	NP Windsor East	Airfield, burnt out	Y	B-25	RAF	FV953FA	6	0	Briza, Vitezslav, Hadravek, Jan, Mares, Jaroslav, Salz, Z. Karel, Turna, Josef, Satola, Josef		Crashed and burned 2 m E of Windsor, at Soldier Rd area, reached 1,000', Two minutes into the flight nose rose sharply and it then nose-dived, burst into flames, and crashed to earth within sight of the airfield hangars, also said to be 2 miles from Windsor
8/11/1943	NP Airfield	Salvaged	N	B-25	RAF	FW340	0	1		Brown, D. R. C.	Hard landing, burst tire, damaged oleo leg, undercarriage pipe line
8/12/1943	NP Oakes	Salvaged	N	B-25	RAF	FL199	0	2		McNabb, H. F., Vince, G. H.	A hard landing flapless in trials, landed on all three wheels at once, "rounded out too low"
8/20/1943	NP Oakes	Salvaged	N	B-25	RAF	FR375	0	1		West, J. H.	Cyclone landing Oakes, had hydraulic line burst, wheels would not lower 1.5 hours, so emergency landing made, plane on its nose

Date	Location	Status	Y/U	Type	Service	Serial	Col A	Col B	Crew	Notes
9/13/1943	Bahamas Water TBD	Insuff. Info.	U	B-25	USAAF	42-65104	0	0		Overdue Greenville SC, during flight to NP
9/13/1943	NP Airfield	Airfield, burnt out	Y	B-25	RAF	FW395, 8552	3	0	Blake, John Leslie Edward, Rafuse, Cedric Cardiner, Goodman, Donald	Airfield crash, taking off from Oakes/Main Field when it swung wildly, crashed into trees, and burst into flames. The aircraft was destroyed, Rafuse was taken alive to RAF hospital, died at 4:30 PM
9/16/1943	Grand Bahama Water	Insuff. Info.	U	B-25	USAAF		0	0		B-25 missing Settlement Point, West End, GB
10/5/1943	Eleuthera Bannerman	Findable by boat or swim from shore	Y	B-25	RAF	FR384CM	0	4	Hastie, R. N., Allen, T. W., McLennan, V. A., Trusson, S. J.	Bannerman Town, "Ditched on a rock, 100 yards from the shore, crew were able to leave the aircraft, rear gunner was unconscious with head injuries and was extracted from the aircraft by the other members, dinghy was launched and the crew paddled ashore, HMS P-339 rescued them, HMS P-89, HMS P-191. Later plane reported missing 77 nm East of NP to Exuma but "had been salvaged by RAF Nassau"

Date	Location	Findability	Recovered	Aircraft	Service	Serial	Col1	Col2	Crew		Notes
11/23/1943	Andros North	Deep, insuff. Info.	N	B-25	RAF	FV952FX	6	0	Brdsky, Peter, Fuchs, Pavel, Krupica, Rupert, Simandl, Josef, Styblik, Miloslav, Tomek, Hanus		Mitchell II, Bahamas/Sea, Crashed at Northwest Channel Light, SW of Chub Cay, near Joulter Cays NE of Andros. Failed to return, signal was received by W/T which terminated abruptly and only the first letter was received which was "F", it was presumed to be the first letter of the aircraft's Cell Sign, signal was received from Miami to the effect that the Coast Guard had reported a plane crashing into the sea near NW Light, Bimini.
12/16/1943	NP Oakes	Airfield	Y	B-25	RAF	FL167AX	0	0			While training took off then landed, took off, then crash-landed
12/23/1943	NP Water East Booby	Findable by boat	Y	B-25	RAF	FR376	6	0	Frye, H. D., McLean, J. C., Wilcox, A. J., Petersen, B. N., Swire, W., Craig, C. F.		Mitchell II ditched in sea 6.5 from NP airfield, plane discovered 3 weeks later in 10 feet water, strong tides, no trace of crew. Athol Island, local on island confirmed crash, showed ASR to disintegrated fuselage
6/6/1944	Eleuthera West Tarpum	Findable by boat, asking fishermen	Y	B-25	RAF	FR	0	3			2 nm N of Tarpum Bay, Eleuthera, all rescued, Doctors arrived 3 hours later on the Grumman Goose or the Crash Boat from Harbour Island arrived, c6 hours later, took crew with a face wound and others to NP overnight; the pilot went asap in a Grumman.

Date	Location	Status	Y/N	Type	Service	ID			Crew	Pilot	Notes
10/28/1944	NP Yamacraw, East Fox Hill	Airfield, burnt out in bush, difficult	Y	B-25	RAF	FW148FL, 42-87474	6	0	Bartlett, Ernest Roy, Carberry, John, Foreman, Arthur Henry, Lewis, Robert Stanley, Woodeson, Leslie Somerville, Bentick, Raymond Cyril Walter		Lost height after bombing run and flew into trees at Yamacraw Hill, SE of airfield. Fox Hill Beach, at bombing range, to the S of Fox Hill Road, smoke seen by civilians. Other planes reported "an aircraft was on fire in swampy bush, disintegrated, difficult to identify aircraft type. Ambulance and fire tender sent. Found it was B-25, which had commenced bombing practice but banked steeply, crashed, and only after hitting the earth caught fire.
11/24/1944	NP Water E Athol I.	Findable by boat	Y	B-25	RAF	HD330 FP, 43-3801	9	0			Aka FP ditched following Leigh Light incident in Montague Bay, Athol Island, same day as FW, ASR on scene, 3801 to RAF as Mitchell II HD330. Collided with Mitchell FW150, crashed into sea
11/24/1944	NP Water E Athol I.	Findable by boat	Y	B-25	RAF	FW150, 42-87477	8	2	Scammell, John, William Thomas, Gamble, George Douglas, Strachan, David Gordon		Mitchell FW ditched Montague Bay, Athol Island area, ASR retrieved 2 survivors, Mitchell II, FW150 dived into the sea off Nassau after colliding with HD330, same unit. (Gamble had sunk U-964 on 16-10-1943). Collided, HD330, crashed in sea off NP.
1/6/1945	NP Windsor	Salvaged	N	B-25	RAF	LK	0	6		Lamb, L.	Crashed S end of Windsor, damaging aircraft, no injuries, off runway

Date	Location	Disposition	Findable	Aircraft	Service	Serial	KIA		Crew		Notes
2/2/1945	NP Oakes	Salvaged	N	B-25	RAFTC	KB470, 45 Group	0	0			Failed swing on field at Oakes, lost undercarriage
2/23/1945	NP Windsor	Salvaged, field crash	N	B-25	RAF	FL994 LA, 41-11702	0	9			Liberator III collided with Liberator GRV BZ746 (wrecked) no KIA this aircraft, but 9 KIA on other, in circuit at Windsor Field, belly-landed; SOC 1.3.45.
4/9/1945	NP Water North	Findable by boat	Y	B-25	RAF	FV946, 30471	7	0	Acton, Colin George, Dumble, David Storar, Hallett, Dennis Peter, Hutchinson, Sidney William, Moule, Thomas,		Ditched into ocean off NP, crashed South of NP, smoke, crashed to the sea south of East Point, NP ASR boat *HMS P-2779* from Montague sent and B-25 FY was airborne at 8:30 PM until 9:32 PM to search, with 2 parachutes found, identified as issued, 2 crew retrieved
4/21/1945	NP Water North	Findable by boat	Y	B-25	RAF	HD308FU	6	0	Beynon, David Edmund, Hamlin, Cyril Reginald, Hanney, Robert Aubrey, Lunam,		Waterborne crash on exercises 5 nm N of NP. ASR boats HMS T-170 and HMS P-191 went to area of an oil patch and found a dinghy which helped match the oil to plane tail # "FU" however they were unable to find survivors.
7/16/1945	NP Airfield	Salvaged	N	B-25	RAF	FL995	0	0			Unnamed truck operator struck rudder of B-24, delaying departure of VIPs to Canada for 3 days

| 2/23/1945 | NP South, Yamacraw | Airfield, burnt out in bush, difficult | Y | B-25D | RAF | BZ746 LM, 42-40465 | 9 | 0 | Hayes, Allan Edward, Holland, Alan, Birch, John Raymond, Birkett, Lawrence Arthur, Cribbes, George Deryk, Tomlinson, Arthur Ian, Jackson, Christopher, Hutchings, Bertie Warren, Richards, Geoffrey Edward Charles | | LM collided with Liberator FL994 in circuit, crashed 3 miles (4.8 km) S of airfield; SOC 1.3.45. Collision, Liberator GRV BZ746 LM (wrecked) |
| 5/19/1946 | NP Oakes | Salvaged | N | B-25J | RAF | KJ583, SN 44-28774 | 0 | 0 | | | Both KJ670, KJ583 were Mitchell B-25J's built 1944. KJ583 was warming up on Oakes Field when it ran away during startup and collided with KJ670. No report of injuries but both aircraft DBR, damaged beyond repair and scrapped (problem: Oakes was shut down by May 1946...) |

Date	Location	Status	Recovered	Aircraft	Service	Serial			Crew	Crew	Notes
5/19/1946	NP Oakes	Salvaged	N	B-25J	RAF	KJ679, SN 44-28774	0	0			Both KJ670, KJ583 were Mitchell B-25J's built 1944. KJ583 was warming up on Oakes Field when it ran away during startup and collided with KJ670. No report of injuries but both aircraft DBR, damaged beyond repair and scrapped (problem: Oakes was shut down by May 1946...)
1/1/1943	Abaco Water Walkers Cay	Deep, economically undiscoverable	N	B-26	USAAF		3	3	Cook, John J., Erickson, Dan M., Mann, Walter	Adams, Aaron R., Creakbean, Ronald A., Wooton, Frederick C.	While in group during training exercise SC to Nassau & back w/o landing port engine stalled then ignited. One man panicked, pilot deliberately stayed at controls to crash land and save men. Witnessed to have crashed, group leader called in a Navy rescue boat. 25 nm E of reef of GB, Little Abaco, and c.32 nm ENE of Tox Town. Ex Myrtle Beach SC crashed at sea, of 6 men 3 KIA and 3 parachuted alive, PBY and PBM from Banana River picked them up, brought back
9/15/1943	NP Airfield	Airfield	Y	B-26	RAF	FB455	0	2		Davidson, W., Blake, W. M.	Undercarriage collapsed, landing off runway to rough coral, complete wreck

Date	Location	Status	Y/N	Type	Service	Serial	#	#	Crew	Crew	Notes
10/1/1943	NP Airfield	Airfield, burnt out	Y	B-26	RAF	FB457	0	0		McGill, F. R., Collmer, J., D'Altroy, J. T., Boyd, G. D.	Copilot raised undercarriage at takeoff, Marauder burnt out. Mistook signal from Captain, raised undercarriage, plane burnt out.
10/13/1943	NP Clifton Lyford	Findable by boat	Y	B-26	RAF	FB454, 35463	4	0	Barber, Roland Henry, Cormack, Douglas Waitt Whitehurst, Durward, Denis, Owen, John Griffith		Marauder, Windsor training takeoff NW, crashed in sea off Lyford Cay, smoke floats, oil patch observed, "caught fire and dove into the sea." 4 persons no message; 2 of the bodies were recovered that day from an RAF rescue launch (ASR).
9/19/1944	NP Airfield	Salvaged	N	B-26	RAF	HD638	0	2		Grant, C. A., Pynn, F. S.	Landed at Windsor, was taxiing, copilot accidentally raised landing gear, buckled lower frames, port propellers
10/17/1944	NP Water Cable Beach	Found	Y	B-26	RAF	HD664	2	0	Wood, Jack, O'Neill, Maurice		Marauder, RAFTC HD664, off Cable Beach Balmoral l, 2 KIA, RCAF. Aircraft located Nov-Dec 2021, both families notified.

	4/7/1943	1/9/1945	5/17/1943	5/7/1943	1/1/1944
Location	Acklins South, Pompey Bay	Bahamas Water TBD	Inagua Water	Inagua	Inagua
Status	Found	Insuff. Info., deep	Salvaged	Deep	Findable on land
	Y	U	N	N	Y
Type	B-26C	B-29	Blimp	C-46	C-46
Branch	USAAF	USAAF	USN	USAAF	USAAF
Serial/Unit	41-34720, 3rd AF, MacDill, FL, 323 Bomb, 453 Bomb		K	41-15180	
	0	10	0	2	1
	4	0	0	0	0
Names	Hunt, James Franklin, Stern, Arnold, Williams, Billy R., Stevens, Ralph E.			Inman, William B., Mitchell, Carter	
Notes	Crash, 4 rescued. Plane photographed, burned out but not secured by USAAF as found by author 8.9.22. All parachuted, 2 south, Stern water, Hunt S of Pompey, he went N, 3 went S Salina Point, rendezvous there Chancy Tynes DC.	5:30 PM on 8th 100 nm E of Morrison, possibly NP to Exuma or Eleuthera, on way to Borinquen, overdue, never found	Blimp seen to go down in sea 6-8 miles West however it later landed in Guantanamo	EAL pilots between Turks & Caicos and Great Inagua (40nm E), port engine afire, plane going down, witnessed by other aircraft; a US mail pouch washed up on Inagua, causing confusion	Inagua: Ventura, Curtiss C-46, body, parachute buried by Mr. Nixon

Date	Location	Status		Type	Service	Serial			Crew	Notes
1/14/1944	Bahamas Water TBD	Insuff. Info., deep	U	C-46	USAAF	MSN19142, 42-100679	1	4		Douglas Skytrain (DC-3) built 1943 Morrison to Borinquen ditched in Bahamas, 4 men rescued, 1 KIA.
6/12/1943	NP Airfield	Salvaged	N	C-47	RAF	FD878	0	5	Quick, W., Saarup, H., Ramsey, L., Davis, R. W., Dawson	Dakota undercarriage retracted on parking, damaging propellors. Ground crew B. L. Dawson was seriously injured as plane collapsed on him, survived
11/10/1943	NP Airfield	Salvaged	N	C-47	RAF	FL528	0	3	Marburgh, J. W., Bruen, J. C., Shergold, K. W.	Dakota hit a stationary truck on apron, damaged port fuselage, flap, and aileron
1/5/1945	NP Airfield	Salvaged	N	C-47	RAF	KK204	0	1	Howes, W. M.	C-47 Dakota taxiing in apron when starboard wingtip struck a Mosquito without causing damage.
6/26/1945	Eleuthera Water West	Findable, Insuff. Info.	Y	C-47	USAAF	Curtis	0	0		Curtiss *en route* between NP, Ship Channel Cay and Eleuthera, missing, never found, though ASR boat *HMS P-191*, B-25 FO searched, no original details
7/19/1943	NP Windsor	Salvaged	N	C-47A	USAAF	43-24012	0	1	Reddoch, John H.	From Memphis MAP, TN, taxiing accident, see FA134 Nassau NP, see C-47A same date

Date	Location	Findability	Y/N	Type	Service	Unit/Serial				Name	Description
5/17/1943	Mayaguana	Findable by boat	Y	C-47B	USN	43-16248	0	2		Marcroft, Sam	*En route* from George Field, IL, to Carib made forced landing c.75 miles off Mayaguana
5/29/1945	Mayaguana	Findable by boat	Y	C-47B	USAAF	43-16248, 20714	0	0			Following engine failure, the DC-3 was ditched into the sea .8 miles off Mayaguana
3/6/1945	Bimini Water North	Deep, insuff. Info.	N	Dauntless	USN	Dauntless	0	0	Douglas SBD		40 nm E of Port Everglades, c.20 nm N of Alice Town, SW of Great Isaac Light, NW Providence Channel Light, entrance (in p.30 Quasar Bermuda Triangle book)
1/11/1946	NP Clifton Fuel	Findable	Y	Depot	RAF	Fuel Hut, 45 Group	0	0			RAF bases' fuel hut 201 caught fire, straining resources
9/1/1944	Exuma Water Great Exuma	Salvaged	N	F-6	USN	F6F82, VF80 Squadron	0	2			USS *Ticonderoga* had to divert from ship and make crash landing at Exuma, uninjured, due to mechanical trouble

Date	Location	Disposition		Type	Service	Serial/Unit			Aircraft	Name	Notes
9/11/1944	Bahamas Water TBD	Deep, insuff. Info.	N	F-6	USN	Dauntless	0	0	Douglas SBD		E of Miami, FL (cited in Quasar's book p.30, on Bermuda Triangle)
9/1/1945	Grand Bahama W Water	Insuff. Info., deep	U	F6F Hellcat	USN	F-6F	0	0			F6F Grumman Hellcat fighter overdue from Vero Beach 15.24 on 40-minute flight seen W of West End
3/8/1945	Abaco Water More's I.	Findable on land, small island, strong chance	Y	FM-2	USN	16775, VF-6, NAS Sanford	0	1	Lockheed Ventura	Fyfield, Herbert S.	"Forced crash landing in Great Abaco Island Area, actually crash landed at Moore's Island and that the pilot is now at Marsh Harbour" "sighted land, having only 10 gals fuel, no suitable airstrip available, he made a wheels-up landing in a clear area which turned out to be Moore's Island, Bahamas."
8/7/1944	NP Airfield	Salvaged	N	Hudson	RAF	EW931	0	1		Hudson, R. S. S.	Starboard wing caught on land while landing, damaging it

Date	Location	Status	Fatal	Aircraft	Service	Serial			Aircraft Type	Crew	Description
12/18/1942	Grand Bahama	Missing, drifted, deep	N	JRF	USAAF		0	0			Memory Rock abandoned US Army plane JRF amphib. Flight to Nassau diverted to see if it was there, could not be located.
7/29/1943	NP Water West	Insuff. Info.	U	Kingfisher	USN		0	0			NW of NP
12/15/1944	NP Windsor	Airfield, burnt out	Y	Mosquito	RAFTC	KB589	0	2	de Havilland DH-98	Lee, Manwaring, A. H.	Swung on takeoff from Windsor, lost undercarriage, caught fire, total loss. Plane swung upon takeoff, became unmanageable, crashed along the runway and burst into flames. Lee, third time only slightly injured and survived, Manwaring seriously injured.
1/30/1945	NP Oakes	Salvaged	N	Mosquito	RAF	KB540, 45 Group	0	1	DH.98 Mosquito	Olchalsky, J. P.	Right side brake locked, caused a ground loop, failed on landing, destroyed (Olchalsky 2.2.45)
2/2/1945	NP Windsor	Salvaged	N	Mosquito	RAF	KB479, 45 Group	0	1	de Havilland DH-98	Olchalsky, J. P.	Swung on takeoff, ground looped, undercarriage collapsed, fuselage torn, propellers broken (Olchalsky 30.1.45)
2/13/1945	NP Oakes	Salvaged	N	Mosquito	RAFTC	KB340, 45 Group	0	1	DE Havilland DH-98	Sodal, A.	Oakes, severe bounces on landing, collapsed undercarriage. Severe damage, aircraft, engines.

Date	Location	Disposition		Aircraft	Service	Serial						Notes
3/7/1945	NP Oakes	Salvaged	N	Mosquito	RAFTC	KB381, 45 Group	0	0	DE Havilland DH-98		Cripps, R. J.	Looped on landing, port wing and engine damaged
3/13/1945	NP Windsor	Salvaged	N	Mosquito	RAF	KB591, 45 Group	0	0	DE Havilland DH-98			Swung in landing at Windsor, lost undercarriage
3/15/1945	NP Oakes	Salvaged	N	Mosquito	RAFTC	KB591, 45 Group	0	0	DE Havilland DH-98		Stonehouse	Swung on landing at Oakes, undercarriage collapsed
12/31/1943	Grand Bahama	Airfield, burnt out	Y	OS2N-1 Kingfisher	USN	BuNo 01218	0	2			Spelletich, Kallman	Plane ex-Banana River, FL crashed taking off from West End *en route* to Walker's Cay, no serious injuries, plane burned
6/22/1943	Grand Bahama Walkers Cay	Salvaged	N	OS2U-3	USN	BuNo 5892	1	1	McDonough, Lester, Sobolak, Franklin			Crashed in water after takeoff due to pilot watching another takeoff, pilot survived, not radio officer, towed to Walker's Cay, Grand Bahama
5/26/1944	Eleuthera Royal I.	Salvaged	N	P20	USN		0	1			Newton	Lt. Newton lost a nacelle or dome from a Leigh Light while on a bombing run dive
7/18/1945	Cat I. Water East	Deep, unfindable	N	PB4Y-2 Privateer	USN	BuNo 59642,	12	0	Bailey, C. M., Mattingly, P. E., Takkurn, F. W., Bower, R. H., Meola,			Last heard 60 nm from ENE of New Bight, Cat I, at 0:25, report giving planes position. Aircraft was patrol bomber, based in Miami, all MIA, KIA deep water.

Date	Location	Status		Type	Navy	Name					Notes
4/26/1944	NP Water East	Insuff. Info., salvaged?	U	PBM	USN	Mariner	0	0			Montague Foreshore, Nassau, NP
5/5/1945	Grand Bahama Water	Salvaged	N	PBM	USN	BuNo 6556, Mariner Hedron 9-2	0	0			Coco Solo, Panama to USA "made forced landing at Settlement Point, GB, was towed to Dinner Key, Miami, FL"
7/12/1945	Grand Bahama Water	Insuff. Info.	U	PBM	USN	Mariner	0	0			PBM was overdue so K-96 airship searched for its Andros, Abaco, GB
8/24/1944	Eleuthera Water Royal I.	Findable by boat if not salvaged	Y	PBM	USN	HMS 339, US Depot Ship, Mariner	0	0			Royal Island, northwest Eleuthera, damaged and towed to harbor?

7/10/1945	9/20/1943	2/12/1943	4/1/1943
NP Water North	Abaco Pelican Bay	Exuma Water TBD	Bimini Water Cat Cay
Deep, insuff. Info.	Findable by boat	Salvaged	Deep, drifted
N	Y	N	N
PBM-3	PBM3s	PBY	PBY
USN	USN	USN	USN
BuNo 6545, CenLant, NAS Banana River	BuNo 6730, VB-208		PBY-5A Catalina
12	0	0	0
0	0	0	0
White, J. B., Lavoy, Eugene Wendall, Lewis, Wesley Elliot, Eisley, James E., Garner, Thomas A., Hurt, John E., Wyatt, Edward J., Oliver, Thomas C., Boyer, Gene S., Slotwick, Bernard M., Winder, Glen L., Wororeck, Stephen			
Flight to Great Exuma, flew FL to Windsor *en route* Exuma, but overwhelmed by severe storm 10 nm N of NP, last reported 8 nm N of Cabbage Beach, Hog/Paradise Island. USN PBM *en route* Banana River (JAX) to Great Exuma never arrived, never found. "Flew into a severe storm in that area and he and his plane and crew went missing"	Landing, water, looped, crashed in Pelican Harbour, SE Great Abaco, N of Little Harbour	PBY ran low on fuel landed for the night; search parties sent out.	Key West Boca Chica to Norfolk landed on water in Bahamas, men waved from wings

Date	Location	Status	U/N	Type	Operator	Serial			Names	Names 2	Remarks
4/19/1943	Berry I.	Salvaged	N	PBY	USN	Catalina	0	2			USN PBY landed off or at Whale Cay, Berry Islands, owned by Joe Carstairs; no need for rescue, must be same PBY reported missing East of Miami
6/16/1943	NP Water East	Salvaged	N	PBY	RAF	FP532	0	2		Baxter, T. A., Davidson, W. J.	Seaplane hit hanger, Pan Am ramp, East Bay Street, Nassau Harbour
8/7/1943	San Salvador	Salvaged	N	PBY	RAF	FP532	0	5	Marburgh, J. W., Uren, P. E., Baxter, T., Moore, E., Clarkson, K. D.		Hit submerged coral head 2.5' under surface on takeoff. Takeoff ex San Sal on rescue mission
11/19/1943	Acklins Pompey Bay	Salvaged	N	PBY	USAAF	J1P-28	0	8			Key West to Great Exuma when due to rough weather landed and sought temporary shelter at Pompey Bay, Acklins SW.
2/12/1944	Bahamas Water TBD	Insuff. Info.	U	PBY	USN	J-2P20	0	1		Bayfield	7 PBY's arrived Exuma from JAX on training flight, this aircraft missing. NOB Exuma sent 6 PBY's Key West, searched, not found

Date	Location	Status		Type	Service	ID			Crew	Notes
3/7/1944	Exuma Water TBD	Insuff. Info.	U	PBY	USN	204-P-9	0	0		Survivors found in life raft by 32-P-10, unclear where, TAG Guantanamo convoy, reported by NOB NAS Exuma
4/1/1944	Andros North West	Salvaged	N	PBY	USN	Catalina	0	0		NW of Andros an RAF plane saw a Catalina, crew in dinghy rowing to land. Not confirmed by later search & rescue aircraft.
6/11/1944	Ragged Island	Findable, good chance, 20 yards of beach, engines in reef	Y	PBY	USN	08536, VPB-2 #1, NAS Jax.	0	13	Bernardy, Paul Charles, Economou, Constantine James, McNair, Henry William, Jenkins, Reginald Everett, Robbins, Leon Elton, Pappas, Peter John, Gutlaw, Lee Imey, Tremblay, Norman Alphones, Jowdy, James Joseph, Birch, William Daniel, Doelle, William Andrew, Storkel, Thomas Edward, Cratty, Gerald Eugene	PBY from NAS JAX landed, emergency at Ragged, rescued by Exuma then Guantanamo. Was over Ragged at just 800' when starboard engine caught fire. Sea landing was made on water off Great Ragged I., with no damage. Then pilot attempted to taxi to shore at a sandy beach. When 20 yards from shore the plane grounded on a reef, all attempts to back off failed, the hull was holed multiple places. 12 men went ashore, salvage crew from Exuma arrived, too late as bottom of aircraft was beyond repair. Taxied to beach, hit trees, and sank. Capt. Edward Lockhart witnessed them, relayed observations to author in 2020

Date	Location	Status	Findable	Type	Service	BuNo/Unit			Notes
3/9/1945	Bahamas Water TBD	Deep, insuff. Info.	N	PBY	USN	Hedron 9/2	0	0	Between Bermuda and US
3/11/1945	Abaco	Deep, insuff. Info.	N	PBY	USN	PBY-4Y1, 38765	14	0	Crashed NW of Little Abaco, NE of GB, Paw Snorkel Rocks, 10 KIA
12/11/1944	NP Water City	Salvaged	N	PBY2	USN	JX494, Coronado	0	0	Broke free of mooring in Nassau Hbr. in storm, damaging starboard elevator; AST re-anchored it
7/19/1944	Eleuthera Water Royal I.	Findable by boat if not salvaged	Y	PBY-3C	USN	BuNo6630, VP-208, VPB-204	0	0	Landed on water off Royal I, SW of Spanish Wells, looped (spun) so badly plane struck off charge, written off. USS *Christiana*, YAG-32 based there, PBM Royal I. VPB-204 there 11/27/44-5/23/45

Date	Location	Status	Findable	Type	Service/Unit	BuNo			Pilot	Description
9/21/1942	Exuma Water	Findable by boat if not salvaged	Y	PBY-5A	USN VP92	7247, 44-40347, 38765	1	0	Finnie, R. J.	Consolidated Catalina 7247, water landing between Georgetown and NAS Stocking Island. Crashed while landing off Stocking Island. The aircraft sunk and was lost.
10/12/1943	Exumas Darby I.	Salvaged	N	PBY	USN	BuNo3235	0	0		PSP3235 sent to investigate aircraft losing altitude one engine afire near Darby I. Exumas
3/15/1944	Exuma Water	Salvaged	N	PBY	USN	BuNo 6567	0	0		PSP from Banana River to San Juan made emergency landing Exuma due to damaged port engine
4/18/1944	Bahamas Water TBD	Insuff. Info.; deep, salvaged	U	PBY	USN	BuNo 6548	0	0		PSP en route PR emergency landing Exuma. Next day search for crash survivors by 210 P1, other aircraft PBY-5A, for 3 days

Date	Location	Status	Findable	Aircraft	Service	ID	#	#	Crew	Notes
7/1/1944	Exuma Water	Findable by boat if not salvaged	Y	PBY	USN	P2-210, 01697, 3255	6	0		PSP 210P2 collided with N-ARB C9463, explosion, fire, patrolling convoys. PSP is a plane and N-ARB a boat and both demolished. 5 boat men KIA, 3 injured, 11 on planes, 4 KIA in crash and 7 injured, 2 of whom died for 9 of 11 KIA.
7/4/1944	Exuma Water	Insuff. Info.	U	PBY	USN	BuNo 45266	0	0		PSP Buno 45266 aided a plane down.
12/7/1944	Exuma Great Base	Salvaged	N	PBY	USN	PB-4 214	0	0		PSP 214 PB4 "damaged on ramp while warming engines... not properly secured."
4/18/1945	NP Windsor	Salvaged	N	PBY	USN	BuNo 6548	0	0		Late night flight San Juan PR-Jax, made emergency landing on NP.
7/20/1943	Abaco	Findable, insuff. info, difficult	Y	PV-1	USN	29631, VB2-1, NAS Sanford	0	5	Whitney, Boyd O. Johnston, Thomas G., Mennes, Emiel L. R., Parrish, George L., Emsley, Albert P.	Fire erupted, lost port engine, Great Abaco ahead, made deferred forced landing from 10 miles away (from west?), stalled belly landing in swamp area, 6 inches water, put the fire out to mainland, procured rescue, no injuries. 3 weeks later aircraft seen in and on side of a lake, turret, engines, tale separated

Date	Location	Status	Y/N/U	Type	Service	BuNo			Names	Description
3/11/1945	NP Water	Insuff. Info.	U	RAF	RAF		0	0		2 dinghies, Liferaft flares by fishermen found by RAF Nassau
7/15/1945	Mayaguana	Insuff. Info.	U	Rafts	USN		0	0		USS *Carter* found life rafts on Mayaguana I. left CVE *Guadalcanal* to retrieve life raft at USN ASR dock on Abrahams Bay
11/24/1943	Grand Bahama Water	Findable by boat	Y	SB2A	USN		2	0	Dean, V.	SB2A crashed West end 11:30 AM, into water 30' deep. Body of radio man V Dean recovered, but not pilot.
12/18/1942	Andros Water North	Salvaged	N	SBC-13	USN	BuNo 0584	0	2	Richards, B. M., Underwood	Ditched out of fuel NW Andros. Passenger Underwood. Army JRF rescued them same day. Planes flipped on back, broken propeller and crumpled top wing. Both salvaged by YP-433 Dec 25, 1942 towed Miami Pier 3, overhauled in San Diego
12/18/1942	Bimini Water East	Salvaged	N	SBC-48	USN	BuNo 0545	0	2	Russon, Z P, Wilson	Fighters on training flights force landed off North Bimini. Both salvaged by YP-433 Dec 25, 1942 towed Miami Pier 3

Date	Location	Status		Operator	ID			Type	Crew	Notes
7/19/1945	Eleuthera Water East	Deep, unfindable	N	TBN	USN		8	0			USN, not a B-24, lost plane from exercise East of Eleuthera, searched 5 days, nil result
2/19/1944	Grand Bahama Walkers Cay	Salvaged	N	USN	USN	BuNo. 09491	0	0			(VS-39) From the January 1, 1944 to February 29, 1944 War Diary of Scouting Squadron 39 (VS-39): "February 19, 1944. From Advance Base, Walker's Cay, Bahamas, BWI: From 11:50 to 12:20 searched for Navy BuNo 09491 forced down two miles west of base. Pilot and crew safe. Plane towed to base by crash boat." Doug Campbell 2.23
3/7/1945	Bimini Water TBD	Deep, insuff. Info.	N	USN	USN	Dauntless	0	1	Douglas SBD		Missing from Lauderdale, 40 miles East (of FLL or Bimini?)
3/26/1944	NP Airfield	Salvaged	N	Ventura	RAF	JT829	0	1		Lee, Fawcett	After landing, tail wheel leg collapsed on taxiing. Fuselage and gunner's nest damaged
9/18/1942	Exuma Water	Salvaged	N		USN	92-P-12	0	0			Forced landing in Exuma, no damage or injury

Date	Location		Findable	Service	Plane ID					Notes
9/24/1942	Exuma Water	Findable by boat if not salvaged	Y	USN	92-P-11	0	0			Unlit harbor landing attempt, Great Exuma, crashed, injuries, plane total loss
3/14/1943	Crooked I. Water North	Deep	N	USN		0	0			Wooden lifeboat picked up by PSP 34P3 "sighted an empty wooden life raft, a PC boat investigated. 25 nm NNE of Landrail Point
3/31/1943	Crooked I. Water Southeast	Insuff. Info.	U	USAAF		0	0			PSP 34P8 out of Guantanamo searched SE of Crooked I. for survivors, Army USAAF bomber
4/11/1943	Grand Bahama Water	Insuff. Info.	U	USN		0	1			Man sighted swimming near wreckage of plane, Great Bahamas Bank, some green lights

5/22/1943	Mayaguana	Findable or Insuff. Info. - inside or outside reef?	Y	USAAF		0	0		Plane reported crashed N of Curtis Creek, Mayaguana at 6 AM by Commissioner, follow up again on May 24, 1943, same incident. Report by messenger from Pirates Well, Mayaguana: "plane crashed on the N side of island some distance to sea in a northerly direction from Curtis Creek about 6:00 AM, Sat May 22. No large boats here at present to investigate." The B-25 was last reported previous day and its limit of endurance would not carry it through 06:00 EWT the following morning, no other planes reported missing.
7/19/1943	Cay Sal Bank	Deep, possible, costly; significant site	N	USN	K-74	1	8	Stessel, Isadore; Eversley, Darnley, Jandrowitz, John, Schmidt, Jonathan L., Bourne, Robert Herbert, Rice, John F., Giddings, Gerrold M., Eckert, Garnet, Kowalski, John W.	K-74 USN blimp sank, See USS *Dahlgren* war diary. U-134/Brosin engaged in a firefight with a large USN airship sent from FL to the Bahamas' Cay Sal Bank to investigate. When K-74's bomb mechanism froze it was doomed, U-134 shot it down, Stessel died swimming towards remote Cay Sal. The only USN airship crew KIA by a U-boat.

Date	Location	Status		Service				Names		Description
8/1/1943	NP Windsor	Salvaged	N	RAF		2	0	Hole, John Francis Seager, Day, Edred Frederick		An engine fire at night drove 2 mechanics in the RAFVR to walk backwards and into active propellers, in death records as multiple injuries
10/1/1943	Grand Bahama Water	Findable, insuff. Info.	Y	USN		0	0			Small plane crashed in 3' water; bombs removed
10/28/1943	Eleuthera West Governors	Salvaged	N	USN		0	0			Floating plane or boat reported ablaze, confusion over if PBY-4 Paw Paw, poss. Canadian freighter MV *Bernadou, en route* PR to Palm Beach.
11/23/1943	Bimini Waters North	Deep, insuff. Info.	N	USN		0	0			Navy Plane crashed 2 nm SW of North Rock Light, Bimini, CGR 7007 proceeded to scene for USCG. Had seen an explosion. Unknown aircraft seen by Bimini locals and US officials to have "crashed in flames" which were circled with no result.

Date	Location	Status			Service	Type					Remarks
12/8/1943	Bimini Water West	Deep	N		USN		0	0			Large flame seen on water, 15 nm NW of Bimini said to be *ENA K* distress signal
6/30/1944	Bimini Water East	Salvaged (?)	N		USN	Grumman	0	0			Small fighter plane found in water East of North Bimini
10/31/1944	Grand Bahama Water West	Deep, insuff. Info.	N		USN		0	1			Pilot ditched in water from Vero Beach FL was seen drifting in a rubber life raft

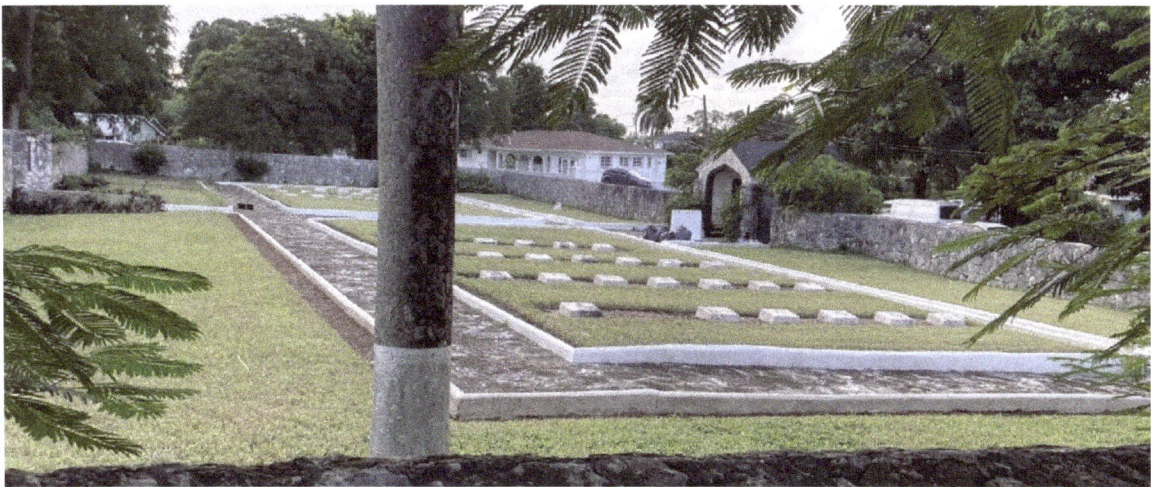

The RAF, or Nassau War Cemetery today, with the Lych Gate to the right, center.

Appendix 2: Names of all Killed in Wartime Air Accident, in The Bahamas

Name	Age	Rank	Date Died	Unit	Service #	Family, Hometown
Barber, Roland Henry	21	Flying Officer	10/13/1943	RAFVR	136158	Son of Roland Arthur and Gladys Mabel Barber, of Northampton.
Bartlett, Ernest Roy	22	Flying Officer	10/27/1944	RAFVR	157831	Son of Albert Henry and Caroline Louise Bartlett, of Edgeware London
Bentick, Raymond Cyril Walter	33	Sergeant	10/28/1944	RAFVR	1603964	Son of Herbert and Charlotte Bentick; husband of Enid Bentick, of Watford Hertfordshire.
Birch, John Raymond	20	Sergeant	2/23/1945	RAFVR	1892417	Son of Edwin James and Mildred Alice Birch, of Gloucester.
Birkett, Laurence Arthur		Flying Officer	2/23/1945	RAFVR	174687	
Blake, John Leslie Edward	20	Sergeant	9/13/1943	RAFVR	1336240	Son of Edward John and Charlotte Stewart Blake, of Portsmouth; stepson of Mrs. A.M.E. Blake, of Liss, Hampshire.
Briza, Vitezslav	23	Sergeant	8/7/1943	RAFVR	787155	Of Czechoslovakia.
Carberry, John	28	Sergeant	10/28/1944	RAFVR	1522659	Son of John and Mary Carberry; husband of Olive

						Carberry, of Sheffield.
Chouteau, Henri	25	Captain	5/30/1943	RAFTC		Son of Henri and Jane Bagnell Chouteau, of St. Louis, Missouri, U.S.A.
Cormack			10/13/1943			
Cribbes, George Deryk	24	Flying Officer	2/23/1945	RAFVR	166098	Son of George Burnett and Sylvia Aida Cribbes, of Buenos Aires, Argentina; husband of Sylvia Mary Cribbes, of Sydenham, London.
Daiken, Alex John		Pilot Officer	3/19/1943	RCAF	J/20616	
Durward			10/13/1943			
Foreman, Arthur Henry	28	Flying Officer	10/28/1944	RAF	55632	Son of David and Louisa Jane Foreman, of Stroxton, Lincolnshire.
Glen, Ian Simpson	26	Sergeant	3/25/1943	RAFVR	1365286	Son of John D.A. and Agnes G.S. Glen, of Stirling. Chartered Accountant.
Goodman, Donald	20	Pilot Officer	9/13/1943	RAFVR	156308	Son of Stanley Jack and Kathleen May Goodman, of Erith. London.
Hadravek, Jan	25	Pilot Officer	8/7/1943	RAFVR	149112	Of Czechoslovakia.
Harris, Albert		Captain	10/28/1944	RAFTC		
Hayes, Allan Edward	22	Flying Officer	2/23/1945	RCAF	J/19172	Son of Cyril E. and Frances Hayes, of Preston, Ontario, Canada; husband

						of Jean Isobel Hayes.
Holland, Alan		Flight Sergeant	2/23/1945	RAFVR	1627769	
Hollowell, Donald Terence		Pilot Officer	3/19/1943	RCAF	T/24107	
Hutchings, Bertie Warren		Flying Officer	2/23/1945	RAFVR	151528	
Jackson, Christopher		Sergeant	2/23/1945	RAFVR	1903874	
Lewis, Robert Stanley	21	Sergeant	10/28/1944	RAFVR	1523173	Son of Ernest and Alice Lewis, of South Shields, Tyne and Wear.
Lyons (Lynes), Joseph Paul	19	Test Observer	5/30/1943	RAFTC		Son of Joseph P. and Lillian C. Lynes, of Hampstead, Province of Quebec, Canada.
Mares, Jaroslav	29	Flight Lieutenant	8/7/1943	RAFVR	101497	Of Czechoslovakia.
Owen, John Griffith	27	Flight Lieutenant	10/13/1943	RAFVR	80066	Son of David Griffith and Olive Eveline Owen of Winklespruit, Natal, South Africa.
Rafuse, Cedric Gardiner	26	Flight Sergeant	9/13/1943	RCAF	R/104322	Son of Norman Willis and Bertha Alice Rafuse, of Nova Scotia, Canada.
Richards, Geoffrey Edward Charles	19	Sergeant	2/23/1945	RAFVR	2225323	Son of George Weaver and Lilian Hazel Richards, of Crosby, Liverpool.
Salz, Z. Karel	31	Sergeant	8/7/1943	RAFVR	788106	Son of Simon and Hilda Salz, of Notting Hill, London. Of Czechoslovakia.

Somerville, Cyril J.		Radio Officer	8/1/1943	RAFTC		Son of Ewart G. and Dorothy A. Somerville, of Sudbury, Ontario Canada; husband of Patricia Jane Somerville.
Sotola, Josef	23	Sergeant	8/7/1943	RAFVR	787341	Of Czechoslovakia.
Tomlinson, Arthur Ian	22	Flying Officer	2/23/1945	RAFVR	165616	Son of Mrs. Margaret Tomlinson, of Galashiels, Borders.
Toone, Reginald Seymour	26	Flying Officer	8/7/1943	RAFVR	125437	Son of Harry Edwin and Annie Elizabeth Toone, of Leamington Spa, Warwickshire.
Turna, Josef	26	Sergeant	8/7/1943	RAFVR	788278	Of Czechoslovakia.
Woodeson, Leslie Somerville	21	Pilot Officer	10/28/1944	RAFVR	165240	Son of Albert James and Mary Jane Woodeson, of Stratford, London.
Zdan, Benjamin Henry		Pilot Officer	3/19/1943	RCAF	J/20606	

Set in hand-hewn Bahamian limestone using a trowel made of the metal of downed aircraft, this memorial tablet at the RAF Cemetery reads "In Memory of The United Nations Airmen Reported Missing from Flying Operations in the Bahamas, 1939-1945." The fact this an untold number of aviators were lost, killed and missing after taking off from Bahamas. Even though they never reached their destinations, they were lost in other lands and not included herein.

Appendix 3: Names of all Killed in The Bahamas While on Wartime Duty

Death Date	SURNAME	FORENAME	Age	RANK	CAUSES OF DEATH, Including Contributors	Nation, Force
12/3/1944	Barker	John Langford Desmond		Flying Officer	Drowned: "drowning by misadventure," in a bathing accident at Nassau, buried w/ honors	RAFVR
10/26/1942	Beeston	Edward James	43	Leading Aircraft man	Drowned: sailing, 4pm. LAC, 88 SP	RAFVR
2/26/1943	Bullard	Baby Girl	1	Civilian, Baby	Plane hit home: B-25 FK176 "on night flying training, crew uninjured. Occupants of house it crashed into all killed."	Bahamian
2/26/1943	Bullard	Louise	19	Seamstress, Civilian, Mother	Plane hit home: B-25 FK176 "on night flying training, crew uninjured. Occupants of house it crashed into all killed."	Bahamian
2/26/1943	Bullard	Charles	24	Laborer, Civilian, Father	Plane hit home: B-25 FK176 "on night flying training, crew uninjured. Occupants of house it crashed into all killed."	Bahamian
4/1/1945	Butler	Joseph Harrison		Aircraft man 2nd Class	Truck crash: He was seriously injured on duty at RAF Nassau when he fell from a moving vehicle,	RAFVR

					dying of his injuries in RAF Hospital	
8/1/1943	Day	Edred Frederick	29	Leading Aircraft man	Propeller: with fellow mechanic Hole "multiple injuries as a result of airplane accident," fire, night, both backed into moving propeller	RAFVR
5/5/1945	Delevea ux	O E		Private	Unknown	NCaribFo rce
11/28/1943	Deveau x	Finley	21	Soldier	Hodgkins Disease: St. Matthew's Parish, Bahamian designated "A" for "African descent"	West India Regiment
3/28/1943	Gouldin g	Anthony Edward	22	Flight Sergeant	Plane crash: Multiple injuries as a result of an aircraft accident.	RAFVR
10/16/1944	Gowans	Henry		Sergeant	Suicide: with revolver at RAF Nassau "from self-inflicted gunshot wound while of unsound mind."	RAF
4/29/1943	Harris	Albert	34	Captain	Plane crash: Head injuries and burns as a result of aircraft accident	RAFFC
6/21/1945	Haskins	William	26	Aircraft man 2nd Class	Operation: under anesthesia for tonsillectomy operation	RAFVR
8/1/1943	Hole	John Francis Seager	25	Corporal	Propeller: with fellow mechanic Day, "multiple injuries as a result of airplane accident," fire, night, both backed into moving propeller	RAFVR

1/11/1944	Jeremiah	Donald	25	Squadron Leader	Addison's Disease: fever in Nassau.	RAF
6/13/1944	Jones	William James	35	Flight Lieutenant	Bus crash: dangerously injured on Nassau Street at 9.10 pm, road accident, dying in RAF station Hospital, Western District.	RAFVR
3/21/1944	Jones	G		Private	Unknown	NCaribForce
1/26/1944	Korn	Charles Byron	33	First Lieutenant, USAM Corps	Strangled	Nassau
3/25/1943	Lumby	James	24	Soldier	Injury: Fractured skull	
7/4/1943	Lytle (Little)	John Henry	26	Leading Aircraftman, Flight Mechanic	Swim accident: fractured cervical vertebrae from bathing accident, died at Bahamas General Hospital, Nassau; "fractured neck."	RAFVR
3/28/1943	Morris	William Frederick	23	Radio Officer	Plane crash: Shock, severe burns, and multiple injuries.	RAFFC Civilian
5/9/1945	Muirhead	William Alexander	21	Aircraftman 1st Class	Road crash: died in the US Army Engineer's hospital, Nassau, injuries sustained in a road accident	RAFVR
8/13/1944	Munroe	Charles	18	Private	Tetanus: St. Matthew's Parish, Bahamian	NCaribForce
1/12/1943	Newell	Geoffrey William		Leading Aircraftman	Road crash: dangerously injured in a road accident at RAF Nassau, died at US Army Engineer's Hospital, of multiple	RAFVR

					injuries to the right leg	
1/31/1943	Page	Frederick Menzies	21	Flight Sergeant	Drowned: boating accident	RAFVR
11/22/1942	Rahming	Charles	27	Defence Force Soldier	Ulcers: perforation of dondenium St. Matthew's Parish, Bahamian	
7/10/1943	Savage	James Robertson	30	Sergeant	Shot: shock from injury cased to stomach, spine and spinal chord caused by bullet	RCAF/Army
3/21/1944	Shelley	Arthur	24	Leading Aircraft man	Shot: accidently shot himself; injuries to brain.	RAFVR
5/9/1945	Sones	Walter George		Leading Aircraft man	Truck crash: struck on the head by a moving RAF lorry	RAFVR
12/28/1943	Toone	Reginald Seymour	26	Flying Officer	Hernia: Internal hernia, fungal fistula	RAF
10/26/1942	Yeldon	Willis Redmond	41	Sergeant	Shot: friendly fire incident in downtown Nassau, this veteran of WWI was visiting and killed by a US MP in altercation. Possible behavioural trigger was PTSD from First War.	Veteran's Guard of Canada

Appendix 4: Aviators Killed and Missing on Duty in The Bahamas

Names of Killed in Action	Date	Location	Type	Branch
Acton, Colin George	4/9/1945	NP Water North	B-25	RAF
Aitken, Philip Raymond	4/25/1944	Eleuthera Water North	B-24	RAF
Allbut, George Robert	6/2/1945	NP Water	B-24	RAF
Anderson, Robert Venable	4/29/1943	NP Windsor	A-30	RAF
Atkins-Tallentire, Durrant	5/21/1943	Andros North	B-25	RAF
Bailey, C. M.	7/18/1945	Cat I. Water East	PB4Y-2	USN
Barber, Roland Henry	10/13/1943	NP Clifton Lyford	B-26	RAF
Bartlett, Ernest Roy	10/28/1944	NP Yamacraw, East Fox Hill	B-25	RAF
Beaulieu, Arthur Joseph	6/28/1943	NP Water West Old Fort Bay	B-25	RAF
Bentick, Raymond Cyril Walter	10/28/1944	NP Yamacraw, East Fox Hill	B-25	RAF
Beynon, David Edmund	4/21/1945	NP Water North	B-25	RAF
Birch, John Raymond	2/23/1945	NP South, Yamacraw	B-25	RAF
Birkett, Lawrence Arthur	2/23/1945	NP South, Yamacraw	B-25	RAF
Blake, John Leslie Edward	9/13/1943	NP Airfield	B-25	RAF
Bower, R. H.	7/18/1945	Cat I. Water East	PB4Y-2	USN
Boyer, Gene S.	7/10/1945	NP Water North	PBM-3	USN
Bradley, D.	7/18/1945	Cat I. Water East	PB4Y-2	USN
Brdsky, Peter, Fuchs	11/23/1943	Andros North	B-25	RAF
Briza, Vitezslav	8/7/1943	NP Windsor East	B-25	RAF
Brooke, Edward B.	1/9/1944	Berry I. Sturrup Cay	B-24	USAAF
Brookes, John West	6/2/1945	NP Water	B-24	RAF
Burchell, Robert Lloyd	4/9/1943	NP Clifton	B-25	RAF
Burns, James Williamson	6/2/1945	NP Water	B-24	RAF
Cameron, Kenneth John	4/25/1944	Eleuthera Water North	B-24	RAF
Carberry, John	10/28/1944	NP Yamacraw, East Fox Hill	B-25	RAF
Carroza, F. M.	7/18/1945	Cat I. Water East	PB4Y-2	USN
Chouteau, Henri	5/30/1943	NP Airfield	A-30	RAF
Cleary, Alastair Grant	5/21/1943	Andros North	B-25	RAF

Cook, John J.	1/1/1943	Abaco Water Walkers Cay	B-26	USAAF
Cormack, Douglas Waitt Whitehurst	10/13/1943	NP Clifton Lyford	B-26	RAF
Craig, C. F.	12/23/1943	NP Water East Booby	B-25	RAF
Cribbes, George Deryk	2/23/1945	NP South, Yamacraw	B-25	RAF
Daiken, Alex John	3/19/1943	NP Airfield	B-25	RAF
Daschuk, Billy James	6/13/1943	NP Windsor	A-30	RAF
Dean, V.	11/24/1943	Grand Bahama Water	SB2A	USN
Dumble, David Storar	4/9/1945	NP Water North	B-25	RAF
Durward, Denis	10/13/1943	NP Clifton Lyford	B-26	RAF
Eisley, James E.	7/10/1945	NP Water North	PBM-3	USN
Erickson, Dan M.	1/1/1943	Abaco Water Walkers Cay	B-26	USAAF
Ernest, William	5/21/1943	Andros North	B-25	RAF
Farnsworth, Ronald	4/9/1943	NP Clifton	B-25	RAF
Fenton, George	4/9/1943	NP Clifton	B-25	RAF
Finnie, R. J.	9/21/1942	Exuma Water	PBY-5	USN
Foreman, Arthur Henry	10/28/1944	NP Yamacraw, East Fox Hill	B-25	RAF
Franks, Robert Henry	6/2/1945	NP Water	B-24	RAF
Frye, H. D.	12/23/1943	NP Water East Booby	B-25	RAF
Fuchs, Pavel	11/23/1943	Andros North	B-25	RAF
Fussell, Denis William	4/25/1944	Eleuthera Water North	B-24	RAF
Gamble, George	11/24/1944	NP Water E Athol I.	B-25	RAF
Garner, Thomas A.	7/10/1945	NP Water North	PBM-3	USN
Gedelian, M. E. G.	5/21/1943	Andros North	B-25	RAF
Glen, Ian Simpson	3/25/1943	NP Airfield	A-30	RAF
Goff, Roy E.	1/9/1944	Berry I. Sturrup Cay	B-24	USAAF
Goodman, Benny Baldwin	4/9/1943	NP Clifton	B-25	RAF
Goodman, Donald	9/13/1943	NP Airfield	B-25	RAF
Gordon, David	11/24/1944	NP Water E Athol I.	B-25	RAF
Guinter, Howard Watson Thomas	5/21/1943	Andros North	B-25	RAF
Hadravek, Jan	8/7/1943	NP Windsor East	B-25	RAF
Hallett, Dennis Peter	4/9/1945	NP Water North	B-25	RAF
Hamilton, Robert B.	1/9/1944	Berry I. Sturrup Cay	B-24	USAAF
Hamlin, Cyril Reginald	4/21/1945	NP Water North	B-25	RAF
Hanney, Robert Aubrey	4/21/1945	NP Water North	B-25	RAF
Harlan, Carl Clifton	7/18/1945	Cat I. Water East	PB4Y-2	USN
Harris, Albert	4/29/1943	NP Windsor	A-30	RAF

Hayes, Alan Edward	2/23/1945	NP South, Yamacraw	B-25	RAF
Holland, Alan	2/23/1945	NP South, Yamacraw	B-25	RAF
Hollowell, Donald Terence	3/18/1943	NP Windsor	A-30	RAF
Hurt, John E.	7/10/1945	NP Water North	PBM-3	USN
Hutchings, Bertie Warren	2/23/1945	NP South, Yamacraw	B-25	RAF
Hutchinson, Sidney William	4/9/1945	NP Water North	B-25	RAF
Inman, William B.	5/7/1943	Inagua	C-46	USAAF
Jackson, Christopher	2/23/1945	NP South, Yamacraw	B-25	RAF
Johnson, Wilfred	6/13/1943	NP Windsor	B-25	RAF
Keayes, James Brian	6/28/1943	NP Water West Old Fort Bay	B-25	RAF
Koepke, John Barth	6/13/1943	NP Windsor	A-30	RAF
Kreple, P.	7/18/1945	Cat I. Water East	PB4Y-2	USN
Krupica, Rupert	11/23/1943	Andros North	B-25	RAF
Lankford, Cyril I.	1/9/1944	Berry I. Sturrup Cay	B-24	USAAF
Lavoy, Eugene Wendall	7/10/1945	NP Water North	PBM-3	USN
Lewis, Robert Stanley	10/28/1944	NP Yamacraw, East Fox Hill	B-25	RAF
Lewis, Wesley Elliot	7/10/1945	NP Water North	PBM-3	USN
Lunam, Donald	4/21/1945	NP Water North	B-25	RAF
Lyons, Joseph Paul	5/30/1943	NP Airfield	A-30	RAF
MacDonald, John Blair	6/2/1945	NP Water	B-24	RAF
Mann, Walter	1/1/1943	Abaco Water Walkers Cay	B-26	USAAF
Mares, Jaroslav	8/7/1943	NP Windsor East	B-25	RAF
Martin, Paul D.	1/9/1944	Berry I. Sturrup Cay	B-24	USAAF
Mattingly, P. E.	7/18/1945	Cat I. Water East	PB4Y-2	USN
McArthur, James Brewer	6/13/1943	NP Windsor	A-30	RAF
McGowan, C. S.	7/18/1945	Cat I. Water East	PB4Y-2	USN
McLaughlin, D. G.	7/18/1945	Cat I. Water East	PB4Y-2	USN
McLean, J. C.	12/23/1943	NP Water East Booby	B-25	RAF
McLean, James Robert	6/21/1943	NP Water East	B-25	RAF
McLean, Robert Forrester	4/21/1945	NP Water North	B-25	RAF
Medos, Floyd J.	1/9/1944	Berry I. Sturrup Cay	B-24	USAAF
Meehan, Robert Paul	6/13/1943	NP Windsor	A-30	RAF
Meola, M. J.	7/18/1945	Cat I. Water East	PB4Y-2	USN
Mitchell, Carter	5/7/1943	Inagua	C-46	USAAF

Morris, William Frederick	3/28/1943	NP Windsor	A-30	RAF
Moule, Thomas	4/9/1945	NP Water North	B-25	RAF
Mulroy, Maurice R.	1/9/1944	Berry I. Sturrup Cay	B-24	USAAF
Neilson, John	6/2/1945	NP Water	B-24	RAF
Ogren, Carl Eric	6/28/1943	NP Water West Old Fort Bay	B-25	RAF
Oliver, Thomas C.	7/10/1945	NP Water North	PBM-3	USN
O'Neill, Maurice Francis	10/17/1944	NP Water Cable Beach	B-26	RAF
Owen, John Griffith	10/13/1943	NP Clifton Lyford	B-26	RAF
Parker, Kenneth Gordon	6/2/1945	NP Water	B-24	RAF
Pearce, Frederick Archibald	4/25/1944	Eleuthera Water North	B-24	RAF
Petersen, B. N.	12/23/1943	NP Water East Booby	B-25	RAF
Powell, Kenneth	4/25/1944	Eleuthera Water North	B-24	RAF
Rafuse, Cedric Cardiner	9/13/1943	NP Airfield	B-25	RAF
Reed, Charles T.	1/9/1944	Berry I. Sturrup Cay	B-24	USAAF
Richards, Geoffrey Edward Charles	2/23/1945	NP South, Yamacraw	B-25	RAF
Rusk, A. M.	11/24/1944	NP Water E Athol I.	B-25	RAF
Salz, Z. Karel	8/7/1943	NP Windsor East	B-25	RAF
Satola, Josef	8/7/1943	NP Windsor East	B-25	RAF
Savage, Andrew M.	1/9/1944	Berry I. Sturrup Cay	B-24	USAAF
Scammell, John	11/24/1944	NP Water E Athol I.	B-25	RAF
Schafer, Gordon Wellsley	4/9/1943	NP Clifton	B-25	RAF
Scott, Edward	4/9/1945	NP Water North	B-25	RAF
Seaforth, Stanley Henry	4/25/1944	Eleuthera Water North	B-24	RAF
Simandl, Josef	11/23/1943	Andros North	B-25	RAF
Slotwick, Bernard M.	7/10/1945	NP Water North	PBM-3	USN
Smart, Charles Leslie	6/28/1943	NP Water West Old Fort Bay	B-25	RAF
Smith, Kenneth Mortimer	4/21/1945	NP Water North	B-25	RAF
Smith, William Francis	4/25/1944	Eleuthera Water North	B-24	RAF
Sobolak, Franklin	6/22/1943	Grand Bahama Walkers Cay	OS2U-3	USN
Somerville, Cyril J.	5/30/1943	NP Airfield	A-30	RAF
Spiller, John William James	4/25/1944	Eleuthera Water North	B-24	RAF
Stessel, Isadore	7/19/1943	Cay Sal Bank	Blimp	USN

Stinson, William Lorne	6/28/1943	NP Water West Old Fort Bay	B-25	RAF
Strachan, Douglas	11/24/1944	NP Water E Athol I.	B-25	RAF
Strong, D. R.	7/18/1945	Cat I. Water East	PB4Y-2	USN
Styblik, Miloslav	11/23/1943	Andros North	B-25	RAF
Swinbanks, Joseph Hancock	6/2/1945	NP Water	B-24	RAF
Swire, W.	12/23/1943	NP Water East Booby	B-25	RAF
Takkurn, F. W.	7/18/1945	Cat I. Water East	PB4Y-2	USN
Thomas, William Vincent	5/21/1943	Andros North	B-25	RAF
Thomas, Peter Henry	4/25/1944	Eleuthera Water North	B-24	RAF
Thomas, William	11/24/1944	NP Water E Athol I.	B-25	RAF
Thompson	7/4/1945	Andros, N Morgans Bluff	B-24	RAF
Thomson, George Somerville	4/29/1943	NP Windsor	A-30	RAF
Tickler, John Earle	6/21/1943	NP Water East	B-25	RAF
Todd, Eric Douglas	5/21/1943	Andros North	B-25	RAF
Tomek, Hanus	11/23/1943	Andros North	B-25	RAF
Tomlinson, Arthur Ian	2/23/1945	NP South, Yamacraw	B-25	RAF
Tompkins, George William	4/9/1943	NP Clifton	B-25	RAF
Torrens, Arthur William	6/28/1943	NP Water West Old Fort Bay	B-25	RAF
Turna, Josef	8/7/1943	NP Windsor East	B-25	RAF
Vallance, John	6/21/1943	NP Water East	B-25	RAF
Wallace, Thomas	6/28/1943	NP Water West Old Fort Bay	B-25	RAF
Walmsley, Elwood Palmes	3/28/1943	NP Windsor	A-30	RAF
Waton, Alvin Bernard	4/9/1943	NP Clifton	B-25	RAF
Webb, Charles F.	1/9/1944	Berry I. Sturrup Cay	B-24	USAAF
White, J. B.	7/10/1945	NP Water North	PBM-3	USN
Wilcox, Thomas	6/13/1943	NP Windsor	A-30	RAF
Wilcox, A. J.	12/23/1943	NP Water East Booby	B-25	RAF
Wild, William	4/9/1945	NP Water North	B-25	RAF
Winder, Glen L.	7/10/1945	NP Water North	PBM-3	USN
Wood, John Walter	10/17/1944	NP Water Cable Beach	B-26	RAF
Woodeson, Leslie Somerville	10/28/1944	NP Yamacraw, East Fox Hill	B-25	RAF
Wororeck, Stephen	7/10/1945	NP Water North	PBM-3	USN

| Wyatt, Edward J. | 7/10/1945 | NP Water North | PBM-3 | USN |
| Zdan, Benjamin Henry | 3/19/1943 | NP Airfield | B-25 | RAF |

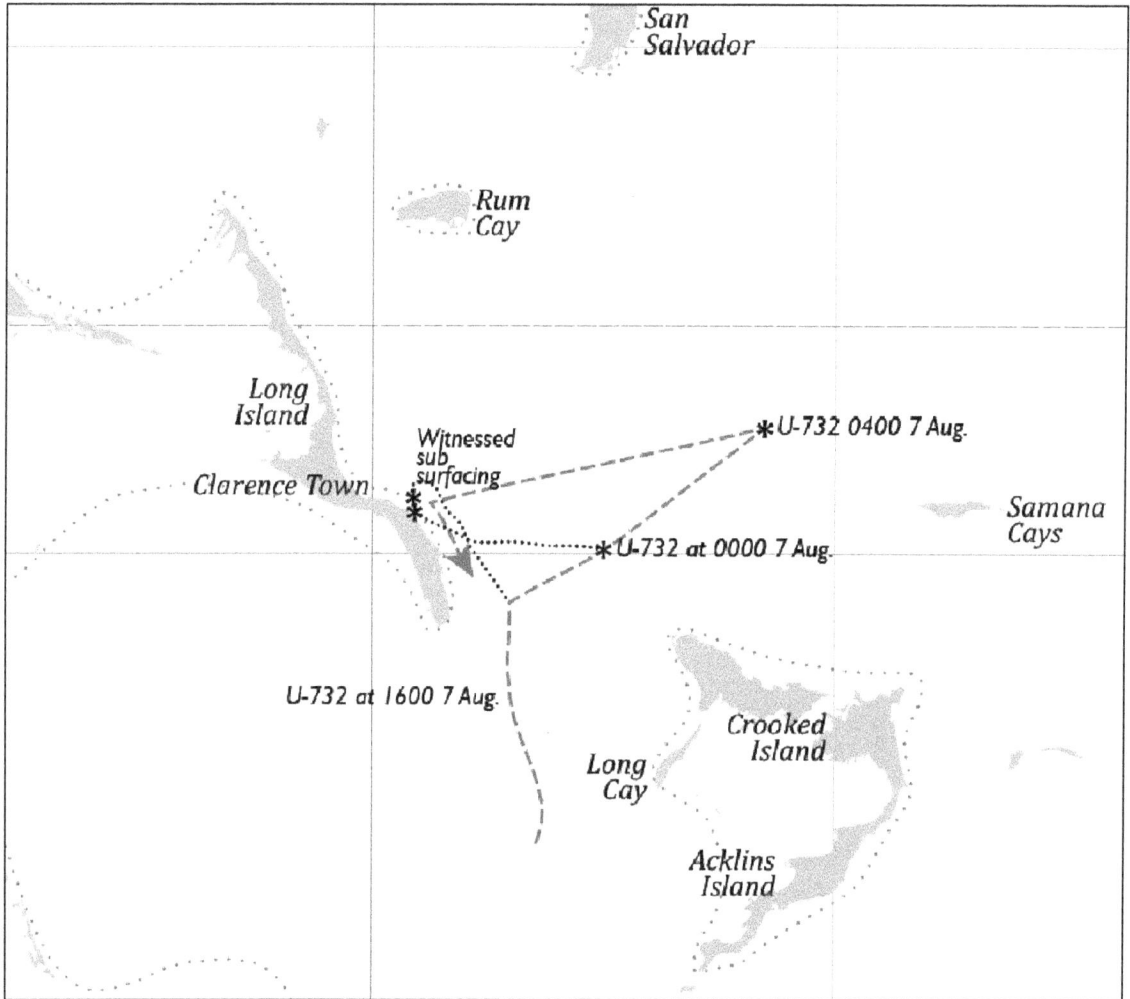

Chart showing the track of U-732 under Carlson as Ancil Rudolph Pratt and friends saw it pass Clarence Town, Long Island Bahamas as children.

Appendix 5: Portraits of Witnesses, Interviewees

Rev. Clerise Cox

Mr. Jonathan "Modi" Dean

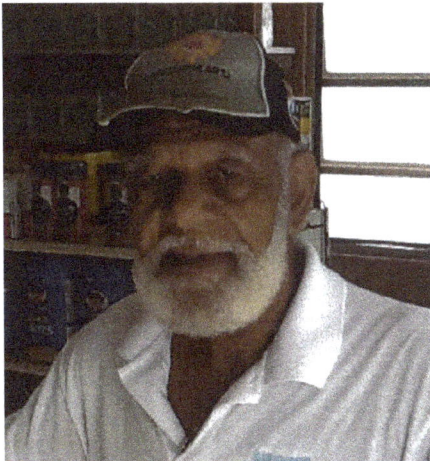

Ancil Rudolph Pratt, Long Island

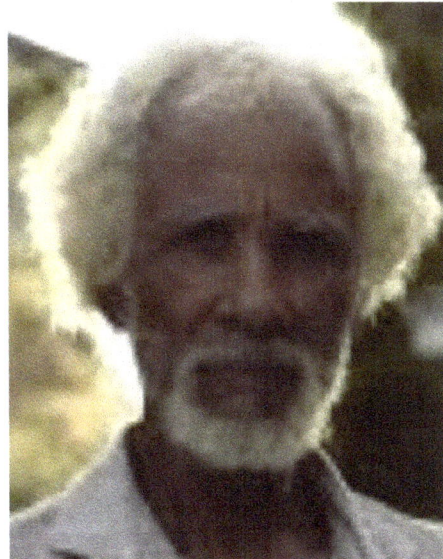

Capt. Edward Lockhart, Sr., Ragged Island

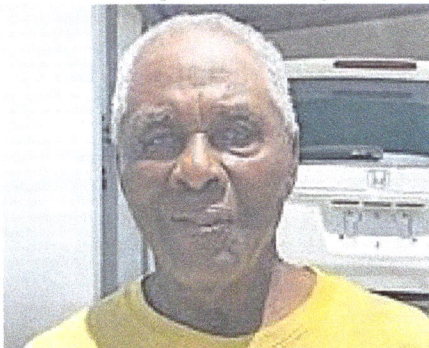

Williamson, Newton, Rev.

Interviewees & Sources

Caldoret, Brita, French artist, photographer journalist, southern Bahamian islands

Campbell, Carl, Rev., Minister and source

Forbes, Geoffrey and Mrs., lighthouse keeper and residents of Salina Point

Forbes, Rev. Rufus residents of Salina Point

Freundt, Rod, AUTEC Kids Facebook page, Andros

Grant, Robin, from Scotland; father served in OTU111, he visited Nassau

Green, Joanne of Green History Search in Guelph, Canada, niece of Jack Wood

Hanna, Stanford, resident of Pompey Bay, Acklins, Bahamas

Hubert, Ronan, Bureau of Aircraft Accidents Archives in Switzerland

Johnson, William R., Jr. (Uncle Bill), Abaco, artist, author, mentor, friend

Lockhart, Edward, Capt., of Ragged Island, ran mailboat *Emmett & Cephas*

Mitchell, Marcus, Eleuthera, former employer & mentor

Moxey, Capt. Joseph, Mango Creek, Andros, thanks to Rev. Carl Campbell

Phythian Mick, Dr., of York; father George was aircraftman on B-25's & ZNS, Nassau

Roker, Hon. Luftus A. resident of Pompey Bay, former member of parliament

Rolle, Rev. Felton, innkeeper, guide, host, friend

Spargur, Eddie, AUTEC Kids Facebook page administrator

Stowe, Michael, US, provided detailed reports of aircraft accident reports

Symonette, R. Craig, shipowner, expert historic craft, mentor

Taylors: Eddins, Limas, Elvin, & managers, officers, on shore, dock, on vessels

Tynes, Mrs. Iris, interviews and emails

Wallace, Phicol, expert on Ragged Island

Williamson, Newton, Rev., Hard Hill, Delectable Bay, Acklins

Wilson, Jacob, mariner, Ragged Island

Appendix 6: Sites in The Bahamas Today

New Providence:
- Montague & Clifton Bay search & rescue base docks, Montague Foreshore & Lyford Cay
- Clifton fuel depot and military sentry outpost, building remains visible, terminal docks
- *Aquamarine*, now Marley Resort, then home of Nepalese prince, Frank Christie
- Royal Nassau Yacht Club, site of accidents and R&R for crew
- Officer's Canteen, opposite fish fry, inland towards Ardastra Gardens
- Bahamas General Hospital, blended with modern buildings, Princess Margaret
- Windsor Field, now Sir Lynden O. Pindling International Airport, out buildings, roads
- Oakes Field, now behind the University of the Bahamas and RBDF and police bases
- Government House and nearby Christ Church Anglican Cathedral, George Street
- Amphibious aircraft ramp downtown Nassau, later Pan Am ramp, now RBDF, BASRA
- Commonwealth War (RAF) Cemetery, Farrington Road and Maxwell Lane
- IODE – Imperial Order of Daughters of Empire, now at Bahamas Historical Society
- St. Andrew's Presbyterian Kirk, Duke, Market, East Hill streets, and other churches
- Hotels: Windsor, British Colonial Hotel, Royal Victoria Hotel Annex is still standing, East Street & Shirley Street, Prince George, Lucerne Hotel (now a bank)

Eleuthera: Harbour Island ASR search and rescue base, and guest house for servicemen

Mayaguana: Remains of dock built by US Navy for search and rescue

Great Exuma: Amphibious aircraft docks and hangars built by US Navy NOB & NAS, fish fry

Long Island: Lochabar Bay, south of Clarence Town; Ancil Pratt saw U-732, Carlsen

Acklins Island: Grave of David Parson at Anderson, Hard Hill Church and school house used to accommodate the 47 survivors of SS *Potlatch* in August 1942 (church recently restored)

Abaco: Norwegian Olaus Johansen of *O. A. Knudsen* buried north of church ruins, Alexandra, Cross Harbour. Plinth commemorating *Daytonian* & *Athelqueen* survivors, Hope Town.

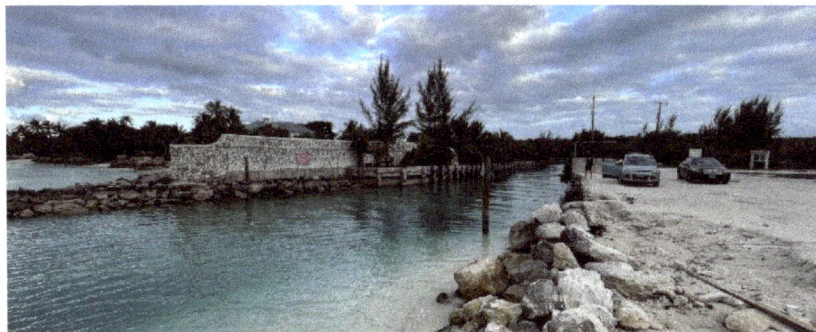

The RAF ASR, Air Search & Rescue boat base in the second, Clifton Bay Lyford Cay Canal, built by H. G. Christie before E. P. Taylor built the club. From this base hundreds of patrols and rescue missions were dispatched from RAF controllers in Windsor Field and Oakes Field during the war. Presently Jaws Beach, Clifton Drive.

A modern tanker approached Clifton Pier to discharge petroleum product for the Bahamas. Distilled spirits – mostly rum – are also exported from the facility which was the allied military's primary source of energy during the war and was carefully guarded. To some extent most of the far west of New Providence was inhabited and patrolled by the RAF.

Cable Beach Manor, built by the Count de Marigny from Mauritius in 1940. In 1943, de Marigny was banished from The Bahamas, and The Manor served as accommodation for RAF Officers. Later owners included Lord Brownlow, and ADC to the Duke of Windsor, Sir Victor Sassoon, of Hong Kong and Cable Beach, then in 1965 it was owned and operated by Jane and Anders Wiberg, the author's parents, until sold in 2018. It was razed in 2021.

An abandoned RAF outbuilding at Windsor Field near the modern national airport.

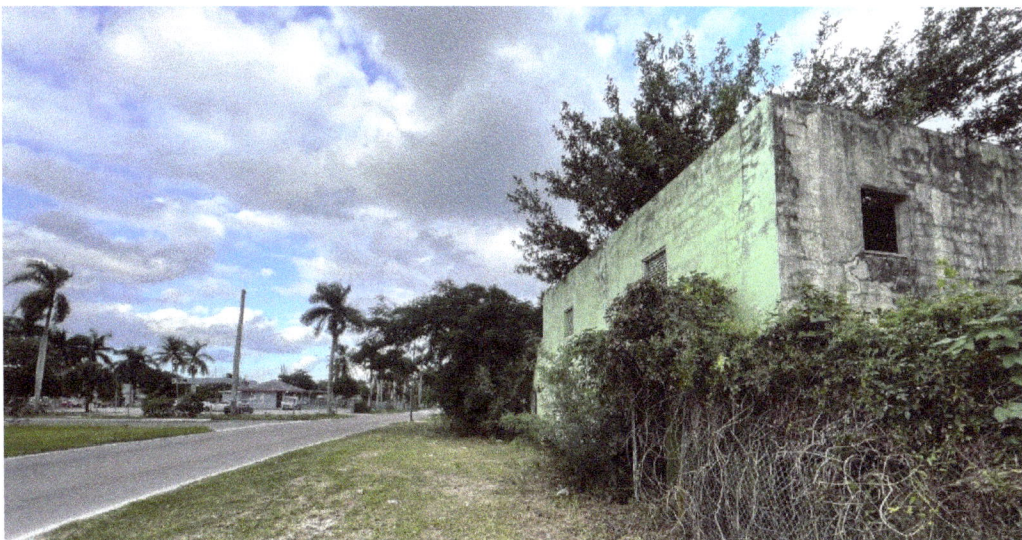

This building and related tanks and extensive pipes and filtration systems were undoubtedly part of a hydro engineering water treatment plant and many decades old and abandoned and very close to the entry to the former domestic terminal where the Taxis would gather. What is not verified is that this was all or RAF vintage, however it seems likely they were.

Historians work with the evidence they are provided. Capt. Paul Aranha suggested that this limestone wall, hand-hewn, "may" be of RAF and World War II vintage, and I am inclined to agree with him. Travelers who utilize the modern airport should recognize this wall connecting the abandoned

Sources & Further Reading

Books

Aranha, Paul C., *Bahamas Airways*, Heartland, Altona, Manitoba, Canada, 2017

Aranha, Paul C., *Island Airman and His Bahama Islands Home*, Media Enterprises Ltd., Bahamas, 2006

Archives Department, Ministry Education *Bahamas During World Wars 1914-18, 1939-45 1985* Department of Archives Exhibition Bahamas

Beruff, Jorge R., Bolivar Fresnada, Jose L. (Eds.) *Puerto Rico en la Segunda Guerra Mundial: Baluarte Del Caribe*, Ediciones Callejon, Libres en Navigante, Inc., San Juan, PR, 2012

Bethel, Tellis. A., Sr., *The Lucayan Islands* (Book 1 of 3), Inspire Publishing, Nassau, Bahamas, 2021

Bethel, Tellis. A., Sr., *The Lucayan Sea* (Book 2/3), Inspire Publishing, Nassau, Bahamas, 2021

Braman, Frederik A., Capt., USN (Ret.), *Cruising by Mailboat, History, Culture and Adventure in The Bahama Islands.*

Campbell, Douglas E., *VPNavy! USN, USMC, USCG and NATS Patrol Aircraft Lost or Damaged During World War II*, Listed by Bureau Numbers, Syneca Research Group, Inc., Southern Pines, NC, US, 2018

Carr, J. Revell, *All Brave Sailors: The Sinking of the Anglo-Saxon*, August 21, 1940, Simon & Schuster, New York, NY, US, 2004

Christie, Carl A., Ocean Bridge, *A History of RAF Ferry Command*, University of Toronto Press, Toronto, Ontario, Canada, 1995

Culmer Jenkins, Olga, Bahamian Memories, *Island Voices of the Twentieth Century*, University Press of Florida, Gainesville, FL, US, 2000

de Quesada, *Alejandro US Coast Guard in World War II,* Osprey Publishing/Random House, UK, 2010

Dean, Ernest Alexander & Woodcock, Gary W., *Island Captain: An Autobiography of a Mail Boat Captain*, White Sound Press, US, 1997

Dodge, Steve, *Abaco History of an Out Island and Its Cays*, 1984, White Sound Press, US

Eccles, Karen E., & McCollin, Debbie., *World War II and the Caribbean*, University of West Indies Press, Kingston, Jamaica, 2017

Eden, Paul, *The Encyclopedia of Aircraft MA of World War II*, Amber Books Ltd., London, UK, 2004 (2021)

Franks, Norman, Images of War, T*he RAF Air Sea Rescue Service in the Second World War*, Pen & Sword Aviation, Barnsley, South Yorkshire, UK, 2016

Gomez Alvarez Maximo, *U-Boats Del III Reich en Cuba* , Carmelo Segura Y. M. A Eugenia Glez. Cintas, Spain, 2009

Griffiths, Geraint, *Into the Blue Diary of RAF Bahamas 1943-45,* lulu.com POD, US, 2009.

Helleberg Fields, Meredith, Ed., *Yachtsman's Guide to the Bahamas*, Tropic Isle Publishers, Inc., Miami, FL, US, 1998 et. al.

Johnson, David Alan, *Yanks in the RAF*, Prometheus Books, Amherst, NY, US, 2015

Johnson, William R. Jr., *Bahama Tales*, With Illustrations by the Author, Lubbers Quarters, Abaco, Bahamas, 2019

Kelshall, Gaylord T. M. *U-Boat War in the Caribbean, 1988/94*, NIP Naval Institute Press US

Klingel, Gilbert, Inagua, *An Island Sojourn*, Lyons & Burford, Guilford, CT, US, 1940, 1997

Lake, Alan, *Flying Units of the RAF,* Airlife Publishing Ltd., Shrewsbury, England, UK, 1999

Lawson, Robert, & Tillman, Barrett, *U.S. Navy Air Combat, 1939-1946*, MBI Publishing Co., Osceola, WI, US, 2000

Lightbourn, Ronald G., *Reminiscing: Photographs of Old Nassau* Vol. II, 2005, Ronald G. Lightbourn, US

Lloyd, Jane, *History of the I.O.D.E. in the Bahamas, 1901-2005*, 2016, Media Enterprises Ltd., Bahamas

Moseley-Moss, Valeria, *Reminiscing: Memories of Old Nassau,* 1999, Ronald G. Lightbourn, Bahamas

Munnings, Harold Alexander Jr. (MD), *Healthcare in the Bahamas,* 2014, Media Enterprises Ltd., Bahamas

Nautical Publications, *Central Bahamas Andros to Exuma Eleuthera*, Maptech Inc., US, 2003.

Nautical, Publications, *Northwest Bahamas Bimini & Berry Abaco*, Nautical Publications GmbH, Germany, 2004.

Neely, Wayne, *The Major Hurricanes to Affect the Bahamas: Personal Recollections of Some of the Greatest Storms to Affect the Bahamas*, Authorhouse, Bahamas, 2006

Partridge, Ewan, & Singfield, Tom, *Wings Over Bermuda, 100 Years of Aviation in the West Atlantic,* National Museum of Bermuda Press, Hamilton, Bermuda, 2014

Parker, Philip M., *Bahamas: Webster's Timeline History 1492-2007*, ICON Group International, US, 2009

Pearce-Jones, Guy, *Two Survived: 70 Days at Sea in Open Boat*, Lyons/Globe Pequot, US, 1940, (1976)

Pearcy, Arthur, Lend-Lease *Aircraft in World War II,* Airlife Publishing Ltd., Shrewsbury, England, UK, 1996

Peggs, Deans A., PhD., *A Short History of the Bahamas*, The Deans Peggs Research Fund, *The Nassau Tribune*, Nassau, N.P., Bahamas, and The Crown Agents, London, UK, 1951

Popov, Nicolas & Dragan, Children of the Sea: Exploring Diversity in the Bahamas, 1988-2000, MacMillan Education Ltd., UK, 2000

Rigg, J. Linton, *Bahama Islands*, D. Van Norstrand Co., Inc., New York, NY, US, 1949

Roberts, Richard Campbell, & Malone, Shelley Boyd, *Nostalgic Nassau, Picture Postcards, 1900-1940,* Nassau Nostalgia, Nassau, N.P., Bahamas, 1991

Rodriguez, Ruth, *Out Island Portraits*, 1946-1956, 1978, Out Island Press, US

Russell, Joe, *Last Schoonerman: The Life of Captain Lou Kenedy*, Nautical Publishing, Far Horizons, US, 2006

Saunders, Gail & Craton, Michael, *Islanders in the Stream* Vol. 2 End of Slavery-2000, University of Georgia Press, US, 2000

Sturtivant, Ray, Hamlin, John, & Halley, James J., R*oyal Air Force Flying Training and Support Units*, An Air-Britain, Upper Norwood, London, UK, 1997

Sherwood, Martyn, *Voyage of the Tai-Mo-Shan*, 1957, Rupert Hart-Davis, UK

Summerscale, Kate, *The Queen of Whale Cay*, 2008, Bloomsbury, Viking, Penguin, UK

Thompson, R. Chester, *The Long Day Wanes: A Memoir of Love and War*, 2006, White Sound Press

Turnquest, Orville, *What Manner of Man is This?,* Grant's Town Press, Bahamas, 2016

Waters, Sydney D., *Ordeal by Sea: New Zealand Shipping Company*, New Zealand Shipping Co. Ltd., New Zealand, 1949

Werner, Herbert A. *Iron Coffins Personal Account of U-Boat WWII* 1969 De Capo Press US

Wiberg, Eric:
> *Åke Wiberg*, Island Books, Boston, MA, 2019
> *Bahamas in World War II: A Chronology, 1939-1945*, Island Books, Boston, MA, 2021
> *U-Boats in the Bahamas*, Island Books, New York, NY, 2015
> *Drifting to the Duchess* (unpublished), Island Books, Boston, MA, US, 2019
> *Mailboats of the Bahamas*, Island Books, Boston, MA, 2020
> *Swan Sinks*, Island Books, Boston, MA, US, 2017

Williams, Darius D., *Rail & Locomotive History of the Bahamas*, White Sound Press, US, 200

Winchester, Jim, *Military Aircraft,* Visual Encyclopedia, Amber Books, London UK, 2009 (2022)

Wynn, Kenneth, *U-boat Operations of the Second World War*, Volume 1 and Volume 2, 1997

Wynne, Lewis N., *Florida at War*, Saint Leo College Press, US, 1993

Young, Everild, *Eleuthera: An Island Called Freedom*, 1966, Regency Press, UK

Zamoyski, Adam, *The Forgotten Few; The Polish Air Force in the Second World War*, Hippocrene Books, New York, 1995

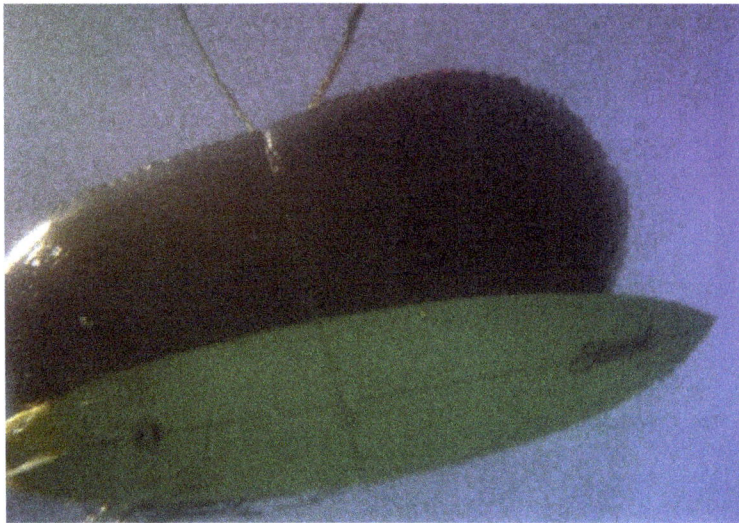

An amateur's concept of heavy-metal salvage equipment; a surfboard and a pool raft. Even together they did not achieve the function. Correct equipment matters.

Primary Sources

The five primary sources for the Daily Diaries Section were:

- o Operational Record Books (ORB) for RAF No. 111 O.T.U., Windsor Field, Nassau
- o Operational Record Books (ORB) for RAF No. 113 Transport Wing, Oakes Field,
- o Gulf Sea Frontier, 7th & 8th US Navy Naval District, Commander, from Sept. 1942
- o Eastern Sea Frontier, temporary USN Defense of East Coast, Dec. 1941-Apr. 1942
- o Base Diaries, all iterations of NAS Great Exuma: NAS, NAF, NAAF, 1942-1945

1) ORBs for RAF 111 O.T.U., Windsor Field, Nassau

Operational Record Books (ORBs) of RAF No. 111 O.T.U., Nassau are kept in The National Archives in Kew, England, outside London. Since these thousands of pages are the bedrock of this book and the reader will naturally wish to know more. I provide the full citations given by professional UK researcher Simon Fowler, author of dozens of books: Summary of Operations Record Books (ORBs) for RAF No. 111 O.T.U. at TNA.: As one group: AIR 29/689, Form 540: Narrative (and unusually detailed) account of the Unit 1942-1945. AIR 29/690 Appendices: 1943 March-July, AIR 29/691: Appendices: 1943 August-December, AIR 29/692, Appendices: 1942 January-June, AIR 29/693 Appendices: 1944 July-December. AIR 29/694: Appendices: 1945 January-August. These are Form

Orange; and are all summaries of sorties [missions] flown by individual aircraft. These reports

are rather uninformative as they mainly consist of navigational details in code. AIR 29/695: Appendices: 1943-1945. These are training syllabuses; details of students; administrative orders, etc. Note: More may be learned by visiting Discovery.nationalarchives.gov.uk. A copy of the complete ORB for 111 O.T.U. has been given digitally and in paper form to the National Archives of the Bahamas for reference.

2) ORBs for RAF 113 Transport Wing, Oakes Field, Nassau. Operational Record Books (ORBs) of RAF No. 113 (Transport) Wing, Oakes Field, Nassau are kept in The National Archives in Kew, England, outside London. It is believed that they, like No. 111 O.T.U., are kept in the AIR 29 group with other RAF records, however this is unconfirmed. Professional UK researcher Simon Fowler, copied them. The reports were originally sent to regional headquarters at the air field in Dorval, Quebec, Canada, near Montreal. There were frequent flights transporting aircraft as well as personnel, between the bases. RAF No. 113 Wing was not in existence long yet they transported thousands of planes around the world on a route southeast of Bahamas to Trinidad, Brazil, Africa and beyond. Note: More may be learned by visiting Discovery.nationalarchives.gov.uk or

contacting Simon Fowler at thesimonfowler@gmail.com.

3) Daily War Diary of Gulf Sea Frontier [GSF], 7th & 8th US Navy Naval District. Located in the National Archives and Records Administration complex in College Park, Maryland, I discovered these on-site while researching U-Boats in the Bahamas in 2009. The first entry can describe them all and reads "Beginning this date, September 14, 1942, the War Diary will include daily maps showing operations a 1200 noon EWT in the Gulf Sea Frontier." On the front is a very detailed chart with color arrows covering the entire Gulf of Mexico, Yucatan Peninsula, and, relevant to this book, the ocean from Havana to Guantanamo, to Key

West to the border of Florida and Georgia. The area specifically covered in a triangle extending east from Florida extends from south of Cay Sal Bahamas, east to the southern tip of Cat Island, and all of the waters north and northeast of Grand Bahamas, Walkers Cay, Abaco, and Eleuthera, In short it covers the Nicholas Channel, the Straits of Florida, the entire east coast of Florida including the Florida Cays.

A "Legend" provides a match to the arrows which covers movements and directions of all vessels, military and civilian, as well as their escorts, air, fixed wing and blimp or airship, and watercraft. It is extremely handy, simple to read and understand, clear and concise and an invaluable tool. Every relevant word and activity have been typed into this study. Note: These documents may be obtained on the site Fold3.com for a fee, or using a professional research firm such as Westmoreland Research, or by visiting NARA near Washington, DC, or by pursuing this link, which they sent:
catalog.archives.gov/id/521028 (which refers specifically to photographs only.

They ought to be with Survivor Statements in the series: Papers of Vice Admiral Homer N. Wallin, compiled 1941 - 1974. Record Group 38: Records of the Office of the Chief of Naval Operations, 1875 - 2006 Entry P-13. National Archives at College Park - Textual Reference (Military) 8601 Adelphi Road, College Park, MD, USA 20740.

4) Daily War Diary of the Eastern Sea Frontier [ESF], US Navy, Dec. 1941-Apr. 1942. This was a short-lived Diary, yet it is filled with the panic, confusion, and dismay of de-facto defeat as the US forces struggle to even understand the extend, veracity and location and capabilities of an enemy they clearly barely understood in the January to April 1942 timeframe while they finally adjusted, in time for the German to go elsewhere to softer targets. As a practical matter, by far the easiest and most cost-efficient method is to visit the entire set, type-set and uploaded by Capt. Jerry Mason (USN, Ret.) and Mrs. Charla Mason at Uboatarchive.net/ESF/ ESFWarDiaryDec41.htm. Officially known as the Eastern Sea Frontier Enemy Action and Distress Diary, these are kept at NARA, outside DC. Department of the Navy. Office of the Chief of Naval Operations. Naval Observatory. 1942-9/18/1947 Record Group 80: General Records of the Department of the Navy, 1804 to 1983.

Note: These documents may be obtained on the site Fold3.com for a fee, or using a professional research firm such as Westmoreland Research, or by visiting NARA near Washington, DC. See also history.navy.mil, archives.gov, an overview is at RG 181 - Naval Districts and Shore Establishments, General Correspondence, Sixth Naval District at Charleston, South Carolina. They ought to be with Survivor Statements in the series: Papers of Vice Admiral Homer N. Wallin, compiled 1941 - 1974. Record Group 38: Records of the Office of the Chief of Naval Operations, 1875 - 2006 Entry P-13. National Archives at College Park - Textual Reference (Military) 8601 Adelphi Road, College Park, MD, USA 20740.

5) Base Diaries for iterations of NAS Great Exuma: NAS, NAF, and NAAF, 1942-1945 Fold3.com in under War Diaries, World War II, 1942 – 1945, and NOB Guantanamo Bay records as well, since NAS, NAF and NAAF mostly reported to NOB Guantanamo.

Articles, Magazines, Booklets, & Pamphlets

Journal of the Bahamas Historical Society:
Aircraft Accident in Bahamas in World War II, Eric Wiberg, Nassau, Bahamas, 2023
Drifting to Duchess Potlatch Carstairs, Eric Wiberg, Nassau, Bahamas, 2015
 U-Boats in the Bahamas, Eric Wiberg, Nassau, Bahamas, 2009
 Bahamas in World War II, Eric Wiberg, Nassau, Bahamas, 2021
Corbeil, Shannon; *Mighty History, Nylon: the reason we won World War II, and started shaving our legs*, April 29, 2020
Heichelbech, Rose, *The Parachute Wedding Dresses of the 1940s Were Really Something Else;* dustyoldthing.com/wwii-parachute-wedding-dresses, 2022 Great Life Publishing
Sundin, Sarah, Aug. 2, 2021, *Make It Do – Stocking Shortages in World War II* sarahsundin.com/make-it-do-stocking-shortages-in-world-war-ii/
Bahamas Historical Society (as publisher):
Pullinger, Diana, artist, Lawlor Jim, text, and Lightbourne, Ronald G., The History of the Bahamas in Pictures, Media Enterprises, Ltd., Nassau, N.P., 2012
Nassau, Bahamas, 1823-4, The Diary of a Physician from the United States visiting the Island of New Providence, Her Majesty's Printers, London, UK, 1968
Department of Archives, Ministry of Education and Culture, The Boat-Building Industry of the Bahamas, Department of Archives Exhibition, 1981, Nassau, N.P., Bahamas
Department of Archives, Ministry of Education and Culture, Bahamas During the World Wars: 1914-18, 1939-45, Department of Archives Exhibition, Nassau, N.P., Bahamas, 1985
Dupuch, Publications, Bahamas Handbook and Businessman's Annual, 1992, various years,
Aranha, Paul C.; Index of all *Bahamas Handbook* articles, Bahamas Historical Society, National Archives
Johnson, William R. Jr., Seapath Bahama Notes & Other Stories, 2003, Tortuga Productions, Bahamas
Nielsen, Jon & Nielsen, Kay, The Bahama Book, A History of the Bahamas from Columbus to the Present (pamphlet), Voyager Press, Dobbs Ferry, NY, US, 1966
Popov, Nicolas & Popov, Dragan:
Island Expedition: Central, Southern Bahamas, Nassau, N.P., Bahamas, 1988
Island Expedition: School at Sea, Nassau, N.P., Bahamas, 1997
Island Expedition: School at Sea Experience, Nassau, N.P., Bahamas, 1994
Wiberg, Eric:
A History of Bahamian Mailboats, 1804 to Present, Powerships, Magazine of Engine-Power Vessels, Steamship Historical Society of America, Warwick, RI, Fall, 2016, p.36
U-Boats in the Bahamas, Journal of the Bahamas Historical Society, Vol. 31, Oct. 2009, p.65
Drifting to Duchess, Potlatch *Carstairs*, Bahamas Historical Society Journal, 2015

Articles in the International Press

The Nassau Tribune Series, Eric Wiberg, bi-weekly column, podcasts, March-Dec., 2023:

Part V: *The Last Flight of a Marauder*, Friday, May 19, 2023
http://www.tribune242.com/news/2023/may/19/eric-wiberg-last-flight-marauder/

Part IV: *20 Accidents at Sea off New Providence*, Friday, May 5, 2023, tribune242.com/news/2023/may/05/eric-wiberg-20-accidents-sea-new-providence/

Part III: *New Providence, 60 Land Accidents*, Friday, April 21, 2023, http://www.tribune242.com/news/2023/apr/21/eric-wiberg-new-providence-60-land-accidents/

Part II: *Wives and bases*, Tuesday, March 24 2023,
http://www.tribune242.com/news/2023/mar/24/eric-wiberg-wives-and-bases/

Part I: *The story of the aircraft lost in The Bahamas*, Friday March 10, 2023,
http://www.tribune242.com/news/2023/mar/10/story-aircraft-lost-bahamas/

INSIGHT: *Acklins gives up its WW2 secrets - in just a few hours*, The Nassau Tribune, August 15, 2022, http://www.tribune242.com/news/2022/aug/15/insight-acklins-gives-its-ww2-secrets-just-few-hou/

INSIGHT: Stories uncovered from the global conflict which touched our shores, *The Nassau Tribune*, Monday, July 4, 2022, http://www.tribune242.com/news/2022/jul /04/insight-stories-uncovered-global-conflict-which-to/

Airmen Mystery Solved, The Nassau Tribune, June 9, 2022,
https://ericwiberg.com/2022/06/nassau-tribune-airmen-mystery-solved

CBC News Canadian Broadcasting Corp., *How a persistent diver in the Bahamas solved a WW II mystery involving a Halifax pilot: B-26 Marauder flown by 2 Canadians in late 1944 crashed off the Bahamas and wasn't found until recently*, Richard Woodbury, Posted: Jun 06, 2022 5:00

Halifax Chronicle, John Demont, *A Bahamian man helps solve a 77-year-old Halifax mystery*, Posted: April 13, 2022, 5:44 a.m.

World War II artifacts donated to the Antiquities, Monuments & Museum Corporation, The Nassau Guardian, February 4, 2022, https://thenassauguardian.com/world-war-ii-artifacts-donated-to-the-antiquities-monuments-museum-corporation/

All articles are available at https://ericwiberg.com/

Websites

Abacoforum.com
AFHRA.af.mil
Aircrewremembered.com
Aircrew-Saltire.org
AirForce.mil.nz
ammcbahamas.com
Ancestry.com
AWM.gov.au
Bahamasferries.com
BahamasNationalArchives.bs
Bradford-marine.com
Convoyweb.org.uk
Crewlist.org.uk
Discovery.nationalarchives.gov.uk
Dupuch.com
Equasis.org
Ericwiberg.com
Facebook.com (groups, travel blogs, etc.)
Findagrave.com
Fold3.com
Google Earth
Gosur.com
Historianaval.org
History.Navy.mil
History.USCG.mil
IWM.org.uk
Littlehousebytheferry.com (Green Turtle Cay blog by Amanda Diedrick)
Marinetraffic.com

Masterbombercraig.wordpress.com
Meandthesea.com (AIDHNC, Cuba)
Media.Defense.gov
Navsource.org (am a contributor)
Newspaperarchives.com
NMB.bm
Number59squadron.com
NYTimes.com
Oldbahamas.com
PBHitoryonline.org
RAFCommands.com
RAFcrewremembered.com
RAFMuseum.org.uk
Sshsa.org (Steamship Historical Society)
Thenassauguardian.com
Therumelier.com (historic photos)
Theshipslist.com
Tore Pa Sporet, Tv.nrk.no
Tribune242.com
Uboat.net
Uboatarchive.net
Ufdc.ufl.edu (Bahamian news digital archive)
Warsailors.com
Whatsonbahamas.com
Wikipedia.org
Worldnavalships.com
Wrecksite.eu

Indices

Aircraft & Vessel Index

General Index

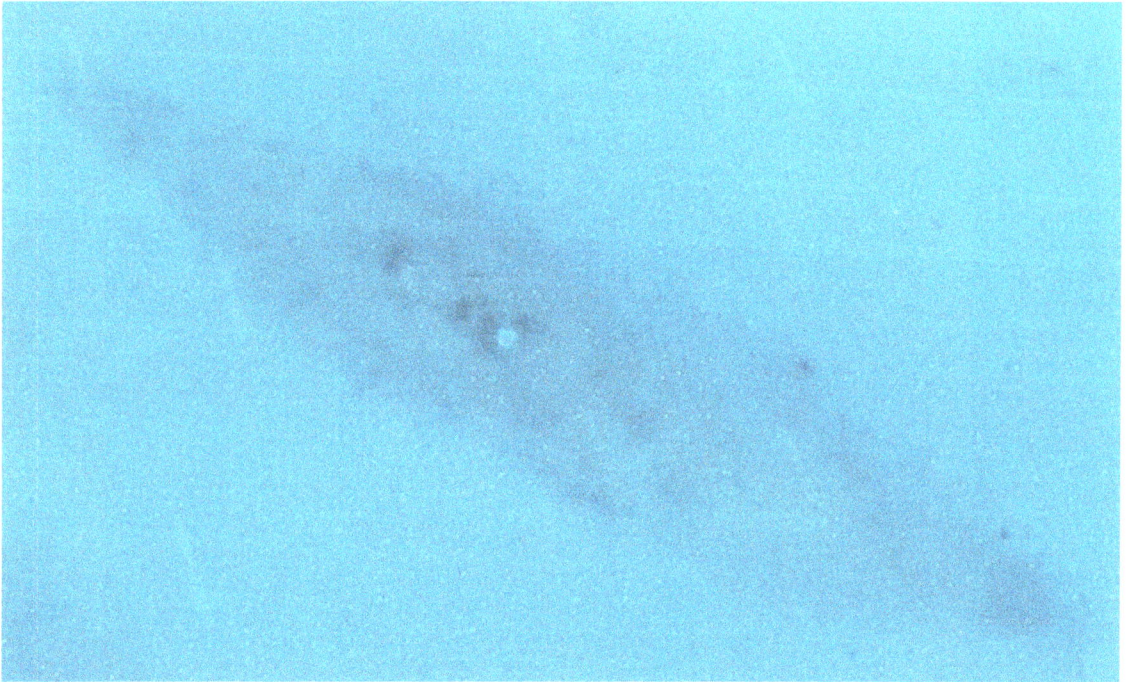

Two Erics were once convinced this was a battleship, submarine or warship lost in the Bahamas. So, after many months of preparation, they set out to find out – it was reef. Not only does this prove that all that glitters is not gold, but also that exertion does not always equate to reward.

Acknowledgements

The one person who made the most adjustments and performed the most yeoman's duty without getting credit is Caitlin. She held down the fort in Boston during at least eight trips to Bahamas in a year, some for a night, yet twice for a month. While I was off sailing and finding planes in Bahamas all of January into early February 2023, Caitlin was moving her parents out of their home and, without any help, putting furniture and thousands of books into a station wagon to cart them up four flights to our apartment in East Boston. For this I feel she deserves a medal and I am certainly grateful for her hard work and eternal good cheer, and for making our home so wonderful in such a short time while juggling so much else personally and professionally. Thank you, Caitlin.

I thank Anders Wiberg (our papa) for always encouraging and supporting me. Furthermore, in Canada I thank genealogist and family of deceased pilot, Jack Wood, and Joanne Green. Though we had not met, she provided very good safety advice during the frenetic, first search phase when no one knew the original purpose, but most would reasonably have doubted the potential outcome. Abdul Rehman Qureshi, founder of Writing Panacea, has been Island Books' chief of operations since 2017. His and Joanne's skills allow me to focus on field research and meaningful writing.

For safety in the field, I often had a companion; I especially thank Jay Marley, John Wiberg, Toby Smith, Charlie Affel, Howard Story, Phicol Wallace, AJ Davis, James Owsley, Rich Ashman, Denis Galipeau, Henrik Gedde Moos, Tony Jermyn, Patrick McGarry, and Renardo D'Arville. The thing about having a wingman is knowing that they will have your back and come and rescue you. Research took place primarily in The Bahamas, UK, US, Canada, and Australia. In the UK, researchers were Carolyn Beckingham, Simon Fowler, Hywel Maslen, and others at RAF Herndon, The National Archives and the Imperial War Museum. Moreover, in London: Lukas Kolff of Bowline Capital; and Nick Fragel, Oxford schoolmate, formerly RAF; and Shona Nicholson at Harris Manchester College, Oxford.

In Nassau, my family and broad support network includes Commander Tellis Bethel, the owners of marinas, boats, hotel/resorts, car rentals, provisioners, my dad for a place to stay, the Orange Hill Resort, Traveler's Rest, Dragan and Nicolas Popov, and my shipmates at Island Expedition who taught me how to interview for oral history. Dr. Harold Alexander Munnings, Jr., and Wayne Nealy, PhD. shared their local expertise.

The local historical community has helped me immensely, including Andrea Major at The Bahamas Historical Society, Jane Lloyd at the IODE, Archivist Leshelle Delaney at the National Archives of The Bahamas, the Willamae Johnson, librarian, and Brendamae Cleare, president, at LJM Maritime Academy, filmmaker Kareem Mortimer, and Dr. Grace Turner and Dr. Chris Curry at the Antiquities, Monuments, and Museums Corporation (AMMC) of The Bahamas, and the leaders of Bahamas Maritime Pilots Association. At *The Nassau Tribune*, to which I have contributed since the 1980s, I thank Editor-in-Chief, Eugene Duffy (RIP) and Stephen Hunt. Several research clients in The Bahamas helped me indirectly and I thank them for their effort. I particularly thank author, historian, mentor Jim Lawlor who hosted my first talk in Nassau and penned a Foreword.

Longtime friends and mentors including Capt. Nigel Bower, Capt. Alan Wardle, Stuart Cove, Lars Carroll, Marcus Mitchell, Stephen Connett, Craig Symonette, Mr. Kendal S. Butler, Capt. Daniel Murray, Marcus Davis and Siren Waerland Davis, Tore Strømøy, Sten Kittelsen, Ian Duthie, Paul Clouting, Godfrey Kelly, Tom Lacy, Jerry Albury, Bjorn Wennerlund, Jerry Albury, Leonardo Ferrisi, D. Sean Nottage, Tim Farrell, Capt. Alexandra Hagerty, Capt. Jim McNamara, Gillian Smith, David Northrup, David Poissant, Dr. Dan Desko, Earl McMillen, Matt, Mike, Bev, and the Oldport Marine team, Capt. Taylor of the *Rookie,* John D. McCown, Lemmie Malcolm, Nikki at the RBYC, Phoebe Hunt & Garry Maidment at *TIDE*, Cory Silken, Jim Fay, Lou Chorney, Kirby Aarsheim, John Appleton, Jonathan Winthrop, Jeff Kimball, Tyson Goodridge, Valerie Simpson, Alan Sutton, John Beard, Fred Hall, Dr. Bob Arnot, Jennifer Malcolm Gerber, Cookie Ross, Robert Moore, and Michael Carvalho, and Kimberly King-Burns, who contributed to my efforts to get to the bottom of nearly 200 mysteries. Doug Campbell, who dug deep to volunteer extraordinary levels of details on US aircraft lost in Bahamas deserves special recognition. Maritime lawyer Patrick Geraghty and Ken Bodnar were instrumental at tracking living relatives of deceased pilots—a thankless and difficult task.

While mentioned elsewhere, those who have owned a vessel recognize what a leap of faith it is to lend or operate and contribute it to volunteers with no certain outcome. I especially would thank those nine individuals who did so. On New Providence my thanks to Amanda Lindroth, *Schooner Queen*, John Wiberg, *Shoal Shaker,* Rich Ashman, *Kimber-L,* Denis Galipeau, Ulric Williams, *Yisel,* and Toby Smith, *Da Skiff.*

For an entire month, my shipmate from *War Baby* in 1992, Howard Story, generously put his 59' Hinckley sloop known as *Parole* at the team's disposal, and we covered 1,200 miles trying to solve six aircraft losses. Thank you, Howard. For a voyage to the White Banks north of the Exumas, I thank Eric Cottell in *TT Providence,* and for meeting us at anchor, showing us directly to an aircraft, and generously supplying us with ice and other victuals; we are all indebted to the entrepreneur, hotelier, and guide Phicol Wallace of the *Lost Key* on Great Ragged Island.

Jean Cote and Suzanne Cote were very helpful in connecting me with experienced artifact researchers amongst the expatriate community in Nassau, for which I am grateful. Mike and Meredith Cassidy, Rick Olney, and the Dawicki family at Northeast Maritime Institute have been encouraging and helpful.

In Canada—in particular Winnipeg, Halifax, Guelph, and Yellowknife, I have been provided wonderful volunteerism and support, importantly from numerous aircraft and aviation history libraries and museums in New Zealand, France, the US, UK, and Canada. I approached every major historic aircraft collection from the Smithsonian's National Air and Space Museum in DC, the National Museum of the US Air Force in Dayton, Ohio, and all of them were very supportive and helpful.

Since I focused on finding all three B-26 Marauders within reach in Bahamas, Kermit Weeks at *Fantasy of Flight* in Polk City, Florida and his team stand out as being exceptionally helpful and inspiring. As he owns the only one airworthy in the world, he even offered me a flight someday. For the wonderful custom-crafted charts, I thank Robert Eller Pratt, a veteran of several decades as a cartographer with *National Geographic.* Since we first worked together roughly 15 years ago Bob's work has made my efforts shine miraculously!

The crew aboard Howard's *Parole (*fka *Mary Sunshine,* fka *Carpe Mañana* as it wended its way from Florida to Maine, then, with me to Bermuda, thereafter Florida, Bahamas, and the Gulf of Mexico included Charles Affel, Patrick McGarry, James Owsley, Tony Jermyn, Leland Dickson, and a few others who helped me out, including Woody. Kent and Petra P.'s visit was very inspiring. I thank Patrick Ogden, Donna Spellman, Peter Cavanaugh, Devin, Joseph, Peter, Alex, and the rest of the Harbour Court team. I thank Merrill Charette, Joshua Levine, Mark Hollingsworth, Mike Smith of B-26 group, Alan R. Crouchman (*Flak Bait*) and Norman Wells of *FlyPast* for their contribution. I am indebted for his interest in my books to BPG.

I am always grateful to an indefatigable support network of friends and family, including Cameron Burrard Clark, Team Fitz (Geoff, Diane), Team Webster (Lora,

Jason, Nate the Great, Abigail, Mia & Graydon), my siblings James, Ann, John, Atle & Gustaf, Lynette, Sofia, and Satu, the McDermids, John & Terrell, Gray & Eve, Fran & Sylvia, Ralph, Mark, Jill, Hoke, Margaret, Tim F., Wickes H., and Kathy Karch and the Pingree family. In Long Island, I'm grateful for Ancil Rudolph Pratt, Angelique, and in research circles; Rainer at Uboat.net, Crewlist.org, artist James Parker Sr., and Jerry & Charla Mason. I also thank Frank, Tom, and friends at the Newburyport Airport as well as the Beverly Massachusetts and Newport Rhode Island municipal airfields, where I spent brief stints watching aircraft and studying their oleo struts to help us identify what we had found.

Individuals whose contributions I wish to recognize include: Rev. Felton Rolle, Rev. Carl Campbell, Capt. Joseph Moxey, Rev. Rufus Forbes, Geoffrey Forbes, Heather Forde Prosa, Capt. J. J. Williams, Macintosh at Marley resort, the family of owners at Nesbitt's, Stephen Smollett, Dr. Michael Pateman, Angela Carroll, Kate Crane, Maria Govan, and my mentor Bill Johnson. Also, I thank the Lands and Surveys Department, Kimberly King-Burns, Dr. James Delgado, and John & Paola Christie. I thank Ann & Peo Rosendahl, Gillian Byles, Capt. Jerry Mason, Michael Barnette, Brock Turner, Steamship Historical Society of the US, Propeller Club of Boston, Manchester Harbor Boat Club, Claire and Sam Cabot, the NYYC Library's Vanessa Cameron, Heather Bain at The Explorers Club and Dickie Bennett of Breaking Ground Heritage in the UK. On the film side in L.A. and New York I extend thanks to Bryan Kestner, Ariel Brozell, Benjamin Stephen, Kevin Delaney and others mentioned herein.

My appreciation to the Dean family of Sandy Point Abaco, Capt. Fred Braman, Rabbi Sholom Bluming, and those who sell my books: Captain's Table, Marci Bond, Princess Street Gallery, and Logos Books. I thank Capt. Roger in Exuma, and many others who answered questions and acted as a guide for me. For help diving on the B-26 wreck in Delaporte Bay, I thank Saoirse Wiberg, Åke Wiberg, Henrik Wiberg (beloved godson), Oliver Wiberg, and our mother, Jane McDermid Wiberg, who taught us to never give up. I appreciate childhood swimming companions Anthony Wilkinson and Frank Baensch. I benefited from the supportive teams at both nautical shops in Sandyport and Cable Beach shopping centers. Meyers' sporting goods were helpful with selling underwater cameras and recommending someone locally who could develop the film.

In Acklins, and responsible for overall management of my frenetic August 2022 visit, was Rev. Felton Rolle. I thank all those in the Pompey Bay community, Rev. Rufus Forbes, Geoffrey Forbes, Constable Forbes, Nicole Fair, Kent Post, Rev. Newton

Williamson, authors; sailors Mari and Fritz Dahmler; German journalists Karolina Kijek and Juan, Capt. Kendres Williams, Honorable Loftus A. Roker, airport team, the team who maintain the Portland Plantation, and Macintyre, the bush guide. At Landrail Point, Andrew Barksdale was always very helpful.

On Moore's Island, Abaco, in Hard Bargain; I thank everyone for such a warm welcome to our entire crew for the duration of our visit. In particular I thank Jonathan "Modi" Dean, other Deans from Sandy Point, minister Rev. Ishmael Williams, Mrs. Williams and a Bishop who doubled as restaurant owner of *Talk of the Town*, Davis and Deans' schoolteacher Mrs. P. Davis, fishermen, guides, residents, and church minister.

Ronan Hubert, president of B3A, Bureau of Aircraft Accidents Archives in Switzerland, has been a great help. Jeremy Cafferata, Esq. President of Freeport Ship Services, has likewise been a constant and selfless support since 2009, when I lived in Freeport briefly. For their encouragement, I thank Eric Wilmott, Jr., Paul King, Jeremy Morris, and Ray D'Arville. The team at Bradford Marine in Freeport (Mike, Dan, et. al.), as well as Williams Marine in Nassau were very helpful, and we did use DockWa for marinas from West End to Flying Fish at Clarence Town.

I would like to thank the couple whose boat we allided with and who were so forgiving, and for the owners whose tender we found washed up, I hope the news finally caught up with you. Shipmates aboard the motor cruiser *Kimber-L*, included skipper Rich Ashman, and divers Lamar Ard and Rusty Schull. For that phase, good friend Nicola Hepburn provided insight into the terrain, as did my older brother John, who had planted the coconuts on Goulding Cay as a teen.

For help with the historic 1930 Wright Brothers aircraft on Great Exuma, the overall mastermind, who introduced his search to Capt. Aranha, who shared it with me was radio enthusiast and aviation researcher Robert 'Bob' Rydzewski of California. Without his continuous attention, support, knowledge, and enthusiasm, this effort would not have lifted off the ground at all and resulted in five site visits in fewer months. On the ground and water, support came from Capt. Steven Cole, Wendy Rowe, guide Renardo D'Arville, Fina Johnson, Luis Simmons, his uncle, conch vendor, Ken Simmons, the Smith brothers of Stuart Manor: fisherman David, builder Ali, and their older brother. Several other helpful residents of Curtis, Rolletown, Steventon pitched in: particularly educators Mrs. Mackenzie and Mrs. Collins.

Many volunteers in the US, Bermuda, Bahamas, and the UK provided insights into 100-year-old aircraft technologies, metallurgy, and history. In Bermuda this included the directs of the National Museum of Bermuda, Elena Strong, PhD., and director emeritus Dr. Edward Harris. At the RAF, esteemed historian Graham Pitchfork wrote my initial Foreword as did Dr. Axel Niestlé, which gave me great credibility. The Imperial Order of the Daughters of Empire (IODE, now shuttered in Bahamas) preserved the history of the RAF Cemetery, as has Capt. Paul Aranha and volunteers from Jane Lloyd, its last president. I thank the leadership and members of the BHS and AMMC.

In south Eleuthera, in January 2023, I was honored to meet with Charles Rolle; Henry McPhee, fish guide, store owner in Tarpum Bay; Chris Maxey, co-founder with Pam of Island School; Capt. John McCarthy on his boat *Big Mac*; Ms. Carey who called her brother the fisherman, the alderman or *de facto* mayor of Tarpum Bay; and family friend Edgar Seligman of Gregory Town, whose family generously bailed me out of a traveling emergency in Ireland in 1991.

For many years of help, the French artist and historian Brita Caldoret opened many doors and always inspired me to keep looking and inquiring about future prospects. The owners of the Lost Key Inn, and Konstantinos Economou and family in Athens, Greece have been helpful, as have Jim Lawrence and Lorraine Parsons at connecting me and Capt. Mrs. Makis & Eleni Kourtesis of Andros. I am always indebted to the Royal Bahamas Defense Force (RBDF) and United States Coast Guard (USCG) as well as the volunteer Bahamas Air Sea Rescue Association (BASRA, including Chris Lloyd) for always being ready to come to the aid of persons like ourselves taking risks on land and water.

At Inagua, I thank the Nixon family and all park wardens, Denise Maycock, and the team at Visit Inagua, the Destination Marketing Organization. For northern Bahamas subsea explorer and US Army veteran Diana Giorgetti has been a great inspiration, as was Chad Silden at his newly-renamed dive ship in Cape Eleuthera. Several persons gave on-the-ground insights into Inagua, including Steve Connett and Marcus Michell, and through his book on shipwrecking there, named *Inagua*, Gilbert Klingel.

For Royal Island; Spanish Wells and North Eleuthera, I carry a copy of Ruth Rodriguez' classic photo book, *Out Island Portraits*. Moreover, with help from friendly St. Andrews classmate Cliff Pinder and his uncle, former mailboat owner Capt. Gurney Elon Pinder; I was able to answer many questions. Other schoolmates who have helped connect me have been Tara Klonaris, Julie D'Arville, Anthony DePuch, Garth & Jolika Buckner, Erika Fezt, Peter Maury, and neighbor Raimond Zeilstra. Realtors

Ashley Brown, the team at H. G. Christie, and Wendy Rowe at Front Rowe Realty in Exuma have all been helpful trying to find me aerial and drone images. I also combed Instagram, Pinterest, eBay, Flickr, and other sites for support.

I am hardly pressed to make much headway in understanding the history of Mayaguana, its vessels, and people without the cheerful help of the Taylor brothers from Pirates Well: Capt. Eddins, Capt. Limas, and Capt. Elvin, as well as their sister, family, and relatives, the Williamsons in Mayaguana, who we met with in 2019. On Acklins Ken Collie and relatives, Hannahs, Capt. Kendres and Capt. J.J. Williams, and Mario Virgill and his brother were most helpful. There is wonderful volunteerism, detailed information, and image flow out of a unique Facebook group called AUTEC/Andros Kids, since 2018. Eddie Spargur has consistently been a friendly and helpful resource for a number of years and in several projects when we finally suit up to search that complex, huge group of islands. I'm sure he and friends will be a significant help.

On the home front in Boston, I thank John Rymes, Steve Tsuchiya, Scott and Campbell Steward, Larry Webster, Jim Nash, Bill & Mrs. Pearsall, Nate Kruska, and Lucinda Jay with photos by her uncle Ray Evans. At Chapman House, Eagle Hill I think Caroline Lee, Tony Bloxham, Chris Rebelo, Ryan Monaghan, Ryan, Julie, Dottie and Tom, and Brendan, Sophie, Chantette Stalworth and Eleanor Bakstad. Nick Young, Ethan, Steve, Grant, Tony, and Stuart Cleary, Trevor White, Brain Fournier, Peter Bang, Ida MacRae, Paul, John, and Katy, Betty Wiberg & family, Bjorn, Sofie, and Joseph Wennerlund, Andrew Allen, Neil Sealy, and Dr. Nicola Virgill-Rolle have been very supportive. Final thanks to Captains Eric Takakjian, Andrew Urs, Charles Fluhr and Taylor as well as Kevin Zhang, Prof. Lin, Jiamin Gao, Shanshan, Mark, Bjorn. Thanks to editor Jacquelyn Austin and Hans Agrawal.

I particularly want to show my appreciation for Henrik Gedde Moos, a former navigation officer, in the Royal Danish Navy who, with his good friend and diving companion, Denis, and my brother, James, was an early believer in this project.

Specific credits for cover design and layout go to Caitlin D. Fitzgerald, interior layout, copy-edits, indexing, cover layout by Abdul Rehman Qureshi, charts by Robert Eller Pratt, photo credits include shipmates Tony Jermyn (most of *Parole* photos not by the author), Charles Affel, James Owsley, Patrick McGarry, Howard Story, Leland Dickerman, Eric Cottell, Toby Smith, Jane Lloyd, Lucinda Jay (for R0y Evans' photos), and Joanne Green.

Sons of RAF Bahamas veterans provided invaluable images: Stephen Smollett, Chris Hoyle, Mick Pythian, Bob Livingstone, nieces Lucy Jay, Joanne Green, and others Family of missing and killed aviators who contributed include those of Alistair Cleary, Jack Wood and Maurice O'Neill, Al Hayes (Geoffrey Hayes, Isobel Crawford), Deryk & Sylvia Cribbes (Vivian Cribbes Guerra), Cyril Sommerville, Henri Chouteau, Ben Zdan & Donald Hollowell, and others. Maps provided by Paul C. Aranha and Bahamas Land & Survey Department. Accommodation & transport in Nassau: Anders Wiberg, Orange Hill Resort. Transport on Eleuthera, Lars Carroll, in Acklins Rev. Felton Rolle.

Journalists and editors who have supported this story include John Demont (*Halifax Chronical*, Saltwire), Richard Woodbury (CBC Canada), editors Eugene Duffy, Stephen Hunt, Rashad Rolle, and Eileen Carron (*Nassau Tribune*), the AMMC, Dr. Michael Pateman, Jim Pennypacker (*Powerships*), Deirdre O'Regan (*Sea History*), Faye Kert (*Le Marin du Nord*), and Phoebe Hunt & Garry Maidment (*TIDE Magazine*), Karolina Kijek, Peggy Groves, Neil Sealy, Erin Niumata Cartwright, and Kate Summerscale.

Archival resources from National Archives of Bahamas, Antiquities Monuments and Museums Commission, The National Archives UK, Australian War Memorial, National Archives and Records Administration of the United States, National Archives of Bermuda, National Museum of Bermuda, Turks and Caicos National Museum, U-Boat Museum Cuxhaven (*Deutsches U-Boot Museum*), and Bertrand Ledan at the Utah Beach Landing Museum (*Musée du Débarquement*).

Backstory of those who lent boats:

Howard Story, *Parole*: 1991 we sailed on *War Baby* in the UK & Ireland. Then in 2021 we made a contact, learned we were both in shipping, and in 2022 sailed in New England and then to Bermuda.

Amanda Lindroth, *Schooner Queen*: She is our uncle Orjan Lindroth's spouse and close to our family. The boat has a touching story, since Orjan bought it for his Schooner Bay, Abaco development, and passed. Our brother John maintains it for Amanda, an interior designer who had owned Rock House in Harbour Island.

Eric Cottell, *TT Providence*: Since the 1980s our families shared orbits, and in the 2000s Eric and I shared interest in shipping, Connecticut, and adventure. This brought us together to motor to the White Banks and investigate what we thought might be a major overturned hull (which was a reef).

John Wiberg, *Shoal Shaker*: John is my older brother and have restored it since 1993, when the family purchased it at Sheriff's auction.

Rich Ashman, *Kimber-L*: Rich reached out to me in mid-2022 simply saying he was tired of searching for things in places where nothing was, and he heard I was good at delivering results. He had a childhood friend's family in common (the Turners) and indeed, on our first day, we found parts of the B-26.

Phicol Wallace, *Lost Key*: Our brother John lived on Ragged Island for months at Phicol Wallace's Bed & Breakfast, named *The Lost Key*. Their friendship and trust was extended to me, to the extent that our payment was not accepted.

Denis Galipeau: When no one, not even I, had any basis of trust in my finding anything—in other words, when it seemed I was a fantasist, brother James put me in touch with Denis and Henrik Gedde Moos, who had military training and experience with finding things at sea. Very generously, they shared their insight, expertise, time, and energy to troll for the plane.

Ulric Williams, *Yisel*: I was probably half an hour from drowning as I struggled with a huge cowling for a B-26 engine plate and just would not give up, despite only having a string and a surfboard. Ulric and his son were motoring past me on a Sunday morning and generously towed me to shore with the sizeable part, causing excitement on shore when it was pulled from the sea for the first time in 80 years.

Toby Smith, *Da Skiff*: A childhood friend and fellow adventurer, Toby, who has been restoring and promoting Paradise Island Lighthouse and the former beach club at Hog Island, took his time to search Delaporte Bay and Cable Beach Bay.

Thanks to he who always earns the final word: much loved and admired musician son, Felix.

About the Author

Born on Manhattan in 1970, Eric Wiberg lived in The Bahamas until 1983, then attended boarding schools in New England and attended university there and in the UK. After skippering a 68' yacht to New Zealand and penning a memoir about it, he ran tanker ships from Singapore for three years, then sailing yachts from Newport until 2005. He continued his maritime career in recruiting, media, and tugs in New York and Connecticut until 2019, when he returned to Boston to write full-time. During the pandemic, he completed 25 books in as many months.

Eric has been finding artifacts internationally since the 1970s. A licensed captain for over 25 years, he has 250,000 miles of surface travel, passports covering the US and EU, a law license, and a master's degree in Marine Affairs. His specialty is tracing the events involving vessels, planes, and the people on them, and tracking and reporting the story behind them. Envisioned as the first in series, this book would not have been possible without the support of crewmates, fellow writer Caitlin, who designed the cover, and son Felix.

www.ingramcontent.com/pod-product-compliance
Lightning Source LLC
Chambersburg PA
CBHW051313020426
42333CB00028B/3316

* 9 7 8 1 7 3 5 6 3 2 4 2 1 *